PREFACES TO SHAKESPEARE'S PLAYS

PREFACES TO SHAKESPEARE'S PLAYS

A. L. Rowse

ORBIS · LONDON

CONTENTS

INTRODUCTION

It has been suggested to me by my publisher that I should bring together in one convenient volume the Introductions to each play in *The Annotated Shakespeare*. I am glad of the opportunity to revise them, sometimes re-writing and adding new material information.

Hitherto, I had not written specifically about the plays, but about Shakespeare's life and the times in which he lived – the perspective in which his life has properly to be seen. Nor is that to be accomplished successfully without a lifetime of research in the Elizabethan age.

My aim all along was to show the real Shakespeare in that perspective and from that knowledge. In solving the problems of the Sonnets, and elucidating the autobiographical facts in them, we now have added a dimension to our knowledge of his life.

My aim in studying the plays is the similar one of throwing light, from our knowledge of the time, upon what went into them. For Shakespeare, like all writers, wrote from his own experience, what he read and felt and thought, his observation of people and events, and what went on around him.

The law of diminishing returns has long been demonstrated in Shakespeare 'criticism': the search for Shakespeare 'sources' has succeeded only in burying him under a mountain of commentary and notes. The inspired commonsense of Dr. Johnson saw that there is a limit to the value of criticism, when often the work 'can draw no aid from critical illustration'; and this thought was echoed by Hazlitt. Let the play speak for itself. My aim is the more useful one of clearing the ground, giving the play its setting, its date and place in Shakespeare's work and in its time, so that the topical and historical, literary and dramatic influences and references can illuminate the play.

The plays need a modicum of annotation – they have already received far too much; we recall Dr. Johnson's warning against 'the rage for saying something when there is nothing to be said'. Nor do we need yet another text of the plays: there are several admirable complete texts, and numerous reliable editions of individual plays.

I recommend the complete Shakespeare edited by C.J. Sisson and his *New Readings in Shakespeare*. He had the inestimable advantages of being widely read in the documentation and social life of the period, so that he was familiar with Elizabethan speech and usage, as also with Elizabethan handwritings. His approach was thus historical, as mine is.

Shakespeare was the most historically minded of all dramatists – one third of his plays are historical. I should have liked to arrange his work in chronological order, to illustrate both its development and the flexible variety of his genius – the 'Johannes Factotum' of Robert Greene's jibe. Here was a man who could turn his hand from history to comedy to tragedy with the greatest ease, in accordance with the opportunities that presented themselves, the challenges and demands upon him, the available resources in the way of actors, his own inclinations, and what would appeal at the moment.

The pattern would work out thus:

1590-1	Titus Andronicus
1591	The Comedy of Errors
1591-2	The Taming of the Shrew
1591-4	The Sonnets
before 1592	1, 2, 3 Henry VI; A Lover's Complaint
1592	Richard III; The Two Gentlemen of Verona; Venus and Adonis
1593	Love's Labour's Lost; The Rape of Lucrece
1594	A Midsummer Night's Dream
1594-5	Romeo and Juliet; Richard II
1596	King John; The Merchant of Venice
1597-8	1, 2 Henry IV
1598	As You Like It
1599	Henry V; Much Ado About Nothing; Julius Caesar
1599-1600	The Merry Wives of Windsor
1600-1	Hamlet; The Phoenix and the Turtle
1601	Twelfth Night
1602	Troilus and Cressida
1603	All's Well That Ends Well
1604	Measure for Measure; Othello
1605-6	Macbeth
1606	King Lear
1607	Antony and Cleopatra
1608	Coriolanus; Pericles
1608-9	Timon of Athens
1609	Cymbeline
1610-11	The Winter's Tale
1611	The Tempest
1612-13	Henry VIII

Convenience before courage: I have arranged the plays chronologically (as far as possible) within the conventional categories. But since Shakespeare was so historically minded, first won fame with his *Henry VI* historical plays, and ended with another, *Henry VIII*, I have dared to place the history plays first.

SHAKESPEARE'S
HISTORIES

The essence of the Renaissance experience was a heightened self-consciousness, a self-awareness: one can see it in painting in the new, unexampled development of portraiture. In England its fullest expression is to be seen in literature with William Shakespeare. The full flowering of the Renaissance impulse was rather late in reaching Britain, impeded as it was by the absorption of the critical Reformation experience. From the 1580s onwards, these twin impulses fused in the national self-consciousness and bounding self-confidence generated by the struggle with Spain – a small half-island country against the world-empire of Philip II's Spain and Portugal combined.

It was not simply rejoicing over the defeat of one Spanish Armada, as literary folk are apt to think; there were three Armadas which met with disaster, in 1588, 1596 and 1597, and the mood of boastful self-confidence (cf. Drake) – or the natural inspiration of patriotism – antedated these events. In the early 1580s, the struggle with Spain, the madrigals, great literature (with Sidney and Spenser), and the Elizabethan drama all begin together.[1]

The dramatists of the English chronicle plays found appealing subjects in England's past, but no one to more purpose than the rather late-comer on the scene, the actor, who was a junior to the university wits. He was thus able to profit immensely from the work of the best of them – those whom in time he would come to rival as artistic equals, Sidney and Spenser, Lyly and Marlowe.

The actor – who was also a poet and a quick-reading man – had two chief store-houses of information open to him: Edward Hall's *The Union of the two noble and illustrious families York and Lancaster* and Holinshed's *Chronicles of England, Scotland and Ireland*. (Raphael Holinshed was a fellow Warwickshire man, but others contributed more extensively to the book.) The second and much fuller edition of Holinshed came out in 1587, the year before the first Armada, just at the right time for the actor, commencing author, to make the utmost use of it. Various editions of Hall had come out long before, in the 1540s and 1550s, and Hall exerted a formative influence in shaping up and giving meaning to the muddled and murderous events of the 15th century, as Holinshed's chronicle of them never could.

For Hall had a dominant theme. The conflict regarding the succession to the throne, which went back to the deposition of Richard II in 1399 and Bolingbroke's assumption of the crown as Henry IV, had ultimately let loose dissension and civil war, with all its horrors, which was settled only by the union of the Lancastrian heir with the Yorkist heiress, Henry VII and his wife, Elizabeth. Beside the horrors there were all the dramas, political and personal. The whole 15th century provided a marvellous storehouse – and we must remember how new and exciting all this was, apart from verbal memory and folk-tradition. For history was not taught at school; education was based on the classics. So that the images and comparisons that spring naturally to Shakespeare's mind, apart from those drawn from nature, are classical; he follows his historians faithfully, even in their mistakes, shaping them up, shortening, cutting for his dramatic purposes.

What distinguishes his history plays from the numerous ordinary chronicle plays is that he sees the pattern, the significance of events – in that like Hall, not Holinshed. From the very beginning, with the *Henry VI* trilogy, he is concerned with the phenomena of social disorder, the appalling consequences of the breakdown of authority, an impotent king like Henry VI or an unstable one like Richard II, the dire necessity of order and obedience, of competence in the ruler, obedience in the subject.

How different Shakespeare was in this respect from the other dramatists! He is more like Sidney and Spenser. Where did he get his extraordinary social concern, his political understanding, his involvement with the problems of kingship? Philip Sidney was a member of the governing class; Spenser was recruited to it. Shakespeare had a thoroughly governing-class attitude to these questions (with its corollary in his view of the people). After all, he regarded himself as a gentleman, which he was through his mother, an Arden; even his father was an alderman, eventually bailiff (i.e. mayor), of Stratford. As an observant boy of six or seven, he would have seen the disturbance triggered by the Northern Rebellion of 1569-70, the recruits raised and sent north, armed from the town's armoury.

Moreover Shakespeare was a family man, grafted into society and undertaking his responsibilities – unlike the inhabitants of literary Bohemia: Robert Greene, living with a whore, sister of a hanged thief, or unmarried Kyd and Marlowe, the latter as unorthodox about religion as he was about sex. These people display no sense of social responsibility and not much political understanding in their work. Shakespeare did to an extent so remarkable that it has come to be fully appreciated only in our own politically and socially disturbed time.

His life fell between two distracted periods: the Wars of the Roses (his grandfather might well have been at Bosworth, as Elizabeth I's was), and the Civil War, during which Shakespeare's daughter entertained Charles I's Queen at New Place. Shakespeare knew too well how thin is the crust of civilisation, how easy for society to break down, to fall into what dark waters beneath. And, a cultivated man who hated cruelty, he knew that social breakdown brought only all the more suffering with it. We in our time have the bitterest reasons for appreciating that, in all the wars and revolutions since the overthrow of European civilisation in 1914, with a second onslaught from the same quarter in 1939.

This overriding theme, with all its consequences, recurs and is demonstrated in play after play, not only the English histories but in the Roman histories, the tragedies and tragi-comedies. For Shakespeare's histories are more like his own tragedies and comedies than they are like other people's histories, let alone the ordinary shapeless chronicle plays. Indeed, it is a tragi-comedy, *Troilus and Cressida*, that most explicitly expresses his views on the necessity of hierarchical order according to social function. Ulysses' famous speech on Degree practically versifies the Homily on Obedience, which Elizabethans had regularly brought home to them in church.

> 'Every degree of people, in their vocation, calling and office, hath appointed to them their duty and order. Some are in high degree, some are in low; some kings and princes, some inferiors and subjects, priests and laymen, masters and servants, fathers and children, husbands and wives, rich and poor – and every one have need of other, so that in all things is to be lauded and praised the goodly order of God, without the which no house, no city, no commonwealth can continue and endure. Take away Kings, princes, rulers, magistrates, judges and such states of God's order, no man shall ride or go by the highway unrobbed, no man shall sleep in his own house or bed unkilled, no man shall keep his wife, children and possessions in quietness.'

Hardly any of the chronicle plays saw into the meaning of events, they merely narrated them: in fact, in spite of their popularity, Shakespeare owed very little to them. He owed much more to Hall, with whose message of national unity and social integration he agreed, and on this basis made his own mixture, never failing to draw the moral, as a good historian should.

The chronicle plays were, however, inspired by patriotism and here Shakespeare agreed with them. There was every reason why he should: the little country was up-and-coming – 'they are people such that mend upon the world.' It was an obvious source of inspiration to all writers and artists to be alive and working at such a time – their work shows it.

Politics and history are two sides of the same coin, and Shakespeare was historically minded, again exceptionally – more so than any other dramatist. Ten of his plays deal with English history, four with Roman, one with Scottish, two with the pre-history of Britain – *King Lear* and *Cymbeline* – which to Elizabethans enjoyed a similar status to that of history proper. Shakespeare's love of the past, with its rich layers of lore, is liable to appear anywhere – in Mercutio's long evocation of it, that crops up unexpectedly like something left over from *A Midsummer Night's Dream*, which is largely created out of this material.

> O, then I see Queen Mab hath been with you.
> She is the fairies' midwife, and she comes
> In shape no bigger than an agate stone
> On the forefinger of an alderman . . .

(Did his father, the alderman, wear such a ring?) Along with the fairy-tale lore comes contemporary social life, as with Bottom and his fellows, or just as the citizens' life of Windsor goes in harness with the legend of Herne's haunted Oak.

> Sometime she gallops o'er a courtier's nose,
> And then dreams he of smelling out a suit;
> And sometime comes she with a tithe-pig's tail,
> Tickling a parson's nose as 'a lies asleep,
> Then dreams he of another benefice.

He was not interested in the future, as secondary artists are – Bernard Shaw for example (even he was better inspired with *St. Joan*), for the past is inspirational and inspires poetry, the future polemics and propaganda.

What made him so absorbed by the problems of kingship – not only the sad stories of the deaths of kings, which lent themselves obviously to pomp and circumstance on the stage? The old tradition that he took 'kingly parts' may offer a clue, for the mimetic faculty of an actor would lead him into the inwardness of the part. John Davies of Hereford saw the point:

> Had'st thou not played some kingly parts in sport,
> Thou hadst been a companion for a king,
> And been a king among the meaner sort.

Did he think of himself as a king? Or, in modern jargon, did he identify? There was no reason why he should not. He was immensely ambitious: as has been pointed out, to challenge all three *genres* of drama at the very beginning of his writing and about the same time – history with *Henry VI*, tragedy with *Titus Andronicus*, comedy with *The Comedy of Errors*. Robert Greene was quite right in spotting the euphoric self-confidence of the actor.

From the first we notice variety, a Protean variety, even within the one category of English history plays. An elastic potentiality is suggested, even in work that is raw and crude; the immeasurable capability of development we learn only later. We shall observe with each play what makes it different from the others. Even within the first trilogy, the Second Part of *Henry VI* is more diverse than the First; the Third differs again in being more a revenge-play. *Richard III* is a grand historical melodrama. *Richard II* is totally different: the most formal and ceremonial, the most lyrical and poetic, of the history plays. *King John* is a reversion to chronicle play; the

11

two parts of *Henry IV*, a superb fusion of history with comedy. *Henry V*, with its prominent Chorus, is epical; *Henry VIII* something of a stately pageant with ceremonial shows.

From the first the ability to plot a play went along with the forward thinking out of the intellectual theme. These capacities rarely went together. Anthony Munday, for example, was highly regarded as a 'plotter', but the rest of him was pedestrian. Shakespeare was a planner in all senses of the word: in his art, as in his life, he brought it off.

In his earlier English history plays he is close in attitude to Daniel's *Civil Wars*, the one contemporary who approaches Shakespeare in historic concern and with a similar political outlook. Shakespeare owed something to this book, though we need not suppose him incapable of thinking up for himself a comparable epic of England's past in the form of drama. For, where Daniel was a sympathetic, reflective mind, the actor-dramatist was all for action, with far greater power. And, later on, we find Daniel learning from Shakespeare.

More remarkably, and yet not unexpectedly, we find Marlowe, from whom Shakespeare gained much, learning from the actor turned dramatist. Marlowe's last and most mature play, *Edward II*, was indebted to *Henry VI* for its wider spread of characterisation, its portrayal of a non-hero in place of the Marlovian concentration upon a Tamburlaine. Indeed, so much attention is paid to uncovering 'sources' for Shakespeare – often with irrelevant pedantry, when Shakespeare could have picked up the ideas anywhere or possibly have thought of them for himself – that we are apt to overlook his influence upon others or their response in competition with him. It was a highly competitive age: hence its achievement. Marlowe's *Edward II* and the admirable *Woodstock* play are indebted to Shakespeare; the Chamberlain's Company's success with *Henry IV* led immediately to the Admiral's commissioning *Sir John Oldcastle* from Munday, Drayton and Hathaway.

Everything shows Shakespeare's essential independence of mind, for all that he providently used everything that came to hand. His greatest debt, however, was to the time in which he lived. France and Italy had no chronicle plays to build on. The Elizabethans had every reason to be proud of their country and of themselves: the age itself inspired them, bore them up and carried them upwards.

---

1. cf. my *The Elizabethan Renaissance*, vol. II *The Cultural Achievement* (Macmillan, London, and Scribner, New York, 1972)

THE FIRST PART OF
King Henry VI
BEFORE 1592

The combination of dramatic effectiveness with the forward planning of a trilogy announced the arrival of a new playwright of power and promise, as also the self-confidence Robert Greene observed in the actor. These plays were immensely successful in the Elizabethan age, and made the actor's name as a dramatist. They have again proved their actability and appeal to audiences in our time, with a certain amount of judicious cutting – for the abounding author simply flowed over.

In the interval these plays have been disconsidered, misconceived and subjected to every kind of absurdity from critics and commentators, even eminent ones like Coleridge. He, however, was hardly a model of common sense. The inspired sense of Dr. Johnson saw that 'in the productions of genius there will be inequality' – particularly in its early productions, we may add; that 'the diction, the versification, and the figures are Shakespeare's'. That is perfectly obvious today with our greater knowledge of Elizabethan usage. It was also apparent to Dr. Johnson, coming to the Second Part of the trilogy that 'this play begins where the former ends, and continues the series of transactions, of which it presupposes the First Part already known. There is sufficient proof that the Second and Third Parts were not written without dependence on the First.' In spite of that mighty sign-post we have had a welter of conjecture and commentary, superfluously confusing the reader, as again with regard to the Sonnets.

A further difficulty arose from the fact that memorial reconstructions of the Second and Third Parts were issued as quartos in 1594 and 1595, while the full text of the trilogy published many years later in the First Folio, 1623, was unsatisfactory. In a way this was understandable, for the printers had complicated materials to work from and added their own mistakes. The very inconsistencies point to the author, for one cannot always remember what one has written; and Shakespeare never had time to tidy up and revise his earliest work. Why should he? – the play was the thing; it had had resounding success, and it had launched him.

—— oOo ——

As always we must keep in mind the two-fold background – that of the stage, dramatic and literary, and that of the events of the time.

The patriotic excitement generated by the struggle with Spain, the mood of national self-confidence, pride and self-glorification – again natural enough in a youthful people on their way up in the world – at the triumph over the Spanish Armada in 1588 expressed itself in a surge of self-consciousness and interest in the nation's past. The expanded edition of Holinshed's *Chronicles*, of 1587, provided keen purveyors of popular entertainment with a storehouse of subjects for dramatisation. A common stock came into existence of subjects, themes and reactions to them, as also of diction and images, largely from the classical education then general. People naturally borrowed from each other, especially those working in proximity as Marlowe and Shakespeare were, in this kaleido-scopic, confused time.

The dominant influence observable in *Henry VI* is Marlowe's. He had patented this grandiloquent poetic diction, in splendid blank verse, in *Tamburlaine*. The actor copied it – indeed he may have had it in his head from acting in it; though already he had his own grandiloquence, which reverberated in the theatre and which Elizabethans relished. One notices already in this early play his characteristic words – his fondness for words ending in 'ive', submissive, intermissive; for words like presage, peruse, periapt. Where Marlowe's blank verse is more splendid at this date, Shakespeare has much more rhyme – he is a natural poet with obvious capacity for development, and greater potentiality for there is more variety and diversity. A couple of scenes in this play are almost wholly in rhymed couplets; these also conclude each scene, often a single speech. And this must have had a useful punctuating effect in the theatre.

Marlowe was the senior, the initiator, the leader; but the influence was not all one way. Before he died, so lamentably, he was influenced in turn by *Henry VI* and wrote his *Edward II*. A purely literary influence, observable in phrases, is Spenser, whose *Faerie Queene* came out this year, 1590. Ubiquitous are the traces of school education in the classics and of Bible and Prayer Book from constant early attendance at church. A number of classical references are traceable to Cooper's *Thesaurus*, the Latin dictionary which Vicar Bretchgirdle had bequeathed for the use of the scholars at Stratford Grammar School – he had christened William in 1564. Other references, to Froissart, for example, show the quick-reading man, adept at picking up tips from everywhere – as an actor would be. Anyhow, the years before 1590 gave time for reading – and Shakespeare continued always to be a reading man, and a rapid one.[1]

—— oOo ——

Though there are touches from Holinshed, the dominant theme in shaping the *Henry VI* plays came from Edward Hall's book, *The Union of the two noble and illustrious families York and Lancaster*, of which there had been several editions in the 1540s. This book elaborated the message of the Tudor dynasty – the ending of the uncivil strife of the War of the Roses in the Lancastrian heir, Henry VII's union with Elizabeth, heiress of the house of York. The conflict between these two houses, unleashed by the imbecility of poor Henry VI, led to the discord and breakdown of social order, which is foreshadowed in this play, is a secondary theme in it and becomes the primary subject of its successors, including *Richard III*. It all went back to the revolution of 1399 and Bolingbroke's ejection of Richard II from the throne; from this exfoliated another quartet of historical plays. One sees what a prodigious planner the actor-dramatist was to become.

In the First Part the main theme is that of the war in France, the conflict unleashed by Charles VI's imbecility (Henry VI's grandfather) and Henry V's astonishing, but ultimately fatal, conquest. Fighting the French was a traditional activity ever since the Norman Conquest (and in spite of the fact that the dynasty was French – even Henry VII was as much French and Welsh as English). The subject immensely appealed to the simple souls of the Elizabethans, to anti-French feeling, the boastful pride in themselves of a young people, the gallant memories of the Hundred Years War, such heroes as 'fighting Talbot'.

Talbot is the popular hero of this play (typically he gave his name to a hunting dog) – and apparently was played by an actor the more appealing for being undersized. Thomas Nashe, himself one of this early group, familiar with Marlowe and Shakespeare, testified to the play's appeal. 'How it would have joyed brave Talbot (the terror of the French) to think that he should triumph again on the stage, and have his bones new embalmed with the tears of ten thousand spectators at least – at several times – who imagine they behold him fresh bleeding.'

The villain of the piece, if we may so call a Saint, is Joan of Arc: she is rendered as the 15th-century soldiers who fought in France thought of her – as a witch and a strumpet. (After all, had she not been condemned as such by the Church? – when she was probably only a chaste, repressed Lesbian.) The tyro of a dramatist gave the groundlings what they expected, though there is no reason to suppose that he knew any better. Except that, when she speaks for herself, the dramatist's sympathy cannot help breaking in:

> Virtuous and holy, chosen from above,
> By inspiration of celestial grace,
> To work exceeding miracles on earth.
> I never had to do with wicked spirits . . .
> A virgin from her tender infancy,
> Chaste and immaculate in very thought,
> Whose maiden blood, thus rigorously effused,
> Will cry for vengeance at the gates of heaven.

Hers is the Shakespearean humanity, thus early expressed, which was true to his nature and paid such dividends later in the sense of dramatic justice. We may also notice the reiteration of v's, conscious or unconscious, that bespeak the natural poet.

Already the characters are more individualised, the scenes more varied, than in Marlowe. The rivalry between Humphrey, Duke of Gloucester, and Cardinal Beaufort is sketched, which will have formidable development in the next play. Suffolk's character is also headed forward, for he is portrayed as falling in love with Margaret of Anjou, whose marriage to Henry VI he negotiated, with fatal consequences. The age of the young King presents a difficulty: a child at the beginning, he has to be ready for marriage at the end. However, that presented no difficulty to Elizabethans, who did not look for probability in their plays but strong scenes.

Of these we have plenty. Perhaps the best remembered today is the plucking of white and red roses in the Temple Garden, for which there is no historical warrant, but from which in the play the rival parties take their emblems: Yorkist white, Lancastrian red. The simple spectacle must have provided something different in the elementary equipment of the early Shakespearean theatre. The gallery above the stage served for walls, battlements, etc. to scale; we know that Hell reverberated below the stage. In this play a chair is brought in two or three times, to carry a sick or dying character. There were ceremonies, several funeral processions and dead marches, a coronation, drums and trumpets, much marching to and fro, fighting of groups or individuals, the confrontation of colours – Gloucester's blue-coats against Winchester's tawny-coats.

The early Elizabethan theatre was crude and rhetorical, but effective: we must remember the redoubled impact upon spectators, when there were no act- or scene-divisions, and – with the stage partly surrounded, partly occupied by spectators – the audience felt themselves part of the action. It is thus absurd to condemn these early plays for being 'episodic' – for, of course, they consist of episodes: strong scenes were what was wanted. What is more remarkable is that there should have been such effective over-all planning, the feat of reducing so many years, indeed decades, of history to some dramatic form. Every opportunity is taken by the practising dramatist to help the illusion of unity: this is the function of forward-looking prophecies, backward-looking curses, dreams and omens. They all help to knit things together, so that in the end each play has the dramatic unity of rise-climax-fall – and that in spite of the refractory material, almost impossible to weld into shape.

—— oOo ——

Not many flecks of Shakespeare's own time occur in this play dealing with events a century and a half before, but there are some. For example, in the 1590s there was some doubt and dispute as to the right policy to pursue. This is reflected in

> One would have lingering wars with little cost;
> Another would fly swift but wanteth wings;

A third thinks, without expense at all,
By guileful fair words peace may be obtained.

(The Queen preferred the third course.)

The Tower was still the country's chief arsenal and storehouse, as when Gloucester says,

I'll to the Tower with all the haste I can
To view th'artillery and munitìon.

The French King hails Joan of Arc as another

Helen, the mother of great Constantine.

The Gild Chapel at Stratford had a wall-painting of this legend; it had fallen to John Shakespeare as burgess to whitewash the painted Doom there (unlikely as he was to have been a Catholic).

In Gloucester's berating the Cardinal, who was bishop of Winchester, he does not fail to rake up the Stews on the South Bank, which were on episcopal property:

Thou that giv'st whores indulgences to sin . . .
Winchester goose!

This meant a venereal swelling in the groin.

We note that Sir William Lucy, of the family at Charlecote, was given a good part. Shakespeare himself is audible in his characteristic grand words, impressive to an audience:

In dumb significants proclaim your thoughts;

or 'with sudden and extemporal speech'; eyes wax dim, 'as drawing to their exigent', etc. Suffolk, speaking of Margaret of Anjou, says:

She's beautiful, and therefore to be wooed;
She is a woman, therefore to be won.

These words are improved on in *Venus and Adonis*, and something very close appears in Marlowe's *Hero and Leander*.

—— oOo ——

The only text of the First Part of King Henry VI is that of the Folio, but its unsatisfactory state means that it requires careful editing. Until quite recently there have been much confusion and superfluous conjectures as to composite authorship. We need not exclude the possibility of the actor apprenticing himself by working over an earlier draft in this First Part. The best editions of all three plays, by Dr. Andrew S. Cairncross,[2] clear up the confusions. Characteristically he retains the reading 'Falstaff' from the Folio, which most editors have corrected to 'Fastolf' from the Chronicles. It does not seem to have occurred to anybody that, in spite of the spelling, Falstaff would have been the popular pronunciation of Fastolf.

Similarly with regard to superfluous annotation, under a misapprehension, take the line:

> Our isle be made a nourish of salt tears.

One editor comments: 'Elizabethan form of "nurse". Three ideas seem to be presented: (a) the men will all be killed, only the women left; (b) the women will nurse their babes at their weeping eyes; (c) England (i.e. the women) will be one "nourish", feeding her offspring (at her weeping eyes) on salt tears (instead of milk).' All nonsense: 'nourish' is a simple misprint for the common Elizabethan word 'marish', i.e. marsh.

---

1. v. my *Shakespeare's Globe: His Moral and Intellectual Outlook* (Weidenfeld & Nicolson, London, 1981); American title *What Shakespeare Read and Thought* (Coward, McCann and Geoghegan, New York, 1981)
2. *Arden Shakespeare* series (Methuen, London)

THE SECOND PART OF
King Henry VI
BEFORE 1592

Dr. Johnson considered the Second Part of the trilogy the best. It marks an improvement on the First in variety and character of action – the wide spread from the feuds and factions at Court around the King, the conjuring of the Duchess of Gloucester, her trial and penance, the killing of Suffolk at sea, the realistic lower-class scenes of Jack Cade's Rising. The characters are also more varied and developed. Henry VI reaches maturity as the kind, saintly man he was, more fit for a monk than a king. This provokes its reaction in his wife, the passionate Margaret of Anjou, whose nerves are on edge at her husband's impotence, while her love for Suffolk comes into the open. The characters of spirited old Salisbury, the ambitious York aiming at the Crown, Suffolk with the arrogance that brought his fate upon him, the uncouth proletarian Cade – all stand out as individuals.

The language also is in keeping. Henry VI's is notably Biblical as becomes him. For the first time Shakespeare gives expression to his attentive ear for lower-class speech – Cade's talk is the most memorable to us in the play. To Peter, the Armourer's man, is given the first malapropism of which Shakespeare was to make such use for jokes, with Bottom, Dogberry, and Mistress Quickly. Peter reports his master as saying that the King was an 'usurer', when he meant 'usurper'. The language of the play as a whole is also more varied, richer, stuffed with classical allusions, mainly from Ovid, not only the favourite *Metamorphoses* but also the *Tristia*. Everywhere is evidence of the actor's verbal receptivity; he not only picked up words and phrases everywhere, making the utmost use of Latin school tags to suggest more classical expertise than he had, but he needed this virtuosity to express his teeming mind. In these early plays we watch him flexing his muscles.

The puns are simple enough – history did not provide such opportunities as the banter of the comedies, but Shakespeare made the utmost of what he could, overdoing it in fact:

> Unto the main! O father, Maine is lost!
> That Maine which by main force Warwick did win:
> Main chance, father, you meant, but I meant Maine,
> Which I will win from France or else be slain.

Less rhyme occurs, but it punctuates speeches no less than scenes. The imagery is more lurid: everybody has been struck by the slaughter-house, butchering and butcher images that constantly occur when Shakespeare thought of the breakdown of social order and civil war. The subconscious associativeness of his mind is hardly less remarkable than his conscious intention: the images cluster together like sea-weed under the water. His subconscious worked for him almost as much as his conscious mind, most fortunate of writers. Dreams are an element in many of the plays.

An image sometimes has an obsessive visual power that suggests recollection:

> And as the butcher takes away the calf,
> And binds the wretch and beats it when it strains,
> Bearing it to the bloody slaughter-house;
> And as the dam runs lowing up and down,
> Looking the way her harmless young one went,
> And can do naught but wail her darling's loss . . .

This was a familiar enough spectacle in the vicinity of Smithfield, or in a country town like Stratford. John Aubrey has been discounted for saying that Shakespeare's father was a butcher, when all the records show that he was a glover. But in a country town the handling of skins would have gone with butchering, in which the glover would lend a hand. Aubrey went on, 'and I have been told heretofore by some of the neighbours that, when he was a boy, he exercised his father's trade; but when he killed a calf he would do it in a high style, and make a speech.' It is in character.

For Shakespeare's grand style thus early we may cite young Clifford's speech towards the end of the play, which foreshadows the Wars of the Roses that will be the subject of the next.

> O! let the vile world end,
> And the premised flames of the last day
> Knit earth and heaven together,
> Now let the general trumpet blow his blast,
> Particularities and petty sounds
> To cease!

And so on – the theme of revenge is developed in accordance with the rules of rhetoric, citations from the Bible and Ovid to round it out.

—— oOo ——

The main theme of this play is the fatal marriage of Henry VI to Margaret of Anjou. She came to him not only without dowry, but her father received Anjou and Maine, which were strategic keys to Normandy and led to its loss. The losses in France sharpened the conflict in England; only a strong king could have imposed order, and Henry VI was not only weak but suffered a complete mental breakdown. One cannot but feel sympathy for him, with all the nasty egos scuffling for place and power around him – no wonder he was sick of it all. In our day, when politicians and Trade Union leaders are so disinterested, we find the slanging matches going on around the King distasteful. Elizabethans did not: they revelled in these declamatory amenities. Elizabethan theatre was highly oratorical and given to stomping about the stage; Shakespeare was to be the leader in the development of a subtler and more natural dramaturgy.

Occasionally passages, especially genealogies, are taken straight out of the Chronicles – prose rapidly versified, as with the argument about the renewal of the French war at the beginning of *Henry V*. Elizabethans were not taught English history at school – it was all the more exciting and new to them; however, they were closer to the tradition – as with the youthful misrule of Prince Hal, we now know, or again with the misdeeds of Richard III.

Shakespeare makes no doubt that the Wars of the Roses were ultimately due to the sin of Bolingbroke in usurping the throne of Richard II. The historian may well think that he blames Bolingbroke too harshly; for (a) Richard became impossible as king and had to be replaced; (b) Bolingbroke was led on not only to claim his rights as Duke of Lancaster but the crown itself as a matter of sheer self-preservation; (c) he was called to the job by the will of the country, so far as it could be expressed by Parliament and Church, and he made a far better king. Richard was the son of Edward III's eldest son, the Black Prince; Edward's second son died young. The third son, Lionel Duke of Clarence, had only a daughter – so the Yorkists derived their claim through the female line. John of Gaunt was the fourth son, but his son was the next heir *in the male line* after Richard. That weighed in the balance too; but it led Henry IV to displace the anointed king: there was the crime. We watch its working out, its nemesis, in these plays as in a Greek tragedy.

We are grateful for a let-up from this sombre theme in the variety of episodes this play presents. We have the interesting scene of the Duchess of Gloucester calling up the spirits. One of these answers to the name of Asnath. There is no reason why this should not be Asmenoth, 'guider of the North', referred to in Greene's *Friar Bacon and Friar Bungay*. May not the episode be partly responsible for Greene's charge of plagiarism against the actor turned dramatist? The episodes of the Armourer, charged with accusing York of treason, provide some comic relief – his last appearance is a drunken scene, with a fight.

The scenes that appeal most today are the realistic ones of Jack Cade's Rising, in which we have Shakespeare's first depiction of the people – upon which subject he never changed, from play to play until the ultimate hardening of the lines in *Coriolanus*. We now realise that – even apart from the Court, the universities and inns of court – his audiences were mainly of the educated upper classes, with whom his derisory picture of the people would be popular. The groundlings, who paid a penny to stand in the pit, were merely a minority. His regular propitiation of the audience is addressed not to the groundlings but to the seated part of it: it was they who made the theatres pay, not the lower orders.

Cade promises the people, almost as if it were a general election:

> There shall be in England seven half-penny loaves sold
> for a penny; the three-hooped pot shall have ten hoops.
> All the realm shall be in common. And when I am king, as
> king I will be –
> ALL: God save your Majesty!
> CADE: I thank you, good people – there shall be no money.
> All shall eat and drink on my score, and I will apparel them
> all in one livery, that they may agree like brothers.
> BUTCHER: The first thing we do, let's kill all the lawyers.

At the next appearance of the mob, in Smithfield, Cade commands:

> Now go some and pull down the Savoy; others to the Inns
> of Court. Down with them all!

This must have been popular. In fact, it had been John of Gaunt's palace of the Savoy that was wrecked in the Peasants' Revolt of 1381, with all its treasures, jewels, tapestries, books and manuscripts. For Elizabethans did not expect the people to care for learning, any more than a society run by Trade Union standards cares for culture. Cade charges Lord Say (builder of beautiful Broughton Castle):

> Thou hast most traitorously corrupted the youth of the realm in
> erecting a grammar school. And whereas, before, our forefathers had
> no other books but the score and the tally, thou hast caused printing
> to be used . . .

This is the beginning of a comic speech, good-humoured enough from Shakespeare; all the same, Cade does not fail to have Lord Say and his son-in-law's heads struck off and brought in upon two poles for demonstration.

The gravamen of Cade's speeches is:

> Henceforward all things shall be in common.

The sixteenth century was well aware of the phenomenon of Communism. The Peasants' Revolt in Germany, of 1526, with the Anabaptist horrors at Münster, had sent a thrill of trepidation throughout Europe, comparable to that aroused by the Bolshevik Revolution of 1917 in Russia, with all that that portended for the world.

Shakespeare is but at the beginning of expounding, through the lessons of history, his conviction that the breakdown of authority and social order leads only to more cruelty and suffering than before. It is not likely that this man, who understood human nature better than anyone, was wrong – the experience of our tragic century has proved how much more right he was about society than liberal and democratic illusions about it, or than Victorian optimists were. We see the consequences of the breakdown in 15th-century England in the next play.

—— oOo ——

Ireland was, as usual, unfortunately topical. In the prolonged conflict with Spain the Elizabethans could not allow the neighbouring island to be conquered by the enemy. A post arrives,

> To signify that rebels there are up,
> And put the Englishmen unto the sword.
> Send succours, lords, and stop the rage betime,
> Before the wound do grow uncurable.

We hear of the 'uncivil kerns of Ireland': this is what the Elizabethans thought them, not having the advantage of our anthropological knowledge to explain a primitive pre-medieval society; 'uncivil' meant not reduced to civility. The 'gallowglass' we hear of are the warrior following of the Celtic tribal chieftains, who kept Northern Ireland and the Hebrides in constant turmoil during Elizabeth's reign.

Places referred to are familiar. York summons his armed following to St. George's Field: this was one of the chief training grounds for the musters at the time, on Bankside between Southwark and Lambeth. Bedlam was on the way out of the City through Bishopsgate to the theatres in Shoreditch; Robert Greene was to be buried there in 1592.

The countryman addicted to out-of-doors sports reveals himself again:

> Believe me, lords, for flying at the brook –

this was the regular term for hawking by the waterside, evidently for waterbirds, duck and mallard.

> I saw not better sport these seven years' day;
> Yet, by your leave, the wind was very high,
> And, ten to one, old Joan had not gone out –

i.e. the old bird had not flown. Capering

> upright like a wild morisco,
> Shaking the bloody darts as he his bells,

takes us back to the Cotswolds, where morris-dancing never died out, and whence its general revival in this century came. And what are we to think of the reference,

> . . . like rich hangings in a homely house?

Rich hangings in a great house were no rarity; but Wilmcote, his mother's home, was exceptional for the large number of hangings in a farmhouse.

There are two texts of this play: that of the Quarto published in 1594 under the title, *The First Part of the Contention of York and Lancaster*, and that of the First Folio, which was based partly upon that and partly upon the Company's fuller transcript of the author's manuscript. This complicated process of transmission gave rise to doubtful readings and much discussion; printers added their mistakes. The confusion has now been largely cleared up and does not anyway detract from enjoyment of the play. For modern production it needs cutting, which is precisely what the Shakespearean actors did, as we see from the shorter Quarto version.

THE THIRD PART OF
King Henry VI
1591

The Third Part of this trilogy is less varied and interesting than the Second; it had such refractory and (to us) more monotonous material to deal with in the ding-dong feuds, slanging-matches and battles of the Wars of the Roses. The dramatist did a most competent job in licking this elongated Chronicle material into shape, foreshortening periods of time for dramatic effect, etc. Nor did this mean that the Third Part was any less effective with the Elizabethans. For Shakespeare gave them a somewhat different mixture and turned out a revenge-play, a kind that was highly popular at the time, with Kyd's *The Spanish Tragedy* and his lost 'Hamlet'. At this same time the practical actor, with his eye on box-office appeal, was turning out another revenge-play, *Titus Andronicus* (going one better than Kyd in horrors), which has many analogies with *3 Henry VI*.

Here revenge is a *leit-motiv*: Clifford specifically declares his motive for killing York's boy, Rutland, in that York killed Clifford's father; the sons of York declare revenge upon Queen Margaret, for York's death, so that here we have the murder of Henry VI in the Tower, while the killing of his son at Tewkesbury is to come in *Richard III*. Richard's character is being carefully prepared here and headed for the next play Shakespeare has in mind. The trilogy is to become a tetralogy, or quartet of plays.

We note further improvement in the verse: the actor is developing rapidly as a poet. Fine, and very long, speeches are characteristic of this play – the most famous being Henry VI's soliloquy reflecting on the misery of his position, the horror of the war and how much better it would be to be a simple country swain. These speeches are developed in accordance with the rules of school rhetoric, *inventio*, *vituperatio*, and all that. Henry's is a refreshing contrast in its preference for rustic simplicity: he is the only person who disclaims such motives as revenge, but is ineffective and therefore becomes a victim. His weakness is a prime cause of the troubles, but the effective power-seekers are – or are to be – no better off. The most malign among them, Richard, will receive his due in the next play. Meanwhile, he says to Warwick:

> Thy brother's blood the thirsty earth hath drunk,
> Broached with the steely point of Clifford's lance;
> And in the very pangs of death he cried,
> Like to a dismal clangor heard from far,
> 'Warwick! Revenge! Brother, revenge my death!'

This recalls Lodge's reminiscence of Kyd's original 'Hamlet': 'the ghost which cried so miserably at the Theatre [i.e. Burbage's in Shoreditch], like an oyster-wife, "Hamlet, revenge!"' The most popular play of 1591 and 1592 was *The Spanish Tragedy*, and in the Third Part of *Henry VI* we find the actor-dramatist competing with Kyd's revenge-play. The word itself occurs more frequently than in any other of his plays, far more than in *Hamlet*. But what an almighty development was to take place between this and that!

Revenge is the dominant theme of *3 Henry VI* (as with *Titus Andronicus*). Nemesis followed for the perpetrators of those historic crimes. The House of Lancaster paid for Henry IV's guilt in regard to Richard II in the Yorkist murders of Henry VI and his son. The Yorkists paid for theirs in the killing of Richard, Duke of York, and later on of Clarence at the hand of his brother, Edward IV. Then Richard III outdid them all with his murders not only of Henry VI but of his brother's great friend Hastings and his brother's children in the Tower. The concept 'Machiavellian' is first applied to him in this play, in a forceful speech which develops his character and foretells the future:

> I can add colours to the chameleon,
> Change shapes with Proteus for advantages,
> And set the murderous Machiavel to school.
> Can I do this, and cannot get a crown?
> Tut! were it further off, I'll pluck it down.

And he did! – a remarkable achievement in its malign way, aided by the chance of his brother's early death.

The play is full of the sudden turns and changes of fortune, the ups and downs of each side in turn – and indeed the wheel of Fortune is a recurring image. This was the dominant theme with Kyd, and witnesses again to his influence, to which Ben Jonson testified; Kyd, Marlowe and the actor were writing in some proximity. The play again has notable reflections, virtual quotations from Marlowe. Here is one from *Tamburlaine*:

> How sweet a thing it is to wear a crown,
> Within whose circuit is Elysium
> And all that poets feign of bliss and joy.

Another line –

> And we are graced with wreaths of victory –

comes from *The Massacre at Paris*, which is also of this very time, for it ends with the murder of Henri III in 1589.

A theme which everyone has commented upon is that so close to Shakespeare's mind and heart: the breakdown of social order and the consequent release of men's aggressiveness and cruelty with the collapse of authority or impotence of government. For all the sympathy with which he is drawn as a man, Henry VI is not let off the responsibility that is laid at his door – by both sides, most bitterly by Queen Margaret, who is driven to fury by his feebleness. We watch her becoming the virago she is destined to be in *Richard III*.

With the anarchy that ensues comes the degeneration of morality, the prevalence of perjury, the breaking of oaths and unscrupulous shifts from side to side. It is the young Richard who proclaims openly,

> An oath is of no moment, being not took
> Before a true and lawful magistrate
> That hath authority over him that swears.
> Henry had none, but did usurp the place.

So the Yorkists break their oath to King Henry, and the compromise he sought to arrange by making York Regent, while retaining merely the title of king for his own life. But neither did this arrangement appeal to Queen Margaret and her son. Both sides were eager to fight and kill: it is a bloody play, and we are presented with much stabbing and killing on stage. At one point we have the horror: 'Enter a Son that hath killed his Father, with the body in his arms', followed shortly by: 'Enter a Father that hath killed his Son, with the body in his arms.'

In short, when authority breaks down anarchy ensues and politics becomes an open, ruthless power-struggle, which it should be the whole purpose of politics to direct in a civilised manner, to canalise men's aggressiveness into beneficent courses, for the good of society. As the Prince of Wales says:

> If that be right which Warwick says is right,
> There is no wrong, but every thing is right.

(The Prince was to be killed at Tewkesbury, Warwick at Barnet within a month of each other in 1471.)

Shakespeare has no illusions about the people, here any more than anywhere else. King Henry says,

> Look, as I blow this feather from my face,
> And as the air blows it to me again,
> Obeying with my wind when I do blow,
> And yielding to another when it blows,
> Commanded always by the greater gust,
> Such is the lightness of you common men.

He goes on to beseech them:

> But do not break your oaths . . .

In vain, of course. For what is the point of beseeching? Power is what they obey, the better if dressed up in a little brief authority, to mitigate the struggle for survival at the bottom of all existence. Of course, there are times in history when people become ungovernable and nothing *can* be done. Henry VI's reign formed one of them; then the naked struggle for survival surfaces in all its reptilian horror.

—— oOo ——

A respite from the struggle is given us in only one or two scenes. King Henry takes time off from the battlefield to moralise like the countryman he fain would be:

> What time the shepherd, blowing of his nails,
> Can neither call it perfect day nor night.

This Cotswold image will come to mind in the country song that ends *Love's Labour's Lost*. How much happier the King would be if he were but a country shepherd tending his flock:

> So many days my ewes have been with young:
> So many weeks ere the poor fools will ean [give birth];
> So many years ere I shall sheer the fleece . . .
> Gives not the hawthorn bush a sweeter shade
> To shepherds looking on their silly sheep,
> Than doth a rich embroidered canopy
> To kings that fear their subjects' treachery?

Or, in modern terms, to politicians, fearing the treachery of colleagues.

> . . . the shepherd's homely curds,
> His cold thin drink out of his leather bottle,
> His wonted sleep under a fresh tree's shade,
> All which secure and sweetly he enjoys,
> Is far beyond a prince's delicates.

Here speak the preferences of the countryman, who achieved success in London, but never lost touch with the country and preferred to return to it.

Another scene that is a let-up from the horrors of high politics and the power-struggle at the top – compare the bloodshed through which Hitler and Stalin, and many others, waded to power in our time – is the scene in which Edward IV seeks to win Elizabeth Woodville, Lady Grey, for mistress and, failing that, woos her for wife. A delightful scene in itself, it is one of the play's quick changes. Quickest of all, and more important to the action, is that in which Warwick, on embassy to Louis XI to arrange a marriage for Edward IV to a French princess, receives the humiliating news of his marriage to the Lancastrian widow. Warwick immediately reverses course and goes over to Queen Margaret and her son: they begin to tread the Calvary that leads to Barnet and Tewkesbury – the Yorkist triumph.

—— oOo ——

It is from this play that comes the line addressed to Queen Margaret,

> O tiger's heart wrapped in a woman's hide!

which Greene parodied with his 'Tiger's heart wrapped in a player's hide', in his attack on Shakespeare and his profession. We need say no more about the matter, except that it is one more indication of the success these plays achieved, which won for him the notice and then the patronage of Southampton. Shortly we find a line from the play reflected in a sonnet: Clarence's

> I will not ruinate my father's house,

is echoed in the early sonnet:

> Seeking that beauteous house to ruinate
> Which to repair should be thy chief desire.

Here is an image,

> Like one that stands upon a promontory
> And spies a far-off shore where he would tread,
> Wishing his foot were equal with his eye,
> And chides the sea, that sunders him from thence –

which has an echo in a Sonnet:

> Let this sad interim like the ocean be
> Which parts the shore, where two contracted new
> Come daily to the banks . . .

The thought is different, the image similar. The rare word 'promontory' is contemporaneously repeated in *Titus Andronicus*. One wonders where he had been touring recently: Dover?, as the Chamberlain's men did later.

Warwickshire is to the fore in the last Act, and places are named which could be familiar to him along the route from London. We have Southam, near Banbury, Dunsmore upon Watling Street, and Daventry, given its old pronunciation of Daintry. Sir John Somerville appears, of the Warwickshire Catholic family which had got into trouble in 1583 for conspiracy against the Queen; this had involved the North Warwickshire Ardens.

Richard's murder of Henry VI in the Tower brings up familiar associations:

29

> So flies the reckless shepherd from the wolf;
> So first the harmless sheep doth yield his fleece,
> And next his throat unto the butcher's knife.

This, significantly enough, suggests acting, for it is immediately followed by –

> What scene of death hath Roscius now to act?

Amid all the metropolitan horrors, as again notably with *Titus*, the countryman speaks – as never with Marlowe – in out-of-door sports: several references to hawking and falconry; we have a brace of greyhounds

> Having the fearful-flying hare in sight –

shortly to be given extended treatment in the description of hare-coursing inserted into *Venus and Adonis*. Park-keepers in a chase in the North discover the poor wandering King, who has crossed the Border from Scotland:

> 1ST KEEPER: Under this thick-grown brake we'll shroud ourselves,
> For through this laund [glade] anon the deer will come;
> And in this covert will we make our stand,
> Culling the principal of all the deer.
> 2ND KEEPER: I'll stay above the hill, so both may shoot.
> 1ST KEEPER: That cannot be: the noise of thy cross-bow
> Will scare the herd, and so my shoot is lost.

The reading, the classical quotations are more than ever from Ovid, a chief favourite with Marlowe too, and from the Bible, less in favour with Marlowe. And we have glimpses of subjects in mind that were later to form plays, especially *Julius Caesar*.

—— oOo ——

An actor's version of the play, suitably cut, was printed in 1595 as the Quarto, *The True Tragedy of Richard Duke of York, and the Death of good King Henry the Sixth*, etc. This, with the Company's transcript from the author's manuscript, formed the basis of the fuller Folio text. Each supplied omissions and emendations from the other, and added dubious readings and errors to the author's natural inconsistencies over such a large canvas. The author seems to have added actors' names he had in mind: in this play, Gabriel, presumably Gabriel Spencer, whom Ben Jonson killed in a duel; also 'Humfrey' and 'Sinklo' or Sinkler, who is named also as appearing in *The Taming of the Shrew*.

King Richard III
1592

Richard III is the first of the plays to hold the stage unbrokenly from Shakespeare's day to this. It has always been popular, and it is easy to see why. It offers exciting drama as such, completely integrated as the chronicle plays of *Henry VI* could not hope to be; though it is the longest, except for *Hamlet*, one's attention is compelled at every moment. Above all, it has the fascination of presenting Shakespeare's first fully developed character as a psychological study. Dr. Johnson spotted the psychotic interest of Richard's character – he is not merely a Machiavellian villain: 'the wickedness of Richard proceeded from his deformity, from the envy that rose at the comparison of his own person with others, and which incited him to disturb the pleasures that he could not partake.'

In short, Richard takes his place as first in the remarkable gallery of psychotic characters – Richard II, Othello and perhaps Iago (to whom Richard is closest akin), Macbeth and Lady Macbeth, King Lear and Leontes – who have their special appeal to modern psycho-analysis. The findings of modern psychology – Oedipus complex, paranoia, schizophrenia – Shakespeare remarkably prefigured. His knowledge of the human personality was not only that of external observation but of an unsurpassed understanding of the intuitive and the subconscious.

This had its first full expression in *Richard III*, whose personality lent itself obviously to the treatment. Shakespeare understood Richard as he was in historic fact with his usual penetration; the only thing he added was a certain gaiety, a self-conscious delight in doing evil, which was not present in the historic Richard, who was a morose, rather grim character, in contrast to his brothers, Edward IV and Clarence, who were both exceptionally handsome men.

The play is sometimes described, depreciatingly, as a melodrama. But this is only Greek for a musical, and it would make a striking modern musical, as *West Side Story* was made out of *Romeo and Juliet* – such is the undying vitality of Shakespeare's creations.

—— oOo ——

Richard has abounding vitality, a marked character of his own, already adumbrated in *3 Henry VI*; this is in its way a source of attraction. Sixteenth century people were fairly close to Richard – after all, it was Elizabeth I's grandfather who had given him his comeuppance – and knew perfectly well what was what about him. Shakespeare's portrait derives, through Holinshed and Hall, mainly from Sir Thomas More. St. Thomas More was a truth-telling man of great political intelligence and close observation, who had still closer sources of information as to Richard's *coup d'état*, his usurpation of his nephew's throne, and his murders of his brother's boys in the Tower. More was a friend of the Earl of Surrey, afterwards Duke of Norfolk, who was in the room when Richard arrested his brother's chief friend, Hastings, and haled him out to summary execution without any pretence at trial. After that there was no turning back, as Richard says in the play – he is so far *in*. More knew Richard FitzJames, Bishop of London, and others who were on the spot; his father, Sir John More, was a young lawyer in the city at the time.

Everybody knew what Richard was and what he had done, though the murders were kept a dark secret, and the details were covered up – More as a trained lawyer ferreted them out. In the ghastly Wars of the Roses people had become familiarised with the killings of opponents – after all Richard was known to have been in the Tower the night that Henry VI was murdered there; but it was not the thing to murder women or children. This was what turned the country's stomach against Richard, and accounted for the defection of his leading supporter, Buckingham. The play itself employs the word 'homicide' for him: the term of the Act of Parliament which condemned him after Bosworth. Actually, at Bosworth, where his army was twice the size of Henry Tudor's, only Richard's cronies fought for him. The Howard 'Jack of Norfolk', whom he had made Duke, was killed with Richard. In Shakespeare's time Norfolk's great-grandson, Lord Henry Howard, in his *Defensative against Supposed Prophecies* (1583), in the decade before the play, gives us the Howard family tradition as to Richard's 'heinous' crime. They knew. Everybody knew. It needs no discussing.

One marked difference is that where More treats Richard with grave and subtle irony, much more searing, Shakespeare treats him with his usual high spirits. The play has even a comic aspect. Richard is a conscious hypocrite, over and over, notably in the scene where he displays such reluctance to assume the burden of the crown. In fact, at the time of his *coup d'état*, Richard did a certain amount of ham-acting, which took in nobody; Buckingham had to play up too. This becomes, as the actor-dramatist describes from experience:

RICHARD: Come cousin, canst thou quake, and change thy colour,
 Murder thy breath in middle of a word,
 And then again begin, and stop again,
 As if thou wert distraught and mad with terror?
BUCKINGHAM: Tut, I can counterfeit the deep tragedian,
 Speak and look back, and pry on every side,
 Tremble and start at wagging of a straw,
 Intending deep suspicion: ghastly looks
 Are at my service, like enforcèd smiles . . .

Elizabethan acting was oratorical and emphatic – needs must with open-air theatres – very gestural and formal.[1]

Shakespeare took obvious delight in exploring the crevices of his tragic hero – for there is something heroic in Richard's ambition and scheming against such odds, and his eventual arriving where he intended to be, as also his fate was tragic. More subtlety appears in his depiction than in any of Shakespeare's characters so far. One notices the element of neurosis in Richard: in his last interview with Buckingham he is beginning to lose control; on receiving the bad news of Buckingham's revolt, he strikes the messenger and then rewards him 'to cure that blow of thine'. Dr. Johnson noticed a subtlety that few notice. In the very first scene Richard says to Clarence:

> Whatso'er you will employ me in,
> Were it to call King Edward's *widow* sister,
> I will perform it.

It is a subtle invitation to speed their brother out of this world: his wife is not yet a widow. At Buckingham's revolt Richard is nerve-racked with anxiety – and no wonder, all that he had done was becoming too much for him. While, in the night before Bosworth, tortured by dreams and the ghosts of his victims – the lights 'burn blue' as in *Julius Caesar* – one can sympathise with him, facing his fearful fate. (The body of an anointed king would never have been so maltreated, as it was after Bosworth, had he not been the criminal he was – led on by the mania for power, like Hitler, who came to a similarly squalid end.)

In spite of this being a one-man play – and so a favourite with great actors, from Burbage onwards – other characters are sufficiently individualised. Queen Margaret appears again in her role of Cassandra; Edward IV's Queen Elizabeth is drawn as the feather-headed light-weight she was, not knowing which way to turn, poor woman. Hastings is the over-confident, lusty extrovert, boon-companion of Edward IV in their womanising. We have no reason to doubt that Richard's disapproval of this was genuine: an unattractive type physically, unlike his two handsome brothers, he was envious and disapproving (again understandably: he is getting his own back). Clarence is the 'false, fleeting, perjured' Clarence: wonderfully good-looking and no good at all. Even his murderers are well-contrasted; the second murderer hasn't the heart to go on with it, and there is a comically realistic passage which is pure Shakespeare on the lower orders:

> I'll not meddle with it: it makes a man a coward. A man cannot steal,
> but it accuseth him; a man cannot swear, but it checks him; a man
> cannot lie with his neighbour's wife, but it detects him.

And so on: 'some certain dregs of conscience are yet within me.'
Richard's answer to that sort of thing is:

> Conscience is but a word that cowards use,
> Devised at first to keep the strong in awe.

His argument is that often advanced at critical junctures – 'the necessity
and state of times.' It is in keeping with the casuistry of high politics, and
testifies to Shakespeare's growing understanding of their inwardness:

> Look what is done cannot be now amended:
> Men shall deal unadvisedly sometimes,
> Which after-hours gives leisure to repent.

What makes this a tragedy rather than a melodrama is that he had been
cruelly tempted and he cruelly fell: if only he had been able to produce the
Princes alive from the Tower, he would have been able to answer his
enemies. He never could: they were dead precisely two years before
Bosworth, never seen alive after August 1483, when Richard sent the
order for their murder from Warwick Castle.

Of the dreams, omens, prophecies, curses that send a shiver down the
spine in these plays, the most justly famous dream – along with Richard's
before Bosworth – is Clarence's in the Tower. He dreams beforehand his
death by drowning:

> Methought I saw a thousand fearful wracks,
> A thousand men that fishes gnawed upon;
> Wedges of gold, great ingots, heaps of pearl,
> Inestimable stones, unvalued jewels,
> All scattered in the bottom of the sea:
> Some lay in dead men's skulls; and in the holes
> Where eyes did once inhabit there were crept,
> As 'twere in scorn of eyes, reflecting gems . . .

This would become in the far future, more concisely:

> Those are pearls that were his eyes.

Brackenbury, Constable of the Tower, comments as Clarence falls asleep:

> Princes have but their titles for their glories,
> An outward honour for an inward toil;
> And for unfelt imaginatìons
> They often feel a world of restless cares
> So that between their titles and low name
> There's nothing differs but the outward fame.

This would become the dominant theme of the second tetralogy – *Richard II, 1 & 2 Henry IV, Henry V.*

We notice from these speeches, indeed from the famous first lines of the play, how rapidly the verse has matured from the *Henry VI* plays: the actor is now writing verse with absolute confidence, conviction and precision:

> Now is the winter of our discontent
> Made glorious summer by this sun of York.

In one of the *Parnassus* plays at Cambridge a few years later, in which the triumphs of the London stage and its authors were made fun of, we see how famous these lines had already become. Burbage is trying out a young scholar for the part:

> BURBAGE: I like your face and the proportion of your body for Richard III. I pray you, Master Philomusus, let me see you act a little of it.

The young scholar immediately fires off with

> Now is the winter of our discontent
> Made glorious by the sun of York.

The line to become most famous was Richard's cry at Bosworth when unhorsed:

> A horse! a horse! My kingdom for a horse!

This line was repeated and parodied again and again. Burbage was so famous in the role he created that when delightful Bishop Corbet was being shown over the battlefield a generation later, the guide quoted it, but 'when he would have said "King Richard died", he "Burbage" cried.'

Success registered itself, too, in London folklore, the kind of story told about those who come across to people's minds as persons, and which they take pleasure in retailing. Manningham wrote in his Diary in 1602: 'Upon a time when Burbage played Richard III there was a citizen grew so far in liking with him that, before she went from the play, she appointed him to come that night unto her by the name of Richard III. Shakespeare, overhearing their conclusion, went before, was entertained and at his game ere Burbage came. The message being brought that Richard III was at the door, Shakespeare caused return to be made that William the Conqueror was before Richard III.'

So popular was the play that there was a continual demand for it in print – which it was not to the interest of Shakespeare or the Company to supply. Somehow, almost certainly through actors, the printers got hold of a shortened, acting version of the play for print as a quarto, which came out in 1597. Between then and 1622 no less than six editions were called for, a number equalled only by the quarto of *1 Henry IV* in which Falstaff figures. It would seem that Richard III and Falstaff were two favourite characters with the Elizabethan public.

Shakespeare himself was so swept up into his subject that the play does not contain many references to anything extraneous. The play is a Marlovian one in the sense of its being dominated by one character and that a Machiavellian villain. I notice a verbal reminiscence of Dr. Faustus's end in Richard's night-thoughts before Bosworth:

> I shall despair. There is no creature loves me;
> And if I die, no soul will pity me.

There is a less obvious echo from Greene's *Farewell to Folly* (1591) in

> My conscience hath a thousand several tongues;

but this may be an Elizabethan commonplace. In the lines –

> Look how my ring encompasseth thy finger,
> Even so thy breast encloseth my poor heart –

I detect the kind of thought running all through the Sonnets contemporaneously. The play can hardly have come long after the Third Part of *Henry VI*; so 1592 would seem to be about right for its date.

—— oOo ——

The Folio text in 1623 of this long play was based upon that of the latest quarto, of 1622, which went back to earlier printed versions, compared with one which had served for a prompt book in the theatre. The result was many misprints and dubious readings, which have provided good game for textual editors. These have never stood in the way of the general enjoyment of Shakespeare's first great play.

---

1. Joseph, Bertram Leon *Elizabethan Acting* (Oxford University Press, London, 1951)

King Richard II
1595

Richard II is an utterly different play from *Richard III*; where that was melodramatic, with a distinctly comic aspect in the drawing of the hero-villain, *Richard II* is a lyrical tragedy, highly poetic, with not a joke in it. Exceptionally, it is all verse, with a great deal of rhyme, not only to punctuate the conclusion of speeches and scenes. The verse has a curious feature, which it shares with *King John*, that followed on the heels of this play: both have a number of sestets, rhyming ab ab cc. The whole tone of *Richard II* – except for the patriotic note which it shares with *King John* – is different: it has more in common with the lyrical tragedy of *Romeo and Juliet*, which it followed.

Not much difficulty about date, which is usually assumed to be 1595. Shakespeare drew on Samuel Daniel's *Civil Wars*, of early 1595; they were kindred spirits, drawn together by association with Florio, and there were mutual exchanges in their work – they were not ashamed to be indebted to one another. At the end of 1595 Sir Edward Hoby wrote inviting Sir Robert Cecil to supper in Canon Row, Westminster, 'where as late as it shall please you a gate for your supper shall be open, and King Richard present himself to your view.' It is probable that this refers to the new play, as it is a more intimate, shorter play, with a smaller cast. Hoby was Lord Chamberlain Hunsdon's son-in-law; the Chamberlain's Men would be available for an evening performance. The busy Robert Cecil, doing all the work of Secretary of State, minuted laconically: 'Readily'.

Shakespeare drew upon Holinshed as usual for his English history, but he also looked up a French chronicle for the events of Richard's reign. The Plantagenet royal house was French; Richard was pro-French, in favour of peace with France. His speech was French, as was the language of the Court until Henry IV and the Lancastrians. Though Richard was king of England, he does not make any of the patriotic speeches: they are given to John of Gaunt.

In historic fact Richard II was an aesthete, like Charles I; both were unsuccessful as rulers, and came to tragic ends in consequence. Again and again we find in Shakespeare this confrontation between a ruler who is a failure politically and the effective political type – an Antony as against Octavius, Henry VI as against York and his sons; here the political type, who has the gift for rule, is Bolingbroke. Richard II is not. In historic fact he was a non-combatant; we may share his preference for peace, but it militated against him in the jungle of medieval politics and war. He was also a neurotic; having been a king since he was a child turned his head. In the last years of his absolutism he would sit in hall wearing his crown, silent, and anyone who caught his gaze had to abase himself. A line in the play suggests that Shakespeare may have known the tradition. Richard, contemplating himself in the glass, says:

> Was this the face
> That like the sun did make beholders wink?

The strain of rule was too much for him. Most important: he could not be trusted. This was a fatal flaw in a monarch, as was the case with Charles I: there must be a last court of appeal whose word everybody can trust and therefore accept. Oliver Cromwell decided that he could not trust Charles I's word. Bolingbroke was in a similar position with Richard II: it was simply the sense of self-preservation, in the struggle for survival, that led him forward from claiming his rights as Duke of Lancaster to taking Richard's throne. Had he not, with a turn in the political tide, or in the ups-and-downs of the bucket which are an image in the play – Richard would have had him by the neck. The Duke of York warns Bolingbroke:

> Take not, good cousin, further than you should,
> Lest you mistake the heavens are over our heads.

Bolingbroke is well aware:

> I know it, uncle, and oppose not myself
> Against their will.

The heavens, i.e. the political tide, were with him.

It was a fundamental mistake on Richard's part to have withheld Bolingbroke's inheritance from him: it created a sense of insecurity throughout the governing class, sufficiently alienated by Richard's misrule already, and gave them an able leader to overthrow his 'tyranny', i.e. irresponsible rule. Coming to the crown, Bolingbroke shows that he has, what Richard had not, this fundamental quality in a real sovereign (cf. George Washington or Abraham Lincoln): *justice of mind*. He does not allow his resentment as a private person, his sense of injury, to influence the justice he metes out as a sovereign. Henry is willing to restore his former enemy, Mowbray:

> Repealed he shall be
> And, though mine enemy, restored again
> To all his former lands and signories.

Aumerle enters into conspiracy against him; as King, Henry judges him:

> Intended, or committed, was this fault?
> If on the first, how heinous e'er it be,
> To win thy after-love I pardon thee.

Such rulers deserve to win: Richard, whatever his good qualities – he was a patron of the arts – was incapable of it: he always acted for personal motives, out of personal resentment, etc. And he would not be advised: historically, so long as his uncle Gaunt was alive to keep things together, Richard kept his throne. After Gaunt's death things went to pieces; Richard surrounded himself with a lot of flatterers. And what a fool he was to go off to Ireland, leaving the coast clear for an injured Bolingbroke to descend upon!

—— oOo ——

The tragedy was not so much in Bolingbroke's usurpation: the country (the 'heavens') called him to the throne – but in Richard's murder. Here we are up against one of those inextricable knots in history, which make for true tragedy: neither side could help himself, each was in the clutch of ineluctable forces. Richard *had* to go; Henry *had* to take his place. We must not forget that Henry was Richard's heir in the male line, and Richard had no children. But so long as Richard remained alive, he was a constant threat to the security of the throne. At the first move to restore him – his friends did him no good, as so often in history – he was made away with.

And that was worse than crime, it was sacrilege against the sacred person of an anointed king. Everybody understood that at the time, when we understand it only with the aid of anthropology. It inflicted a terrible sense of guilt upon a medieval person such as Henry IV, and may well have been a factor in the disease that afflicted him. The divinity that shrouds the sacramental person of a monarch is expressed in the famous lines:

> Not all the water in the rough rude sea
> Can wash the balm off from an anointed king.

It is the same anthropological necessity whether among the peoples in what used to be darkest Africa, or in the enlightened and rationalistic United States: the assassination of a President arouses quasi-religious horror.

The sequel was, as Richard's chief supporter, the Bishop of Carlisle, prophesied:

> The blood of English shall manure the ground
> And future ages groan for this foul act . . .
> And in this seat of peace tumultous wars
> Shall kin with kin and kind with kind confound.

This was given its chance with the next incapable ruler to succeed, Henry's grandson, Henry VI.

Popularity is a weapon in the political game, as all politicians know; some command it with ease. Others cannot, however well they have deserved of the state: Churchill never could, until the state was in dire peril. Bolingbroke deliberately cultivated popularity, and was rewarded on his entry into London:

> Whilst he, from the one side to the other turning,
> Bareheaded, lower than his proud steed's neck,
> Bespake them thus, 'I thank you, countrymen.'

The common people, whom Richard had never considered, threw 'dust upon his sacred head' – anthropologically, a fallen king becomes a sacrificial victim. One of his followers knows what to think of that, and of them:

> And that's the wavering commons; for their love
> Lies in their purses, and whoso empties them,
> By so much fills their hearts with deadly hate.

(Shakespeare never lets up in his reflections on them.) Power is what matters in politics; Richard knew that well enough:

> Yet I well remember
> The favours of these men. Were they not mine?
> Did they not sometime cry 'All hail' to me?

Very well – then he should have kept a more careful grip on the levers of power.

Having lost it, he takes refuge in self-pity – and Shakespeare gives him most of the poetry of the play, and much of the sympathy. It is usual to find the man, under the king, more appealing than he deserves: in my view anyone who loses control in circumstances so favourable to him deserves what he gets. Dr. Johnson, though tender at heart, felt something of this. 'It seems to be the design of the poet to raise Richard to esteem in his fall, and consequently to interest the reader in his favour. He gives him only passive fortitude, the virtue of a confessor rather than of a king. In his prosperity we saw him imperious and oppressive, but in his distress he is wise, patient, and pious.' Even this is an overgenerous judgement: one knows what Richard would have done to Bolingbroke, whom he had treated with conspicuous injustice, if he had had the chance.

Shakespeare did his best for him: he turned the aesthete into a poet. Many beautiful passages occur in which Richard indulges his self-pity.

—— oOo ——

Patriotism was an element in the play's appeal. The exuberant jubilation of a small people – only half an island, as Pope Sixtus V said admiringly – who had come through the test of the struggle with the Spanish world-empire, led to a spirit of pride, self-confidence and boasting that went with youthfulness. Gaunt is given this theme to celebrate, not the King:

> This happy breed of men, this little world,
> This precious stone set in the silver sea,
> Which serves it in the office of a wall,
> Or as a moat defensive to a house,
> Against the envy of less happier lands.

In my time at school we learnt it by heart, and had reason to believe it – no point in it today. Gaunt's splendid apostrophe, developed in accordance with school rhetoric, 'even in American performances', we learn, 'usually evokes a solid round of applause' – but that must have been after the comparably heroic experience of 1940-45.

> England, bound in with the triumphant sea,
> Whose rocky shore beats back the envious siege
> Of wat'ry Neptune, is now bound in with shame

– as it might be, a supine and work-shy demotic society.

Elizabethan England was apt to be choosy about immigrants, selecting only the best, and – like all youthful peoples – anti-foreign. For all that Italy provided such inspiration in the arts, ordinary Protestants looked on her as a school of vice, particularly in its more sophisticated forms – whoring after

> Report of fashions in proud Italy,
> Whose manners still our tardy apish nation
> Limps after in base imitation –

i.e. the English were backward, slow to catch up.

Richard II had a topical significance which is hard for us to catch. With Elizabeth I, as with Richard II, the succession was an open question, much in men's minds but dangerous to touch. Essex, darling of the people, pursued popularity; some people thought of him as another Bolingbroke. Richard noted his behaviour much as Elizabeth did Essex's, and

> Observed his courtship to the common people;
> How he did seem to dive into their hearts
> With humble and familiar courtesy . . .
> Wooing poor craftsmen with the craft of smiles.
> Off goes his bonnet to an oyster-wench;
> A brace of draymen bid God speed him well . . .
> As were our England in reversion his.

A follower of Essex, Sir John Hayward, dedicated his account of Boling-broke's assumption of the crown to Essex, rather too obviously, and was sent to the Tower for it. Some joke about Richard II passed between Essex and Sir Robert Cecil, to what effect we do not know. On the eve of Essex's Rebellion in 1601, his agents bribed the Company at the Globe to put on *Richard II*, then an old play, but with its deposition scene to suggest ideas to the audience. The government did not blame the players, but the Queen was furious: 'I am Richard II, know ye not that? This tragedy was played forty times in open streets and houses.'

It was popular, if not as much so as *Richard III*. Three quartos of it appeared in rapid succession in 1597 and 1598; but the deposition scene was censored, until James I had been safely on the throne for some years.

—— oOo ——

As in every one of Shakespeare's works, plays, poems, or sonnets, we find revealing references to his profession:

> As in a theatre the eyes of men,
> After a well-graced actor leaves the stage,
> Are idly bent on him that enters next,
> Thinking his prattle to be tedious . . .

That brings him immediately before us: we know that he was well-graced as an actor himself.

It is usual to compare *Richard II* with *Edward II*; actually there is much less of Marlowe's influence in this than there was in *Richard III*, and a world of difference in tone and atmosphere. The one reflection we may detect is where Bolingbroke charges Richard's favourites, Bushy and Green:

> You have in manner with your sinful hours
> Made a divorce betwixt his Queen and him,
> Broke the possession of a royal bed,
> And stained the beauty of a fair Queen's cheeks
> With tears drawn from her eyes by your foul wrongs.

There is no warrant for this in historic fact: Richard's Queen was at the time a child of eight. Shakespeare is thinking of Edward II's neglect of *his* Queen for his lover, Gaveston. No homosexual interest appears in Shake-speare, though in life Richard doted on Robert de Vere, and made him, absurdly, Duke of Ireland. Richard's grand passion is rigorously excluded; this aspect of things did not appeal to the heterosexual, family man – as it did to Marlowe, Bacon and the Earl of Oxford.

We see the subjects of past and future plays teeming in his mind, in 'the sad stories of the deaths of kings':

> How some have been deposed, some slain in war,
> Some haunted by the ghosts they have deposed,
> Some poisoned by their wives, some sleeping killed –

we recognise Kyd's Hamlet waiting to leap out and take shape in the most wonderful play ever written.

Music has a place in *Richard II*: one reference reminds us of the Sonnets:

> Or like a cunning instrument cased up
> Or, being open, put into his hands
> That knows no touch to tune the harmony.

This was not the case with the Lady of the Sonnets –

> How oft, my music, when thou music play'st –

with her fingers touching the jacks of the virginals. Shakespeare's immense sensitiveness to music must have added to her spell over him; and, perhaps significantly, with his unconscious associativeness of mind that betrays him to us, an echo from the Sonnets follows:

> Four lagging winters and four wanton springs.

That experience was not far away in 1595.

—— oOo ——

The text offers no particular problems. A good text was put out in 1597, subsequently reprinted, but without the deposition scene, so long as Elizabeth I lived and the succession was open. This was inserted in a fourth quarto of 1608, but from a faulty copy. This was corrected when it came to the Folio.

King John
1596

King John is different again from *Richard II*, though linked to it by the patriotic speeches about England and the sea, given to Richard Coeur-de-Lion's Bastard Faulconbridge, which echo those of John of Gaunt in the previous play. Where that was a lyrical tragedy, *King John* is a straight chronicle play. It is also coupled with *Richard II* in language, in particular, as we have noticed, by the feature of rhyming sestets which occur in both.

King John is a mature play, even more so than its predecessor: in characterisation, with the powerful characters of the Bastard and Constance, young Arthur's mother. And it is mature in language and in thought; the Bastard's famous speech on Commodity, i.e. political convenience or expediency, shows considered political observation, as does his engaging cynicism in general. So also does the convoluted casuistry of Cardinal Pandulph, verging on sophistry. This is not an early play.

Indeed we have an indication of date in the reference

> So, by a roaring tempest on the flood,
> A whole armado of convicted sail
> Is scattered and disjoined from fellowship.

This is precisely what happened to the second Armada, of the late summer of 1596, which was dispersed by tempest before it reached the English coast.

There had been plays on the subject of King John before, going back to the Protestant rant of the ex-friar John Bale. The subject was an obvious one in the common stock of subjects and themes from the English past, which expressed Elizabethan national pride and Renaissance self-consciousness. Shakespeare took an anonymous play ready to hand, *The Troublesome Reign of John, King of England*, and based himself on that. Holinshed also was drawn upon, with Foxe's *Martyrs* and the Book of Homilies read in church. His real source, as with any creative writer, was his own knowledge and experience, and his genius lit up the pedestrian draft he worked from, though some inferior fossils of it remain.

One thing that is characteristic of him – we are given none of the Protestant tirades of the time, much to the fore in Bale and Foxe. Shakespeare concerned himself with neither the religious nor political propaganda of the time; in that way he was a safe writer, who never got into trouble. This bespoke his nature; not only his courtly tact – he was above the vulgar passions that agitated ordinary people about politics and religion. His passion was human beings in their essence, their characters and conflicts, man as such.

Thus we have an outstanding portrayal of a very masculine type in Coeur-de-Lion's Bastard. Shakespeare created him with affection – he is more real to us than anybody in the play, with his downright, rather colloquial language: a no-nonsense fellow, akin to the too masculine Hotspur in *1 Henry IV*. The Bastard, from the fact of his birth, is an Outsider; this gives him the angle from which to observe society, its conventions and pretences. His first long speech is a comment on Elizabethan society much to the point, with its

> dialogue of compliment,
> And talking of the Alps and Apennines,
> The Pyrenean and the River Po –

this was 'worshipful', i.e. upper-class, society. It fitted his 'mounting spirit', his aim to move upwards, very well;

> For he is but a bastard to the time
> That doth not smack of observatiòn.

The precise meaning of this is a little difficult for us to catch; it suggests that not to pay attention to what other people are up to is out of keeping with the time.

With regard to them the Bastard has no illusions, as his speech on Commodity, the most famous in the play, makes clear. Commodity means people's self-interest, the sense of their own advantage and convenience, what they can gain, which deflects them from the straight course of justice and virtue, and makes the world run with the bias. (The image is from the gentlemanly game of bowls.) The world's bent this way

> Makes it take head from all indifferency,

i.e. deflects it from impartiality, always in the direction of self-interest. The Bastard has the candour to ask why he himself rails so against Commodity, and answers:

> But for because he hath not wooed me yet.

Such a candid confession is rare and charms us. The importance of his diagnosis for the action is that

> Since kings break faith upon Commodity,
> *Gain*, be my lord – for I will worship thee!

This expresses Shakespeare's mature thought about society – it hardly differs from Marx or Pareto on the subject. The Bastard's attitude on the humbug bandied about by the great – by the King of France, the Duke of Austria and Cardinal Pandulph, the Legate from Rome – on the political issues, King John's heretical taking of Church lands and his nephew's inheritance, his willingness to patch up a peace at his nephew's expense – is three times expressed thus:

> And being a calf's-skin on his recreant limbs.

A calf's-skin was the fool's livery, and this is what the Bastard awards those eminent politicians, humbugs all. They do not care about the rights and wrongs of poor young Arthur, for all that he was the son and heir of John's older brother: the boy is but a pawn in the world's game of political Commodity.

—— oOo ——

Constance, Arthur's widowed mother, reacts against the trafficking and bargaining, the *Kuh-handel*, with natural resentment. Her character too is fully developed; it progresses from her forlorn widowed state to apprehension, then anger and resentment at betrayal; lastly, driven crazy by grief, she becomes a virago like Queen Margaret in the earlier plays. The boy Arthur is charmingly portrayed, if a trifle too knowingly for our taste: that and the sentiment of his appeal to Hubert not to put out his eyes had strong appeal to the emotional Elizabethan audience. There would have been two well-trained boy-actors for those parts.

For us, who realise what was behind the boy's death, it has a more affecting appeal; for this summer saw the death of Shakespeare's own, and only, boy at Stratford at the age of eleven.

> Grief fills the room up of my absent child,
> Lies in his bed, walks up and down with me,
> Puts on his pretty looks, repeats his words,
> Remembers me of all his gracious parts,
> Stuffs out his vacant garments with his form.

The mother asks the Cardinal, who after all was a priest, whether it is true

> That we shall see and know our friends in heaven.
> If that be true, I shall see my boy again.

This is the father in William Shakespeare speaking; that Stratford was in his mind, or possibly he was writing at Stratford, we can tell – for immediately after talk of young Arthur's death, we have:

> I saw a smith stand with his hammer, thus,
> The whilst his iron did on the anvil cool,

> With open mouth swallowing a tailor's news;
> Who, with his shears and measure in his hand,
> Standing on slippers which his nimble haste
> Had falsely thrust upon contràry feet.

A neighbour in Henley Street was Hornby, the blacksmith; was there a tailor there too? Not improbably.

Other personal touches bespeak him. We are accustomed to the frequent images from his profession. The men of Angers

> . . . stand securely on their battlements
> As in a theatre, whence they gape and point
> At your industrious scenes and acts of death.

The soldiers on the battlements, so frequently referred to in these warring plays, would be up in the gallery looking down on the stage.

We have often noted his liking for grand, resounding words: 'expedient' march for swift march; 'his marches are expedient to this town'; for words ending in 'ure', creature, rondure, expressure. We have comments characteristic of him:

> For new-made honour doth forget men's names.

Again,

> Let not the world see fear and sad distrust
> Govern the motion of a kingly eye;

for 'inferior eyes borrow their behaviours from the great'. The 'lusty English' are described as 'like a jolly troop of huntsmen'. More important is the phrase that expresses Elizabethan thought on the soul:

> . . . his pure brain,
> Which some suppose the soul's frail dwelling-house.

—— oOo ——

Patriotism is the main argument of the play. The internal division between King John and his barons, plus the King's defiance of Rome, exposed the country to the French invasion. No opportunity is taken to inveigh against Rome, though the Legate Pandulph's statement of the issue is exposed as a tissue of unconvincing sophistry. A little expression is given to anti-French sentiment, notably the inconstancy imputed to the French and their readiness to break oaths. This reflected once more the bad impression made by Henry of Navarre's desertion of the Protestant cause.

Several salutes to England's chief defence in the sea, and the spirit of adventure overseas, are completely in line with the country's mood in the 1580s and early 1590s:

> . . . that pale, white-faced shore
> Whose foot spurns back the ocean's roaring tides
> And coops from other lands her islanders.

The islanders were adventuring abroad, voyaging, marauding, colonising, joining expeditions to fight on the Continent:

> . . . all the unsettled humours of the land,
> Rash, inconsiderate, fiery voluntaries . . .
> Have sold their fortunes at their native homes,
> Bearing their birthrights proudly on their backs,
> To make a hazard of new fortunes.

This was not only a commonplace of the time but common experience.

The moral of the play is that of all the early historical plays and is the expression of the nation's mood in the struggle with Spain: in unity lies strength, internal dissension exposes the country to social disorder and, in *King John*, to foreign invasion. The theme is set out in speeches which are a direct continuation of those of Gaunt in *Richard II*. The concluding lines summing up the play are justly famous:

> This England never did, nor never shall,
> Lie at the proud foot of a conqueror
> But when it first did help to wound itself . . .
> Come the three corners of the world in arms
> And we shall shock them! Naught shall make us rue
> If England to itself do rest but true!

The play was first printed in the First Folio; the text offers no problem. The absence of earlier printed versions or records of performance suggest that it was not one of the most popular plays. Nor is it an inspired play – coming from its author's inner spirit and answering to his romantic, lyrical nature – as its predecessor was. Sisson observes that here Shakespeare's 'heart was not in his work . . . his subject did not awaken in him the "Muse of fire"'; that it was in fact 'task-work'.

The material was rather refractory, and Shakespeare was hampered by the task he set himself of revising the anonymous *Troublesome Reign of King John*. We may observe, however, that it is when he gives reign to his own imagination, with his creation of the Bastard Faulconbridge and with the child Arthur and his mother, that the work takes flight.

THE FIRST PART OF
King Henry IV
1597-8

The two parts of *Henry IV* are the apogee of Shakespeare's English history plays; yet they differ from all the others in being almost equally chronicle plays and comedies. As such, in their mixture of history with fiction they are the ancestor of the historical novel; while Falstaff, their grand comic creation, is the progenitor of a type which abounds in English literature.

We must note the continuity provided by the dramatist's provident, planning mind. The action of *Henry IV* springs from Richard II's historic deposition; but even before becoming king Bolingbroke laments the 'unthrifty' course of his son and heir Prince Henry. He is sowing his wild oats with the old reprobate Falstaff and his boon companions; even so, at his first appearance with them, his regal future is foreshadowed:

> I know you all, and will awhile uphold
> The unyoked humour of your idleness . . .
> So when this loose behaviour I throw off,
> And pay the debt I never promised,
> By how much better than my word I am . . .
> My reformation, glittering o'er my fault,
> Shall show more goodly, and attract more eyes
> Than that which hath no foil to set it off.

In the event, he will 'redeem the time when men think least I will'. But the Prince, underneath his escapades, is not joyous like Falstaff; though engaging in their pranks, he is really detached from them, cool, controlled and contemptuous. He is really a political type like his father and unlike his cousin Richard (whom, in real life, he was fond of as a boy – to add to the tragedy); the Prince is quite consistent with the hero-king he became – he shows his quality already on the battlefield of Shrewsbury.

Though the Prince in his salad days can rival Falstaff in the virtuosity of his abuse – Falstaff was his butt – after the comic exploit of robbing the King's receivers upon Gadshill, he restores the money and with interest. We are deeply touched by the interview between the troubled father and his wayward son, between the King with all his anxieties and cares and the carefree Prince. The Prince answers his father's searching reproaches:

> Do not think so, you shall not find it so;
> And God forgive them that so much have swayed
> Your Majesty's good thoughts away from me!

He promises:

> I will redeem all this on Percy's head,
> And in the closing of some glorious day
> Be bold to tell you that I am your son.

He kept his word.

—— oOo ——

It is usual to regard Hotspur (Percy) with favour, as a gallant English fellow. His nickname tells us that he is in truth a hot-head, all for action regardless of consequences, ready to risk everything on a single throw. Though not one of the meek, he will inherit six feet of English earth. Nor is he one to take telling or learn from experience:

> By heaven, methinks it were an easy leap
> To pluck bright Honour from the pale-faced moon,
> Or dive into the bottom of the deep,
> Whose fathom-line could never touch the ground,
> And pluck up drownèd Honour by the locks,
> So he that doth redeem her thence might wear
> Without co-rival all her dignities.

He is most insensitive and rude to Glendower, as the English are apt to be to Celts – and it is most impolitic of him, for Glendower is his chief ally; he is dependent upon the support of the Welsh in the rebellion against Henry IV. Glendower claims, with the psychic sense of a Celt:

> at my nativity
> The front of heaven was full of fiery shapes,
> Of burning cressets, and at my birth
> The frame and huge foundation of the earth
> Shaked like a coward.

Hotspur replies, with English common sense:

> Why, so it would have done
> At the same season if your mother's cat
> Had but kittened, though yourself had never been born.

And he goes on at the leader of the Welsh resistance like that. Glendower boasts:

> Three times hath Henry Bolingbroke made head
> Against my power: thrice from the banks of Wye
> And sandy-bottomed Severn have I sent him
> Bootless home, and weather-beaten back.

Hotspur laughs at him:

> Home without boots, and in foul weather too!
> How scapes he agues, in the devil's name?

Now the strange thing is that, in historic fact, Henry IV three times mounted powerful invasions of Wales and each time was thwarted by exceptional bad weather. No wonder Glendower fancied that the elements fought for him – and actually there seem to have been some portents around the time of the birth of this leader with his authentic charisma. Moreover, the Welsh belief in his legend, or aura, was a fighting factor not to be disregarded; Hotspur had not the political sense to see that. The Welsh resistance went on for years, and the English never captured its leader; he died, no one knows where, as strangely as he had lived.

He is a legend in Wales. He was a Welsh *mage*: Hotspur was a brave fool.

—— oOo ——

Falstaff is at the Antipodes from Hotspur: he is a coward, but he is certainly no fool. Take the point of Honour, for which Hotspur would throw away his life. On the battlefield Falstaff catechises the concept thus:

> Can Honour set to a leg? No. Or an arm? No. Or take away the grief of a wound? No. Honour hath no skill in surgery then? No. What is Honour? A word. What is that word Honour? What is Honour? Air. Who hath it? He that died a-Wednesday. Doth he feel it? No. Doth he hear it? No. 'Tis insensible then? Yea, to the dead. But will it not live with the living? No. Therefore I'll none of it. Honour is a mere scutcheon . . .

Falstaff encounters a dead body:

> Soft! Who are you? Sir Walter Blunt – there's Honour for you.

Falstaff's option is: 'Give me life, which if I can save, so; if not, Honour comes unlooked for, and there's an end.' When he found himself attacked by a 'termagant Scot', he counterfeited death. 'To counterfeit dying, when a man thereby liveth, is to be no counterfeit, but the true and perfect image of life indeed. The better part of valour is discretion, in the which better part I have saved my life.'

Can one doubt that his creation spoke for his creator, that prudent non-combatant? No blame attaches to Henry IV and his sons on that score, for they fought for self-preservation. And, of course, Falstaff preserved himself by not fighting.

The main theme is the rebellion against Henry IV by the Percies, who had helped him to the throne and now thought themselves insufficiently regarded. They linked up with the Welsh and the Mortimers to make a dangerous combination, which only Henry's rapid march to Shrewsbury succeeded in forestalling before they could unite their forces. It is not usual to appreciate the politic types in Shakespeare: they have less popular appeal. A more sophisticated judgment can appreciate Henry IV better: he was the right man to occupy the throne. He was an appealing contrast to Richard:

> The skipping King, he ambled up and down,
> With shallow jesters and rash bavin wits . . .
> Mingled his royalty with capering fools,
> Had his great name profanèd with their scorns . . .

While he, when only Bolingbroke, knew how to make himself scarce and the more valued;

> And then I stole all courtesy from heaven,
> And dressed myself in such humility
> That I did pluck allegiance from men's hearts.

It is the subsidiary subject of Falstaff, however, which has captured the world's heart. We do not need to academicise him – ludicrous to add to his weight with 'critical' comment: far better to let him speak for himself.

The contemporary background, however, could do with some elucidation. Falstaff's is that of Elizabethan social life, never more recognisable than in the scenes from low life at the Boar's Head in East Cheap or on the highway, as readers of Simon Forman will know. Shakespeare renders it all with absolute veracity: he knew it well – in Bishopsgate and Silver Street he lodged not far from Cheapside. Impossible to surpass the depiction of the carriers in the inn-yard at Rochester – quite Dickensian, but Elizabethan: 'An it be not four by the day I'll be hanged – Charles's wain [i.e. the Plough] is over the new chimney, and yet our horse not packed.' That is how they told the time.

Hotspur describes, with contempt, a foppish young aristocrat, but of Shakespeare's time who had plenty of opportunity of observing such fantastics at Court:

> He was perfumèd like a milliner,
> And twixt his finger and his thumb he held
> A pouncet-box, which ever and anon
> He gave his nose and took't away again –

in short, a popinjay, like the fantastic Earl of Oxford.

We come closer still to Shakespeare with 'any alderman's thumb-ring' – wasn't his father Alderman Shakespeare? We see the son who has gone up in the world in Hotspur's reproof to his wife for saying 'in good sooth':

Not yours, in good sooth! Heart, you swear like a comfit-maker's wife – 'Not you, in good sooth'!, and 'As true as I live'!, and 'As God shall mend me'!, and 'As sure as day'!

These were all middle-class expressions, not suitable for a Lady Percy.

In addition to the historical reading that went into the play we have a laugh at Euphuism in Falstaff's 'though the camomile, the more it is trodden on the faster it grows, yet youth, the more it is wasted the sooner it wears.' And so on. Falstaff and Prince Henry put on an act of the King examining the Prince on the particulars of his life – greatly to the admiration of the hostess of the Boar's Head:

O Jesu, he doth it as like one of these harlotry players as ever I see!

No less endearing is a phrase 'reaped like a stubble-land at harvest-home' – as one has seen the stubbles on the slopes above Stratford.

Warwickshire is given a good show again – as Cotswold occurred in *Richard II* with no particular necessity. Falstaff, making for Coventry: 'we'll to Sutton Co'fil' tonight', evidently the way Sutton Coldfield was pronounced. But he would not march his mouldy recruits through the city, they would make such a bad impression, with only one shirt among them, and that 'stolen from my host at St. Albans, or the red-nose innkeeper of Daintry' (Daventry).

—— oOo ——

The immense popularity of Falstaff appears in contemporary references, as well as in the demand for printed versions of the play. A quarto of the First Part appeared in 1598, and altogether six printings – equalled only by *Richard III* – before the great Folio of 1623. For Falstaff Shakespeare originally used the historic name of Sir John Oldcastle, the famous Lollard who had married into the Cobham family and died for his religious faith. The portrayal of their family precursor as the drunken, thieving old reprobate of the play, gave offence to Lord Cobham. Shakespeare changed the names of Oldcastle, Harvey and Russell to Falstaff, Bardolph and Peto. Lord Cobham lived in Blackfriars, so did Lady Russell, Robert Cecil's censorious aunt, who disapproved of players, especially those playing within the precincts.

Jokes about Falstaff circulated in the Essex-Southampton circle – evidently they bore some relevance to the Cobhams that is lost to us. The immense success of the play meant that it was shortly followed by imitations. Shakespeare already had his sequel in mind.

Text and date offer no problems, since the quartos printed good texts, though a few relics of the original names remained. It is obvious that *The Merry Wives of Windsor* came after the Second Part of *Henry IV*, since it assumes that the audience is already familiar with Justice Shallow.

THE SECOND PART OF
King Henry IV
1597-8

The Second Part of *Henry IV* followed immediately upon the heels of the First. We must always keep in mind what a practical man of the theatre Shakespeare was: he would naturally want to sound again the notes that had been so successful with the First Part. Elizabethan usage was flexible and pragmatic in this regard, not rigid. He had it in mind to tell the whole story of Henry V, as Prince and King, since he was such a hero to the Elizabethans. This would mean, in dramatic form a trilogy, the third – the heroic – part, *Henry V*, varying in character from the two parts of *Henry IV*. These two, though two halves of one story, worked out somewhat differently. The Second Part did not have the dramatic conflict culminating on the battlefield of Shrewsbury and so did not grip the audience to the same extent.

All the same, it is a mistake to depreciate this Part, for it presents brilliant scenes, as effective as and more touching than the First Part; if it has less dramatic urgency, it has more poetry and pathos, more elbow-room for depictions of contemporary Elizabethan life in town and country, in East Cheap and on the Cotswolds, and also – in the absence of the Prince – far more sex and bawdy talk, in which the dramatist was a virtuoso. It is precisely these naughty scenes that give us, as has been well said, 'an irresistible impression of reality, a sense that we are in touch with the living pulse of Shakespeare's England.'[1] That is the point – they exhibit contemporary life as much as anything of Ben Jonson's and are even more living today.

Again, on the historical side, the portrayal of England's past, 'Shakespeare's presentation of history in drama is on the whole far truer to history than that of any of his predecessors.' This is true of Richard II, Henry IV, Henry V, Henry VI and Richard III. This is not surprising, for though Shakespeare did not have the advantages of being a professor of history or an historical researcher, he had a more penetrating understanding of human beings, their characters and conflicts, their agonising temptations and dilemmas. K.B. McFarlane, a leading authority on the 15th century, which Shakespeare chiefly dealt with, describes him as after all our greatest historian.

—— oOo ——

The Elizabethans were fascinated by the compelling personality of Henry V, which to the outer world seemed to fall into two halves: the 'unthrifty'

Prince and the hero-King. And yet he was no schizophrenic: the subtle psychologist saw that there was consistency, in spite of appearances, and the deft dramatist provided for it in his plays.

In this play the Prince is on his way to assuming the burden of kingship and taking upon him the character of a king. (Shakespeare would not have known that on the day of his father's death Henry spent the whole night alone in Westminster Abbey with an anchorite, and underwent something like a religious conversion. A medieval man, like his father, he would already have been impregnated by belief and open to such an experience, just as his father longed to die on crusade.)

The father has never had such an appeal; and yet, to anyone who understands the imperious necessities of rule and the harsh exigencies of politics, Henry IV has great pathos. In the end, he was broken by them, perhaps too by the burden of guilt his conscience carried. Anyone can appreciate the tension in the father-son relationship, especially when the father is a king and the son his heir (cf. in our time that between George V and his Prince of Wales.) It has life's irony in it too, for the Prince was more fond of the dead Richard than he was of his own father. Shakespeare may not have known that, but he intuited, what he makes Falstaff say, that the King's blood was cold and the Prince inherited it.

And yet the son was loyal: he broke Falstaff's head for comparing the King to a singing-man of Windsor. Henry IV suffered from a succession of strokes. But it was not for the heir to put on an outward expression of grief:

> I tell thee, it is not meet that I should be sad now my father is sick.
> Albeit I could tell to thee . . . I could be sad, and sad indeed too . . .
> Let the end try the man: my heart bleeds inwardly that my father is
> so sick.

The father's heart also bleeds inwardly that his son is set on such courses: politic as ever, he manages to 'sever' the Prince from Falstaff for a while, sending them off in different directions. What was it that the Prince saw so much in Falstaff? The old rascal tells us: it was his function to keep the Prince in a continual laughter (it should be played as such).

No laughter in the King's care-worn life, and his reproaches to his son are searing:

> Thou hast sealed up my expectatiòn.
> Thy life did manifest thou lovedst me not,
> And thou wilt have me die assured of it.

This is when the King is dying and the Prince, thinking him already dead, takes away the crown from his pillow. There follows the wonderful scene in which each is faced with the reality of life and death, understanding and reconciliation at last before the King lays down the cares of this world.

Whether this unexampled episode – so moving on the stage – was historic fact or no, it is certainly symbolic. For during one of Henry's previous illnesses, the Prince in historic fact had taken hold of the government; the King had recovered, and dismissed him from the Council. The King confessed to Warwick, quoting Richard's prophecy what an ill time of care Henry would have as king,

> Though then, God knows, I had no such intent,
> But that necessity so bowed the state
> That I and greatness were compelled to kiss.

This was probably the historic truth. Henry then asks the question that is the kernel of the whole matter:

> . . . Are these things then necessities?

Warwick, loyal to both, amid all the treacheries of high politics, defended the Prince to his father and tried to explain – a very human situation we all know:

> My gracious lord, you look beyond him quite:
> The Prince but studies his companiòns
> Like a strange tongue . . . So, like gross terms,
> The Prince will in the perfectness of time
> Cast off his followers.

Now, facing death, the King lays bare his soul to his son:

> God knows, my son,
> By what bypaths and indirect crooked ways
> I met this crown. And I myself know well
> How troublesome it sat upon my head.
> To thee it shall descend with better quiet,
> Better opinion, better confirmation,
> For all the soil of the achievement goes
> With me into the earth.

Henry's life of care and toil had laid the foundations for a firmer hold for his son as king; even so, his last counsel, prudent and cautious as ever, was –

> Yet, though thou stand'st more sure than I could do,
> Thou art not firm enough, since griefs are green.

Henry had longed to wipe out the stain of his guilt by going on crusade to the Holy Land. Did Shakespeare know that, as a young man, Henry had already gone on crusade with the Teutonic Knights against the heathen of early Prussia?

Thus we are led up to the accession of the young Henry as King. The mask drops; the real man, the politic son of his cold father, stands forth and shows his quality as ruler – shows 'indifferency', the Elizabethan word for impartiality, justice of mind. Though the Chief Justice had rebuked him and 'sent to prison the immediate heir of England', the new King confirms him in office and wishes him increase of honour, and that, if a son of his own should offend, the Chief Justice would similarly commit him.

A great deal of fuss has been made by people of no political understanding about the relegation of Falstaff. Of course he had to be relegated; when he stood to 'leer upon' the new-crowned Henry V, he expected to be able to bestow office and favours upon his rascally crew of thieves and rogues. It does not seem to have been noticed that, as King, Henry treats the shameless old ruffian generously:

> For competence of life I will allow you,
> That lack of means enforce you not to evils.
> And, as we hear you do reform yourselves,
> We will, according to your strengths and qualities,
> Give you advancement.

—— oOo ——

The main action in this play, the Northern rebellion of Northumberland and Archbishop Scrope, is less interesting than the father-son relationship of King and Prince. These together occupy less space than the low life scenes around Falstaff, Justice Shallow and the *habitués* of the Boar's Head. Talk about social realism! – if this is what Marxists want in literature, these scenes are beyond compare. They have too their poetry and pathos, for all their disgrace and bawdiness. They have veracious vividness and intense humanity.

Despite the cursing and swearing, the brawling and bad language of the rogues and their whore, one cannot but be touched when Doll Tearsheet says at length:

> Come, I'll be friends with thee, Jack. Thou art going to the wars, and whether I shall ever see thee again or no, there is nobody cares.

And Falstaff is reduced to confessing,

> I am old, I am old.
> DOLL: I love thee better than I love e'er a scurvy young boy of
> them all.

The pathos is much the same with Justice Shallow in his Gloucestershire home, old age creeping on and he remembering the days of his youth:

> There was I, and little John Doit of Staffordshire, and black George Barnes, and Francis Pickbone, and Will Squele, a Cotswold man: you had not four such swinge-bucklers in all the Inns o'Court again. And I may say to you we knew where the bonarobas were . . . Jesu, Jesu, the mad days that I have spent! And to see how many of my old acquaintance are dead!

Then Falstaff:

> We have heard the chimes at midnight, Master Shallow.

—— oOo ——

Gloucestershire lies in part on the western slopes of the Cotswolds, we notice Shakespeare's kindly remembrance of the familiar places. Shallow's young cousin (Elizabethan for nephew), William, 'is become a good scholar. He is at Oxford still . . . 'a must, then, to the Inns o'Court shortly.' This was the regular course for a young gentleman of expectations. We hear of William Visor of Woncot's case against Clement Perkes of the Hill. Woncot was the regular pronunciation of Woodmancote, the Hill is Stinchcombe Hill. 'Goodman Puff of Barson' – this was how Barcheston was pronounced, where the famous Sheldon tapestries were made. A Gloucestershire place-name, Dumbleton, is used for a person's surname. Hinckley is a Warwickshire town near Coventry.

At Stratford at this very time Shakespeare was repairing New Place which he had recently bought; so we find:

> When we mean to build
> We first survey the plot, then draw the model.
> And when we see the figure of the house,
> Then must we rate the cost of the erection,
> Which, if we find outweighs ability,
> What do we then but draw anew the model
> In fewer offices, or at least desist
> To build at all?

How like the prudent actor, and unlike his father! The money had been made, not by teaching school –

> like a school broke up,
> Each hurries toward his home and sporting-place –

but by the stage:

> And let this world no longer be a stage
> To feed contention in a lingering act.

Shakespeare's observation-post as an actor and his upward move in society enabled him to spot, and spit, its pretences – such as with

> those that are kin to the king, for they never prick their finger but they say, 'There's some of the king's blood spilt.' 'How comes that?', says he that takes upon him not to conceive. The answer is as ready as a borrower's cap, 'I am the king's poor cousin, sir.'

The fools that people are and Shakespeare saw through everybody! He gives it to an Archbishop to describe the common people:

> An habitation giddy and unsure
> Hath he that buildeth on the vulgar heart.

They had been all in favour of Bolingbroke; now–

> Thou, beastly feeder, art so full of him
> That thou provok'st thyself to cast him up.

—— oOo ——

The Epilogue is important for the explanation it gives. It would seem that originally it was spoken by Shakespeare, for he says 'what I have to say is of my own making, and what indeed I should say will, I doubt, prove mine own marring. Be it known unto you, as it is very well, I was lately here in the end of a displeasing play, to pray your patience for it and to promise you a better.' We do not know what play that was; he goes on, 'I meant indeed to pay you with this', and he prays their favour for his new piece with his usual courtesy. He promises to continue the story 'with Sir John in it, and make you merry with fair Katherine of France. Where, for anything I know, Falstaff shall die of a sweat, unless already 'a be killed with your hard opinions.' Then came the disclaimer, to meet the objections of the Cobhams: 'for Oldcastle died a martyr, and this is not the man.'

A good text was printed in the quarto of 1600, probably printed from Shakespeare's own manuscript, with the omission of references to Richard II's deposition. These were supplied in the full text of the Folio.

---

1. *The Warwick Shakespeare* edition, edited by Charles Harold Herford, pages ix-x (Blackie, London, 1893). This old edition of the play has this to recommend it – that the editor was not only a scholar but had a mind on a level with the subject.

King Henry V
1599

King Henry V is different again from its predecessors, *1 & 2 Henry IV*, as those were from what went before: we see what variety Shakespeare achieved within the *genre* of the history play. Yet in this kind his imagination had to work within a given framework, and accept the limitations of events, whatever liberties he took with chronology to give his material dramatic shape. With *Henry V* the dramatist is particularly conscious of the limitations, the difficulty of representing war on the stage, the crossing of the sea, siege and battlefied. He says as much, and introduced a new feature for the purpose: a Chorus, which speaks a Prologue to each act and ends the play with an Epilogue. These sound a particularly personal note, and were no doubt spoken by the actor-author himself. They help to give this play its individual character.

It has not the obvious dramatic conflicts of Henry IV's mortal struggles to gain and retain the crown, or the tension of his unhappy relationship with his son. Henry V is very much master in his own house, as his father prophesied he would be. Before setting out across the Channel for Agincourt he has the affair of the Cambridge-Scrope conspiracy to settle, but that serves mainly to link the action with what has gone before; later, in Henry's meditations we are given a further link with Richard II. All the same, there *is* dramatic conflict – the war with France; this is given heroic emphasis by the smallness of the English army at Agincourt (the archers who wrought such havoc were Welsh), against the vastly superior forces of outdated, heavy French chivalry.

The subject of the play is heroic valour, the achievement of a king who was a hero to the Elizabethans. Once more it answered to the mood of a small people proud and shrilly confident at the figure they were making in the world. The year 1596 had seen the capture of Spain's Atlantic fortress of Cadiz – it was a famous victory: would Spaniards not have boasted if they had captured Plymouth?

Professor Dover Wilson says that '*Henry V* is a play which men of action have been wont silently to admire, and literary men, at any rate during the last hundred and thirty years, volubly to contemn.' So much the worse for the literary men: it condemns them of lack of imagination, which they most stand in need of in their profession. Dover Wilson found that the play spoke for him, when he went abroad to serve his country in the small Expeditionary Force of 1914. Again on 6 June 1944, when the landing craft were nearing the coast of France, to liberate Europe, a Yorkshire captain – who fell in action – repeated to his men the words of Henry V before Agincourt. Those of us who remember D-day in 1944, and have not forgotten what those men died for, think of it still in those terms:

This day is called the Feast of Crispian:
He that outlives this day, and comes safe home,
Will stand a-tiptoe when this day is named,
And rouse him at the name of Crispian.
He that shall live this day, and see old age,
Will yearly on the vigil feast his neighbours,
And say, 'Tomorrow is Saint Crispian.'

—— oOo ——

The Chorus points the changing scenes of the action for us, but it also describes the theatre and gives us precise indications of what was going on in Shakespeare's own time.

> But pardon, gentles all –

a characteristic note with him –

The flat unraisèd spirits that hath dared
On this unworthy scaffold to bring forth
So great an object. Can this cockpit hold
The vasty fields of France? Or may we cram
Within this wooden O the very casques
That did affright the air at Agincourt?

The wooden O was the Globe Theatre which the Burbages had just erected on the South Bank of the Thames, taking the timbers of the old Theatre in Shoreditch, which had done such good service and given Shakespeare his opportunities earlier. Henceforth the Globe was to be the permanent home of the Company, indisputably the first now in London, the Admiral's taking second place. The audience were bidden to imagine the two monarchies confronting each other 'within the girdle of these walls', and to jump over the years contracted in the play:

for the which supply,
Admit me Chorus to this history,
Who Prologue-like your humble patience pray,
Gently to hear, kindly to judge, our play.

With that he left the stage.

At each appearance as Chorus he woos the audience – 'We'll not offend one stomach with our play'; next time – 'Still be kind, And eke out our performance with your mind.' Before the fourth Act we have:

The armourers, accomplishing the knights,

(the very word 'accomplishing' is a Shakespeare signature)

> With busy hammers closing rivets up,
> Give dreadful note of preparatiòn.

This was contemporary; for, in 1599, the largest English army that had ever been sent to Ireland, was being fitted out to retrieve the disaster of the Yellow Ford in Ulster the year before. The next Chorus describes the historic send-off the ever-popular Essex was given by the city, in similar terms to those of Simon Forman who watched it.[1]

> How London doth pour out her citizens:
> The Mayor and all his brethren in best sort,
> Like to the senators of th'antique Rome,
> With the plebeians swarming at their heels,
> Go forth and fetch their conquering Caesar in.

Julius Caesar, his next play, was already shaping in his mind; then comes the reference to Essex, whom Southampton was accompanying to Ireland (to be cashiered by the Queen):

> As, by a lower but loving likelihood
> Were now the General of our gracious Empress –
> As in good time he may – from Ireland coming,
> Bringing rebellion broachèd on his sword,
> How many would the peaceful city quit
> To welcome him!

The hopes placed on Essex were to be falsified: he made a fiasco in Ireland, and returned to ultimate ruin, very nearly bringing Southampton to the scaffold with him. The year is supposed to be that of Agincourt, 1415, but it is also 1599.

The expectations of Essex were high, before that fiasco, and he remained always the darling of the people. There is something of this in the depiction of Henry V, particularly in his night watch; for Essex was known, in the Normandy campaign, for going the rounds at night, keeping the watch, and rubbing shoulders with the common soldier.

It used to be held that Shakespeare so 'transmuted' the events of his time that one could not recognise them in his work. We now know that this was nonsense; but it needs a proper knowledge of the time to be able to recognise them – in the Sonnets, as in the plays. Dr. Johnson was right: it would be quite contrary to a real writer not to incorporate his experience of life and use the people he observed in his work.

Our great critic alerts us to something significant even when he mis-conceives. Of the Prologue Dr. Johnson says, 'Shakespeare does not seem to set distance enough between the performers and spectators.' He clearly did not know that the Elizabethan stage jutted out into the pit, while the galleries which held most of the audience crowded round three sides of it: this eliminated distance and absorbed spectators into the play, in one integrated ritual – with the exciting effect we know from Nashe, much more intimately than in the theatre today. But Johnson is right in commenting upon the dramatist's inconsistencies: 'this poet is always more careful about the present than the future, about his audience than his readers.' Of course; as we have pointed out all along, with him the play came first, readers were secondary. The dramatic approach is primary. Again, Johnson notices the passing phrase, 'now speak we on our cue', and comments: 'this phrase the author learned among players, and has imparted it to kings.'

—— oOo ——

Dominant in the play is the development of Henry's character as king. A good critic has noted how much it deepens in the self-revelation before Agincourt, when facing the question of responsibility for the deaths of his fighting men. 'Every subject's duty is the King's, but every subject's soul is his own': Dr. Johnson thought this 'a very just distinction, and the whole argument is well followed and properly concluded.' We do not need to go into the tedious question of the rights and wrongs of the war, but merely point out that it was a renewal of the war, which had been only suspended by Richard II's truce and Henry IV's chronic difficulties; that Henry V, like all the Plantagenets, was more than half-French and his claim to the French throne was about as good as its occupant's. It was six of one side to half-a-dozen of the other.

Henry was taking advantage of the divisions within France to advance what he considered his just claims. What is unhistorical is that Archbishop Chichele urged on the war in order to deflect an attack on the Church and its lands.

The Archbishop does mention Henry's conversion:

> The courses of his youth promised it not.
> The breath no sooner left his father's body
> But that his wildness, mortified in him,
> Seemed to die too.

This was historically true. It prepares us for the most moving passages of the play, the wonderful night-scene before Agincourt, when the King moves among his men disguised as a common soldier, argues the rights and wrongs of it all with another, Michael Williams, and then withdraws to have it out with himself and to pray before battle is joined. Williams is given a very fair argument for the ordinary man's point of view:

> But if the cause be not good, the King himself hath a heavy
> reckoning to make, when all those legs and arms and heads, chopped
> off in a battle, shall join together at the latter day and cry all,
> 'We died at such a place' . . . I am afeared there are few die well that
> die in a battle, for how can they charitably dispose of anything when
> blood is their argument? Now, if these men do not die well, it will be
> a black matter for the King that led them to it.

Henry carefully considers this from every angle in a convincing argument;
the simple answer is that everybody is responsible for his own soul. But
how about men's lives?

This is the subject of Henry's meditation when left alone by himself,
and we are given the famous soliloquy:

> Upon the King! Let us our lives, our souls,
> Our debts, our careful wives,
> Our children, and our sins, lay on the King!
> We must bear all. O hard condition,
> Twin-born with greatness, subject to the breath
> Of every fool, whose sense no more can feel
> But his own wringing!

I fear that this betrays, as usual, Shakespeare's opinion of the average man
– he had a thoroughly upper-class point of view. But Shakespeare has no
illusions either about kings (sc. political leaders, Presidents, what not).

> And what have kings that privates have not too,
> Save ceremony, save general ceremony?

This leads to a splendid oration on Ceremony – like that on Commodity in
King John, or on Rumour in *2 Henry IV*, or Falstaff on Honour. Shakespeare
sees through ceremony, as he saw through everything:

> Art thou aught else but place, degree, and form,
> Creating awe and fear in other men?

Not having had the advantage of a course in anthropology, Shakespeare
hardly even allows ceremony the plea of social necessity. When, shortly
before Charles I's execution, Cromwellians ceased to kneel to him and
kiss his hand, he observed that it was not material, only a matter of custom
after all. But they did not fail to heap upon him as King the responsibility
for the Civil War and kill him for it – a sacrificial victim. As, in a way,
Richard II had been.

In dismissing the 'good old knight', Sir Thomas Erpingham, to pray
alone, Henry offers up

Not today, O Lord,
O not today, think not upon the fault
My father made in compassing the crown!

We are given, by the hand of a master, sufficient contrasts to vary and lighten the concentration upon the epic themes of the play. Falstaff's end is affectingly reported: Mistress Quickly, in character, is able to tell us, 'Nay, sure, he's not in hell: he's in Arthur's bosom, if ever man went to Arthur's bosom', i.e. for Abraham's bosom. And that was well: it would never have done to have had *him* in the play, as Shakespeare had intended but saw to be quite impossible once he got to work on it. Falstaff's cronies go to France as camp-followers, behave as badly as might be expected, filching and stealing, and get their comeuppance. Pistol has quite a part, with his extraordinary, inflated rhodomontade: one wonders, rather, whether he was meant to be quite right in the head.

It is a funny scene where the gallant Welsh captain, Fluellen, makes him eat a leek for his bombastic insults. Fluellen is English for Llewelyn, since the English cannot pronounce the Welsh inflected 'll'. He is well informed about classic military discipline; this is thought to come from Dudley Digges's manual *Stratioticos* – quite likely, since Shakespeare knew the Digges family. The rendering of Welsh, Scotch and Irish accents we are given, with Captains Fluellen, Jamie, and MacMorris, are effective and bespeak the mimetic observation of the actor, while the dramatist suggests their different national characteristics with skilled economy. Bardolph's trick of saying every now and then, 'And that's the humour of it', is obviously a joke on Ben Jonson, whose *Every Man in his Humour* Shakespeare had played in the year before.

Henry's love-scenes with Katherine of France (ancestress of the Tudors, by the way) have their own charm. They are in French, simple enough, and broken English. We know that Shakespeare could read French; no doubt he wrote these, with their grammatical solecisms, but he may have been helped by the French household in which he lodged in Silver Street, and was on terms of confidence with Madame Montjoy. The French herald's name, Montjoy, was ready to hand in the chronicle. Henry's marriage with Katherine produced Henry VI, who inherited her father's neurotic imbecility; Henry V's triumph in France led to his early death and the long agony of the English extrusion from France, which ruined his son's reign and helped on the Wars of the Roses.

The wheel came full circle: things were as they were before. Such is political activity.

—— oOo ——

We have noticed contemporary Elizabethan life showing through the texture of the play. Here is the Irish kern again: 'you rode like a kern of

Ireland, your French hose off, and in your strait strossers', i.e. bare-legged. Pistol is described, like another Parolles: 'a gull, a fool, a rogue, that now and then goes to the wars, to grace himself at his return into London under the form of a soldier. And such fellows are perfect in the great commanders' names, and they will learn you by rote where services were done: at such and such a sconce, at such a breach, at such a convoy; who came off bravely, who was shot, who disgraced, what terms the enemy stood on', etc. 'But you must learn to know such slanders of the age, or else you may be marvellously mistook.' Shakespeare knew such types about London: unlikely to be mistaken, he observed them for his own purpose.

Here is another stage reference. 'Bardolph and Nym had ten times more valour than this roaring devil i'th'old play, that everyone may pare his nails with a wooden dagger' – an incident in the old moralities Shakespeare would have known from boyhood. The sudden turn-round and repentance of the conspirators, Cambridge, Scrope and Grey, is very much of the Elizabethan stage – we might almost call it stagey.

—— oOo ——

Personal touches we note in Shakespeare's expert praise of the horse – it takes us back once more to the Sonnets and plodding away wearily from his friend and patron. Still more do we recognise him in the frequently expressed thought:

> There is some soul of goodness in things evil,
> Would men observingly distil it out . . .
> Thus may we gather honey from the weed.

Famous lines have entered into the consciousness of all who speak the language:

> Once more unto the breach, dear friends –

like Henry's father's,

> Uneasy lies the head that wears a crown.

We recognise the characteristic lordly words: crescive for growing, congreeted for met together, rivage for shore, legerity for quickness, etc. The caricature of the French and the anti-French sentiments were for the groundlings: we need not suppose that they speak for William Shakespeare.

The Epilogue takes the form of a sonnet, and we can see him delivering it, for he says, with the usual gentlemanly self-deprecation:

> Thus far, with rough and all-unable pen,
> Our bending author hath pursued the story.

Opportunity should always be taken in the theatre to present the Chorus as the actor-dramatist himself, politely bowing. He then refers to his *Henry VI* plays:

> Which oft our stage hath shown; and, for their sake,
> In your fair minds let this acceptance take.

The main sources for the play were two: Holinshed, which Shakespeare had open before him for the first Act, since some of it, expounding Henry's claim to the French throne, is chronicle simply versified. The second was the anonymous play, *The Famous Victories of Henry the Fifth*, the form of which the busy actor-dramatist followed for convenience, as he had with *The Troublesome Reign of King John*.

The authoritative text in the First Folio is a good one, almost certainly from the author's manuscript. A poor quarto was printed in 1600, a shortened version put together by actors, perhaps for provincial performances. Occasionally a reading in this clarifies a dubious phrase – for example, the most famous emendation in Shakespeare: the Folio misprint, 'a Table of green fields', which the quarto reported as 'talk of flowers' – 'play with flowers' appears a line or two before. In the 18th century Theobald emended this to ''a babbled of green fields' – quite unnecessarily. Anyone familiar with Elizabethan script would recognise the reading to be simply. ''a talked of green fields'. As in mathematics, the simplest explanation is always best.

1. *v.* my *Simon Forman: Sex and Society in Shakespeare's Age*, page 220 (Weidenfeld and Nicolson, London, 1974); American title *Sex and Society in Shakespeare's Age: Simon Forman the Astrologer* (Scribner, New York, 1975)

King Henry VIII

1612-13

Henry VIII is Shakespeare's last play. There is a certain propriety, typical of the planning mind we have observed all through his work, that he should round off his production, as he had begun, with a chronicle play on English history. It gave him the opportunity to pronounce his valediction, his real farewell, to the Elizabethan age – of which, all unknown, he would in time become the brightest jewel in its crown – in Cranmer's famous prophecy in baptising the infant Princess Elizabeth. With this the play ends: the wheel has come full circle.

It is much influenced by masque, which had come to the fore at James I's Court – as with several of Shakespeare's later plays. This one offers great opportunities for pomp, ceremonies and processions. Thus it is without dramatic dynamism: the main interest is in the portraits it presents of Cardinal Wolsey and Queen Catherine. And these have attracted the finest actors, so that the play has always been popular.

One misses perhaps Shakespeare's characteristic attack: the mood is a more passive one, of observation, sympathy, reflection, almost resignation. That would be natural enough; after his life of constant effort as actor and dramatist, touring, producing, writing, he was a tired man. *Henry VIII* was written in 1612-13; after that, though he lived for another three years, he wrote no more. He was content to enjoy his well-earned retirement, as the gentleman of Stratford, with an occasional visit to London to keep his hand in the Company's affairs.

Dr. Johnson expresses a very favourable judgment of the play, as 'one of those which still keep possession of the stage, by the splendour of its pageantry . . . Yet pomp is not the only merit of this play. The meek sorrows and virtuous distress of Catherine have furnished some scenes which may be justly numbered among the greatest efforts of tragedy.' This is perhaps too encomiastic; yet Johnson goes further, to say of Catherine's last scene when dying that 'it is, above any other part of Shakespeare's tragedies, and perhaps above any scene of any other poet, tender and pathetic, without gods or furies, or poisons or precipices, without the help of romantic circumstances, without improbable sallies of poetical lamentation, and without any throes of tumultuous misery.'

It is the chaste classicism of the Augustan age that speaks: I suspect that it is precisely the absence of Shakespeare's romantic *fougue* that makes the Doctor so enthusiastic. At the same time actresses have found this a noble part, and artists, notably Blake, have been inspired by the dying Queen's vision of heavenly spirits. Wolsey's part has a number of famous passages which have sunk into our communal memory:

> Had I but served my God with half the zeal
> I served my king, he would not in mine age
> Have left me naked to mine enemies.

Or,

> Farewell! A long farewell to all my greatness!

There follows an oration, developed in accordance with the rules of rhetoric, such as we often observe, on the stages of man's life; and ending on the wretchedness of him who depends on princes' favour:

> And when he falls, he falls like Lucifer,
> Never to hope again.

Or we have Wolsey's earlier premonition:

> I shall fall
> Like a bright exhalation in the evening,
> And no man see me more.

—— oOo ——

A prime difficulty with *Henry VIII* is the character of the King: he posed an insurmountable problem for the dramatist; for he was still a controversial figure – in the way that Richard III was not (everybody knew the truth about him) – and it was hardly possible to tell the whole truth about Henry. After all, he was Queen Elizabeth's father, though he killed her mother, and was to kill her cousin, Catherine Howard. Nothing of this in the play.

The situation was rather like that with Stalin in Soviet Russia, an overpowering personality, without which the country might not have pulled through its revolution, yet a capricious and cruel monarch. Also, like Stalin, a *faux-bonhomme*. Only a few years before the play, Robert Cecil, James I's chief minister, then Lord Salisbury, in a speech to the Lords openly condemned Henry's cruelty – much as Krushchev spoke up about Stalin's.

Even so, it was not for a dramatist to condemn Elizabeth I's father, and something of the traditional 'bluff King Hal' comes through – for he remained popular in spite of his misdeeds. He retains his regal dignity (in real life he was very keen on that); we have his quick changes of mood, his impulsiveness, his characteristic (and rather alarming) 'Ha! Ha!'

Henry VIII inherited his characteristics from his Yorkist stock. He was like his burly grandfather, Edward IV, who killed his brother, Clarence; his great-uncle was Richard III, who killed his nephews; Henry killed two of his wives, besides various other members of his family – his cousin, Clarence's daughter, the aged Countess of Salisbury, her son, and another cousin, the Marquis of Exeter.

Not much of this appeared in the first half of Henry's life – except for Buckingham's execution, with which the play begins – until the crisis of the Reformation, though Wolsey and Sir Thomas More (another victim) knew perfectly what kind of man Henry was. The Reformation was yet another subject that could not be handled in the play – yet it was the backbone of Henry's reign:

> Majestic lord that broke the bonds of Rome.

Thus the play wants integration. In place of that, we are given a series of effective scenes, skilfully linked, pulling together disparate events over the years. Shakespeare took advantage of what could be made dramatic use of – for example, Bishop Gardiner's attempt to 'frame' Archbishop Cranmer, which Henry personally frustrated; and then resolved to give the story a ceremonial end with the baptism of Elizabeth.

—— oOo ——

The tact we have observed all through Shakespeare's career would have prevented him from touching on these controversial issues anyway: he steered clear of them. It was enough to have to deal with the divorce of Catherine of Aragon, which he does with much sympathy in his portrait of her and managing to save the 'honour' – or, at any rate, dignity – of the King.

The dramatist had paid his meed of tributes to Henry and Anne Boleyn's daughter, though with none of the outrageous flattery with which many of the poets treated her; as in everything, he retained his essential independence and dignity – as in his relations with his patron. In the event the Queen had condemned Southampton to death and incarcerated him in the Tower, until her own death freed him. It was observed that her favourite dramatist paid no poetic tribute on her passing. Now, ten years later, at the end of his own career, he could look back over it all and see in the perspective of time – as a prophecy – what her reign had been:

> She shall be loved and feared. Her own shall bless her;
> Her foes shake like a field of beaten corn . . .
> In her days every man shall eat in safety
> Under his own vine what he plants, and sing
> The merry songs of peace to all his neighbours.

The tribute is to the internal peace which Elizabeth kept so successfully throughout the course of her long reign.

The oration goes on with no less tact to salute her successor. The ashes of the maiden phoenix would create another heir, 'as great in fame as she was' (forsooth!):

> Wherever the bright sun of heaven shall shine,
> His honour and the greatness of his name
> Shall be, and make new nations . . .

This was already coming to pass: Jamestown had been founded but a few years before, with Southampton a promoter (hence Hampton Roads and Hampton River) to take a leading part later in the colonisation of Virginia.

The existence of the New World is signalled by the old master in an unmistakable piece of bawdy at the Princess's christening. There is such a crowd that the Porter cries,

> What should you do, but knock 'em down by the dozens? Is this Moorfields to muster in? Or have we some strange Indian with the great tool come to Court, the women so besiege us? Bless me, what a fry of fornication is at door! On my Christian conscience, this one christening will beget a thousand.

His man reports,

> There is a fellow somewhat near the door, he should be a brazier by his face, for, o'my conscience, twenty of the dog-days now reign in's nose.

Isn't that a rather touching tribute to Bardolph, whose red nose was his prominant feature, after all the years? Or perhaps the same actor, whose appurtenance it was, was still with the Company. Then the Porter again:

> There are the youths that thunder at a play-house and fight for bitten apples, that no audience but the tribulation of Tower-Hill, or the limbs of Limehouse, are able to endure.

—— oOo ——

Norfolk's description of how Wolsey takes his fall out of favour with the King, reminds us how gestural Elizabethan acting was:

> Some strange commotion
> Is in his brain: he bites his lip, and starts;
> Stops on a sudden, looks upon the ground,
> Then lays his finger on his temple; straight
> Springs out into fast gait; then stops again,
> Strikes his breast hard, and anon he casts
> His eye against the moon.

Traces of fairly recent tradition about Wolsey make a full character of him, more sympathetic too than that generally entertained by either Protestants or Catholics. In the play he is said to have had a 'witchery in's tongue', which exerted a spell over the King. The Cardinal certainly was an eloquent speaker; but the truth was that, for the first half of the reign, he did Henry's work for him: he administered the country with immense energy and ability. A couple of famous lines describe him:

> Lofty and sour to them that loved him not,
> But to those that sought him, sweet as summer.

Shakespeare gives him historical justice – more so than anyone, except his gentleman-attendant, George Cavendish, who knew him best and wrote his life:

> Though from an humble stock . . .
> Exceeding wise, fair-spoken and persuading.

An earlier historic tradition is mentioned that related to Richard III. Buckingham's father had been Richard's chief supporter in taking the throne from his nephew, perhaps understandably; but his stomach had been turned, like everybody else's, by the murder of the Princes, and Buckingham turned against him. When rounded up at Salisbury, if he had been brought before Richard, the Duke had meant to knife him – suspicious Richard was careful not to give him that chance. With that we go back to Shakespeare's first memorable success with an historic character. Richard's great-nephew, who was just as cruel, comes off less effectively in this last play.

—— oOo ——

The Prologue has a similar appeal to that of *Henry V*:

> Think ye see
> The very persons of our noble story
> As they were living . . .

And it assures the audience that they will find truth in what they see and hear:

> I come no more to make you laugh; things now
> That bear a weighty and a serious brow,
> Sad, high, and working, full of state and woe,
> Such noble scenes as draw the eye to flow.

The Epilogue has the regular making up to the audience, especially to the women:

> If they smile,
> And say 'twill do, I know, within a while
> All the best men are ours; for 'tis ill hap
> If they hold when their ladies bid 'em clap.

The play was produced with exceptional pomp and magnificence, 'even to the matting of the stage; the Knights of the Order with their Georges and garters, and Guards with their embroidered coats, and the like: sufficient in truth within a while to make greatness very familiar.' We see how the theatre had gone up in public estimation and prosperity, carrying its creators and leaders upward with it, from those early days when, as Greene said, the players had been glad to carry their playing fardel a-footback.

At the performance on 29 June 1613, when chambers were shot off to greet the King's entry to Cardinal Wolsey's masque, the thatch around the Globe caught fire and the theatre was burnt to the ground. Though it rose again, like a phoenix from its ashes, rebuilt more splendidly than before, it marked a term and almost symbolically illuminated the end of Shakespeare's work in the theatre.

—— oOo ——

Many business documents must have been lost, so that we have not those of the Burbages as we have Henslowe's. But, thank heaven, the scripts of the plays, so far as we know, were safe. The text of *Henry VIII*, as it appeared in the Folio, was a tidy one, with many more detailed stage-directions than usual, consistently with the dramatist being retired in the country and giving full instructions for production.

SHAKESPEARE'S
COMEDIES

Dr. Johnson, greatest of Shakespearean critics – for there we have a mind on a level with the author he is criticising – observed that comedy was what came naturally first to Shakespeare. Comedy was instinctive with him; he had to work, the deepening experience of life aiding, towards tragedy. 'In his comic scenes, he seems to produce without labour what no labour can improve.'

This was in keeping with his nature, as Robert Greene and John Aubrey observed, and as he described himself in the character of Berowne:

> but a merrier man . . .
> I never spent an hour's talk withal.
> His eye begets occasion for his wit;
> For every object that the one doth catch
> The other turns to a mirth-moving jest.

His earlier comedies are full of merriment and give an impression of a euphoric nature. They are running over with high spirits; one sees it in the wit-combats, the verbal quibbles and endless punning which appealed so much to Elizabethans. This aspect of his genius helped him to gain popularity with them – the 'facetious grace' to which Chettle paid tribute. It is the one aspect that has dated most and appeals least to us – as Ben Jonson observed from close to, Shakespeare could hardly stop himself from running over.

What, then, was the nature of his contribution to comedy, what was its character, and how did it differ from others? It is not easy to state briefly, for this author was above all so Protean, so various and diverse, as well as diverting.

We may diagnose that his first essential contribution to Elizabethan comedy was to shape it up, give it shapely dramatic form. Hitherto comedies, rather rustic and rude, were apt to be wanting in form – indeed much of the traditional drama in every kind was apt to be shapeless. This was not true of the courtly comedy of Lyly, from whom Shakespeare learned. In observing his development we must pay attention to what Ben Jonson tells us, who knew him so well:

> how far thou didst our Lyly outshine,
> Or sporting Kyd, or Marlowe's mighty line.

For his comedy he learned most from Lyly, chiefly from *Endimion*: the banter of Sir Tophas and his page gave the model for that of Armado and Moth; the constables of the watch gave a hint for Dogberry and Verges, as the fairies pinching Corsites black and blue for that of Falstaff in *The Merry Wives*.

Lyly, Kyd and Marlowe were the dominant influences upon his early work; but more important was the discipline of the theatre itself. No writer was ever more a man of the theatre – not even Molière – and he owed his skill in construction, his technique, the sense of the scene, the nucleus from which he worked, to his life's experience as an actor. His poetic power grew with the demands of the theatre for expression.

Even more important was his sense of character. Others had that too, notably Jonson; but none of the world's writers has ever had so penetrating or so various a sense of character – from the simplest, most foolish and light-hearted to the most tragic and profound; no writer has created such a gallery of living, memorable characters with such instinctive sympathy and understanding as he. Here is his supreme achievement.

Then all is expressed with marvellous virtuosity as to language. He was very lordly about language. The actor's profession doubled his literary facility – one notices the astonishing increase of command from the Sonnets, say, to *Troilus and Cressida* or *Antony and Cleopatra*. His vocabulary was twice that of the normal educated Englishman; but his actor's memory picked up words and phrases from everywhere, as his eye and ear noted 'humours' and characters.

So his third specific contribution is style, in the widest sense of the term, expressing the mimetic personality of an actor, though with greater literary ambition than he has been credited with. For he was determined to stake his claim as an educated poet, to challenge fame with others, and was recognised as such even by Cambridge dons like Gabriel Harvey.

His earliest comedy, like his earliest tragedy, came out of his schooling; Elizabethan scholars took their standard of comedy from Plautus, and of tragedy partly from Seneca, though even more from tragic stories in the classics. But from the first his creations expressed his own personality; it is not only that he added elements, invented new characters, but suffused the whole with his own atmosphere. We may call it romantic, for it is compounded of emotion and poetry. With Jonson's comedy the appeal is to the intellect, and he saved his poetry for his poetic and tragic works. His comedies are essentially prose works, where in Shakespeare even the prose is poetic.

They differ too in the effect of their comedy. Jonson laughs at, and bids us laugh at, his creatures. Shakespeare is subtler and more ambivalent: we both laugh at and with his creations. What we owe to his laughter has been well put by an American critic. 'Not only does he laugh as all England laughed, but he believes as all England believes; and no more of the critical spirit is there in him than must needs be in one so well-balanced and sane. And not a single ideal, ethical judgment, or custom of his time does he question . . . By choice he accepted life.' The result is that his imagination is the more embracing. He had quite as much wit as Jonson or Molière, but the appeal to intellect is narrowing and inhibiting: Shakespeare kept both paths, indeed all possibilities, open. He gives us as searing a portrait of a Pandarus, as complete an exposure of a Parolles or a Lucio, as any intellectual satire could provide. There is plenty to disapprove of in Falstaff, but we are left with the feeling that the old rogue is irresistible. Shakespeare's humour inclines to the kindly. He knew quite as well as Swift the depths and universality of human folly and wickedness, but, unlike Swift, he gives humanity the benefit of the doubt.

In short, Shakespeare's comedy provides a catharsis no less effective than his tragedy: laughter is a release from tensions, a warming of the heart, gives one a feeling of good fellowship with our fellow-men, quite apart from reducing pride and showing us a mirror of our less noble selves.

Justice has never been done – the Victorians could not face it – to the enormously bawdy aspect, and content, of Shakespeare. Yet the salty humour has been a preservative through the centuries, one of the forces that have kept him alive. For sex is a force, indeed the life-force; and Shakespeare is the sexiest, bawdiest of all great writers. Nothing snooping and prurient, just the normal, highly-sexed heterosexual's enjoyment of 'the facts of life'. The more one knows of Elizabethan language the more one appreciates not only the direct fun and frolics, but the constant innuendos and puns with their physical suggestions, laughable, rueful, rollicking. Some of it, no doubt, was for the groundlings and helped his never-dying appeal to his audience; but it is a mistake to put it down merely to the audience, as Robert Bridges did, who as a Victorian aesthete of the purest water, was shocked by it. However, such is the nature of life – and without it there would not be life as we know it on the planet. It is absolutely part of the nature of the man, a nature as comprehensive and comprehending as any in literature.

This is a part of the completeness of his characters: he suggests them to us in the round, instead of restricting them to one humour as in *Volpone* or *Le Misanthrope*. These are in consequence less appealing, where Shakespeare's characters are open-ended, leave more to our minds; he followed his intuition and his watchful observation of human nature, unlimited by theory, for theorising is always restrictive and often inhibiting. Hence the enormous variety of his creations, the many permutations and combinations that exfoliated from a few basic patterns. The elemental situations in life are perhaps few enough, and the emotions involved not many; we watch Shakespeare repeating the situations, or the plot, refining upon them, improving, usually elaborating with his own additions to the story, until the prentice-work of *The Comedy of Errors* becomes the masterpiece that is *Twelfth Night*.

The dominant theme is that of love: another reason for regarding his work as 'romantic', going back to traditional romance; love in various aspects and forms, unrequited or requited, frustrated or fulfilled, mistaken or misjudged, competitive, crossed by mischance or magic, rivalled by the power and claims of friendship. Again, as with any real writer, this reflected the man and his experience. Ben Jonson was not interested in love, and he was not successful in marriage.

Marked progress was suddenly made from 1592 to 1593: something inspiring, and immediately maturing, had supervened. 'Might there not be something personal behind it after all? About the time the dramatist was composing his *Two Gentlemen* the poet was beginning to address sonnet-letters to his friend who, when introduced to the poet's lady, plays the traitor as Proteus does and is freely forgiven as Valentine forgives Proteus. But we "ask and ask".'

But we do not need to ask and ask, as Matthew Arnold did; we know: Arnold did not. We turn again to Dr. Johnson for enlightening common sense: 'I am always inclined to believe that Shakespeare has more allusions to particular facts and persons than his readers commonly suppose.' Of course – as with any real writer; and after two centuries of intensive research into the Elizabethan age we are in a much better position to know – William Shakespeare did not need to read up friendship in Cicero's *De Amicitia*.

We now know that the inspiration for, and subject of, *The Two Gentlemen of Verona*, is entirely autobiographical. The theme is the conflict between the claims of friendship and love; the experience that went into the play is the rivalry between the hopelessly smitten actor-dramatist and the more eminently available young patron for the favours of Emilia Lanier. And this, as we shall see, is recognisably corroborated by the related Sonnets of the same date, 1592.

We should recognise that *everything* of William Shakespeare's experience went into his work. This was natural enough, with his limited experience, compared with, say, an aristocrat like Sir Philip Sidney, or university men like Peele and Lyly, Robert Greene, Nashe, Marlowe, in regard to whom he candidly expressed deference, a sense of inferiority towards the 'learnèd'. But it is also in keeping with his own nature, which was candid, if tactful and gentlemanly – as Ben Jonson described it, 'open, honest [i.e. honourable] and free.'

So we should always be on the alert for the autobiographical element in this most autobiographical of writers, in the Plays no less than in the poems – the only one among the Elizabethan dramatists indeed to write his autobiography, in the Sonnets.

Love's Labour's Lost is more sophisticated because of the personal experience that had supervened: the introduction into a cultivated aristo-cratic circle to which Shakespeare's genius responded with alacrity and which gave him inspiration. He also tells us, in Berowne's famous speech, what he meant by love and why he attached such importance to it: as an enhancement of life, a sharpening of all the senses, of eye, ear, touch, taste; as inspiration, doubling the powers to achieve, leading men on to conquer new realms of experience. Women's eyes:

> They are the books, the arts, the academes,
> That show, contain, and nourish all the world.

Such faith is, of course, liable to disenchantment; nor did it fail to appear in the sequel – and that experience again goes into the work.

All is grist to the dramatist's mill, all his experience is in his work. Hence his knowledge of the human heart, and the force of his expression of it – even when he is at play, as in *The Taming of the Shrew*, which no one is likely to forget, as they might forget the first two comedies. The *Shrew* is a very original exercise on the theme of how to tame a woman. There is a stronger element of realism in this play than we usually realise, for the theme was a traditional one in his day, and the actuality is reinforced by the Stratford background of the Induction. It is followed by something totally different, a magical play, *A Midsummer Night's Dream*. Though this swims in the usual element of love – in this case doubly crossed and led astray, in both human couples and in the Fairy King and Queen – perhaps most memorable are the fairy tale of Beauty and the Beast, transformed into Titania and Bottom, and the recognisable realism of Bottom and his fellows, for all that they are caricatured.

We perceive that we have to add to the other major elements in Shakespeare's genius the convincing realism with which he drew lower-class life, for all the caricature, the malapropisms and lapses which he observed in it or with which he endowed it. There is a kind of poetic surrealism in the doubled reality of Lance and his Dog, Bottom the Weaver and his rude mechanicals, Dogberry and Verges, Elbow and Pompey.

All this came out of the native tradition – no one was closer to the heart of it, or had it more at heart, than this Warwickshire man, from the heart of England. The mixture, still more the bordering of the comic with the tragic, was condemned by Philip Sidney, to whose poetic impulse Shakespeare owed much. Sidney's pre-judgment was based on the classics; he did not live long enough to see the triumphs of the native tradition in the drama of the 1590s. Again, with the dramatist's instinctive respect for tradition – and what a harvest he reaped from it! – Shakespeare carried forward and developed the rôle of the Fool, clown or jester. This came not only from the earlier forms of drama but from the actual life of great houses – one more realistic stroke. It enabled him to counterpoint the behaviour of the clown's betters with occasional sharp commentary.

He distinguishes between the professional clown and the 'country clown', the ordinary rustic simpleton. They are all part of a common humanity: 'Shakespeare was too wise not to know that for most of the purposes of human life stupidity is a most valuable element. He had nothing of the impatience which sharp logical minds habitually feel when they come across those who do not apprehend their quick and precise deductions.' Thus Walter Bagehot, himself a sharp, logical mind. Few things are more remarkable than Shakespeare's patience in this direction – such a contrast with Swift at the opposite pole. It belongs to the dramatist's realm of 'negative capability'; like Burke, he appreciated the adhesive uses of simplicity, prejudice, stupidity, ordinary human foolishness. A society of rationalist intellectuals (never so rational as they suppose) could never stick together for long.

And what could be more kindly and humane, after the fiasco of Bottom's play, than the comment: 'the best in this kind are but shadows, and the worst are no worse, if imagination amend them.' There, behind the compassionate imagination, is the double-minded suggestiveness of the man, for it is an epigraph, which holds universally, on his profession.

The farcical enters largely into the early comedies. It is usual to dis-consider farce, as drama concerned *only* to excite laughter; but it is absurd to do so, when we have a better appreciation of the cathartic, indeed therapeutic, function of laughter. And William Shakespeare – with a proper mixture of innate modesty and satisfaction in his achievement – would be the last person to do so. *The Comedy of Errors* (except for the original framework into which it is put) is pure farce, as it was enacted that farcical night at Gray's Inn at Christmas 1594. *The Taming of the Shrew* is farce, for all that its ending with its moral is serious; not to appreciate that is anachronistic, for it is in keeping with what Elizabethans thought, as usual with Shakespeare. Again, towards the end of this period, *The Merry Wives of Windsor* is farce, though again how different: middle-class, bourgeois farce, featuring the townsfolk he knew so well at Stratford, the Fords and Pages as it might be the Quineys and Sadlers – with consequences that might be expected from having Sir John Falstaff plumped down in the midst of them.

For all this, the potentiality of tragedy is implicit in the comedy, as one can see in *The Rape of Lucrece* alongside the high spirits and comedy of *Venus and Adonis* (the tragic ending of which has to be taken with a grain of salt: it was intended as a moral for Southampton). *The Merchant of Venice* and *Much Ado* may well be regarded as tragi-comedies, something again different. For a considerable part of the action *The Merchant* borders on tragedy; and, though the cruder Elizabethans saw Shylock as a comic figure, there is a tragic element in him too – Shakespeare's attitude is ambivalent, as so often. He does not close down on us, as the domineering Ben did: he leaves the matter open.

As You Like It is different again – nothing tragic in that: it is a romantic pastoral play, for which the dramatist took his subject from Lodge's pastoral novel, *Rosalind*. But Shakespeare filled it with his own feeling for the woodland, his own Forest of Arden (rather than Ardennes), and there are more than the usual personal or autobiographical flecks in it. We must never forget that, though the stories sometimes come from Italian sources and the plays are often given an appealing Italian colouring in places and names, they are all indefeasibly English. It is Elizabethan England, town or country, that is portrayed – never more so than in *The Merchant of Venice*. To anyone who knows the ways of the port of London at the time, the merchants and their shipping, their argosies and the risks they took, it is all there. Even the character of Shylock has its contemporary starting point at home in Marlowe's Barabas and the actual Dr. Lopez.

We observe the development to the last of the romantic comedies in *Twelfth Night*, filled with music and melancholy. Something of the situation is repeated from *The Two Gentlemen*, with further echoes in human nature and wider, more varied characterisation. Once more there is the typical Shakespearean mixture: the serious and complex theme of love, taking different forms and at cross-purposes, frustration, misconception, what not – all mitigated by the realism, if caricatured, of Sir Toby Belch and his cronies and the ambivalent character of Malvolio. (Once more Shakespeare leaves us to think what we will about *him* – there is no doubt about the others.)

In this play Viola appears as a boy for most of the time she is on stage, as again did the heroine of *As You Like It*. We must remember how dominant an importance casting had for this most practical of dramatists, an actor himself, who lived in and by the theatre. Disguising female characters as boys, in the intrigue of the plot, was a most convenient ploy when the women's parts were taken by boys – and how talented, precocious and well-trained Elizabethan boy-actors were! The actor-dramatist worked with the materials he had at hand, not in the vacuum of the critic. One effect may be seen in the transformation of the rôle of the Fool with the departure of the rumbustious extrovert Will Kemp, and the arrival of the introvert, reflective Armin, for whom the parts of Feste, Lavache and the philosophic Fool in *Lear* were written.

Everyone notices the melancholy with which the theme of love is endued in *Twelfth Night*; we have the sense that something is ending, as indeed his romantic comedy ends with it. After the War of the Theatres of 1600-2, and the horrid experiences in the background that was yet close to Shakespeare – Southampton condemned to death, in the Tower, Essex executed – things were never the same. Shakespearean comedy was over, the future lay with Jonson's.

We can see something of the influence of the younger master upon the older, always willing to learn from anybody – as he had from Lyly, Kyd, Marlowe. *Troilus and Cressida* is an extraordinary play by all counts – no wonder 'criticism' has been foiled by it; it is a disturbing, as it is a disturbed, play, by an author whose nerves and temper are on edge. Nothing of the 'happy', genial Shakespeare in this. Yet, perhaps by the very fact of his being so disturbed, it contains some of his most brilliant writing and profound reflections on society. It also contains some of his most savage – and that is unlike the nature of the man we know: he did not go this way again until he wrote *Timon*, and, significantly, he left that unfinished.

With *All's Well* and *Measure for Measure* we have something different again: they are hardly comedies, though they are brought to happy endings. Again, though they go together, they are quite different. *All's Well* is a kind of morality; perhaps Shakespeare is harking back to the morality-plays of his youth. At the same time it has a considerable element, which has gone unnoticed, of the personal and actual: close observation and his own experience have gone into it – perhaps too close for aesthetic comfort (for creation, one needs a certain distance).

We may regard the play as experimental, something new; if so, the experiment was justified in the masterly, and more moving, *Measure for Measure* that followed. This play, for most of its action, borders on the tragic; but, with *Hamlet* three years before, we are already in the world of the great tragedies.

The Comedy of Errors
1591

This is the earliest of Shakespeare's comedies, and it is significant that it was based on Plautus, for it was from Plautus chiefly that Elizabethans learned their Latin comedy at school – and grammar school education was largely in Latin. In writing the play Shakespeare was recalling and revivifying what he had learned at school, and had probably used when he taught briefly in a country school. Moreover there is a caricature of a schoolmaster, one of several in his work, in Doctor Pinch. He based his play on the *Menaechmi* (*The Two Men Called Menaechmus*) of Plautus, and adapted another scene from Plautus's *Amphitruo*. With characteristic ingenuity and high spirits he doubled the chief characters, and added more, to increase the confusions of mistaken identity upon which the play pivots.

Even so, the play is the shortest of all the plays, and would have been briefer still in the continuous performance, unbroken by divisions into Acts and Scenes, which Elizabethan plays received. So it was particularly suited to be followed by a jig – dancing with gesture and song – as was frequent on the stage, or to provide an item in a sequence of revels, at Christmas time or some festive occasion.

We happen to know that it was performed at a Grand Night at Gray's Inn on 28 December 1594, amid much rowdy junketing that added more confusion to that presented in the play. We learn that 'after such sports a *Comedy of Errors* – like to Plautus' *Menaechmi* – was played by the players. So that night was begun and continued to the end in nothing but confusion and errors; whereupon it was ever afterwards called "the Night of Errors".'

It would seem that there had been an afternoon performance that same Innocents' day before the Queen at Greenwich – we may imagine the bargeful of players coming up-river with the tide to perform again at night, and appreciate how hard-worked the Chamberlain's men were, Shakespeare among them. At this time the aristocratic Francis Bacon was an active member of the Inn, who took a hand in its entertainments – though he could hardly have been a greater contrast to the actor-dramatist, as a son of a Lord Keeper and nephew of the Lord Treasurer; a known homosexual; a genius in prose, law and science.

—— oOo ——

The play had been written two or three years earlier, along with Shakespeare's first popular success with his *Henry VI* plays. There are contemporary touches that relate it firmly to those early 1590's, when England had to come to the aid of the Protestant Henry of Navarre fighting for his legitimate right to succeed Henri III, assassinated in 1589, on the throne of France.

In a comic passage comparing England and her neighbours to different parts of the body, a character sees France as 'armed and reverted, making war against her heir.' Henry of Navarre was the heir to the throne, whom the country as a whole did not accept till 1594, with the surrender of Paris. The use of the word 'heir' is perfectly understandable, if loosely used: there is no point in arguing about it. Shakespeare was not writing a piece of historical research and never bothered about that kind of thing. The reference was perfectly clear to the audience. America and the Indies are named for the treasure of which Elizabethans were so envious, 'declining their rich aspect to the hot breath of Spain, who sent whole armadas of carracks.' Here is a reference to the quite recent Armada of 1588, very fresh in everybody's memory.

The passage is underscored – a kind of double talk – by suggestions off-colour or rather bawdy. 'In what part of her body stands Ireland?' 'Marry, sir, in her buttocks – I found it out by the bogs.' Ireland was good for a joke, or rather more than a joke, to the Elizabethans, as today. Scotland is characterised by her barrenness, 'hard in the palm of the hand': the country was poor, and therefore penurious. 'Where stood Belgia, the Netherlands?' 'O, sir, I did not look so low!' – with appropriate gestures. It is Shakespeare all over, even thus early.

Moreover, behind Ephesus and Syracuse, the top-dressing or colouring of the play, we find as usual the contemporary scene familiar to the audience. The action is set going by the trade dispute between Ephesus and Syracuse, placing an embargo on all traffic between them; an old merchant has been caught in the conflict, in the enemy town, and condemned to death.

> The enmity and discord which of late
> Sprung from the rancorous outrage of your Duke
> To merchants, our well-dealing countrymen,
> Who, wanting guilders to redeem their lives,
> Have sealed his rigorous statutes with their bloods.

In the circumstances of the long-continuing war with Spain Elizabethans were all too familiar with trade-embargoes and their consequences. The old trade with Spain was disrupted; there had been a prolonged embargo on trade between England and her chief market abroad, the Netherlands, when the Duke of Alba ruled there – and that this was at the back of Shakespeare's mind shows itself in the word 'guilders'.

The *real* life of the age is revealed in many touches, obvious to those instructed in it. The foreign merchant visiting the city tells his man that, till dinner-time,

> I'll view the manners of the town,
> Peruse the traders, gaze upon the buildings,
> And then return and sleep within mine inn.

We are reminded of the visit of Navarre's follower, the Duc de Biron, in 1600 when Sir Walter Ralegh conducted him round the sights of London, and to Westminster to view the tombs in the Abbey, etc.

Far more important is the atmosphere of witchery in which the characters think themselves caught, so great is the confusion between their crossed identities and cross-purposes: they are driven almost to doubt their own identity.

> They say this town is full of cozenage:
> As, nimble jugglers that deceive the eye,
> Dark-working sorcerers that change the mind,
> Soul-killing witches that deform the body,
> Disguisèd cheaters, prating mountebanks,
> And many such-like liberties of sin.

This is recognisably Elizabethan London – as we see it revealed nakedly, for example, in Forman's Case-Books. Witchery and being bewitched were ever-present and ready to Elizabethan minds, increasing the impact and probabilism of a play so improbable in its action to us. We do not have to go, with some literary commentators, to St Paul's Epistle to the Ephesians when we know the facts of life in Elizabethan London.

Even the reference to Lapland sorcerers –

> Sure, these are but imaginary wiles,
> And Lapland sorcerers inhabit here –

is a commonplace of the voyagers to Russia by the Northern sea-route, reported in Hakluyt's *Principal Navigations* recently printed, which Shakespeare – like the rapid reader and writer he was – looked into, as we know.

—— oOo ——

We do not need to waste time discussing what kind of label to attach to this play – Shakespeare set no store by such pedantry, as he takes the trouble to inform us later in *Hamlet*. In his work he constantly transcended the bounds, and transgressed against the rules, beloved by critics, of dull categories. This, however, is the only play in which the label 'Comedy' appears in the title, but a great deal of the action is farcical; there is much knock-about, slapstick, and beating to appeal to the groundlings.

Shakespeare has given a romantic setting in the story of the aged merchant, Egeon, the threat to his life, and the resolution into all's well at the end. As Quiller-Couch, a creative writer himself, well understood: 'in this early play Shakespeare already discloses his propensity for infusing romance into each or every "form" of drama: that unique propensity which in his later work makes him so magical and so hard to define.' Exactly, that is the point, and 'Q.' drives it home: 'there is no line of demarcation – all such lines, or attempts at them, are a professional humbug of criticism.' If this appears too scathing, from a good critic to lesser ones, we may say simply that categories, rough as they are, are conveniences, to be held as such.

The play is by no means empty of content, as people may be misled into thinking with so much farce in it. We have the real theme of the strains of marriage, in the discussion between the two sisters, Luciana and Adriana. Whatever it expresses in the strains of Shakespeare's own married life, with himself so much away from home, living a double life in London, sympathy is tilted towards the woman's side (unlike Marlowe or Ben Jonson):

> Alas, poor women! make us but believe,
> Being compact of credit, that you love us –
> Though others have the arm, show us the sleeve,
> We in your motion turn, and you may move us.

The sympathy shines through the smile of irony. The theme of men's primacy was shortly to provide the stuff of *The Taming of the Shrew:*

> Why, headstrong liberty is lashed with woe . . .
> Men –

this is Luciana speaking –

> Are masters to their females, and their lords.

—— oOo ——

Many revealing flecks bring the personality of the author home to us. Several references to hunting the deer and the hounds bring this out-of-doors countryman before us, and corroborate what we know of him externally. We recognise the man speaking in so characteristic a thought as

> The pleasing punishment that women bear;

or the grandiloquence that annoyed Robert Greene in such a phrase as we have already quoted, '*peruse* the traders' for simply look them over.

A mere line –

> What needs all that, and a pair of stocks in the town?

– brings the country town of the time vividly before us. Dr. Pinch, the schoolmaster, is also a conjurer: he can exorcise, deliver the poor mixed-up characters out of the confusion in which they are caught. Quite so: for he is a clerk, if not in holy orders yet a reading man. He is described in terms that make one think his part was taken by the lean and skinny Sinkler, who seems to have come along with Shakespeare via Strange's and Pembroke's men to the Lord Chamberlain's Company:

> a hungry, lean-faced villain,
> A mere anatomy, a mountebank,
> A threadbare juggler, and a fortune-teller,
> A needy, hollow-eyed, sharp-looking wretch,
> A living-dead man. This pernicious slave . . .

Elizabethans enjoyed that kind of baiting.

At the end the complicated confusions of the play are straightened out; all is made plain in recognition and reconciliation at the neighbouring abbey. Outside the walls is

> the melancholy vale,
> The place of death and sorry execution,
> Behind the ditches of the abbey here.

James Burbage, Lord Chamberlain Hunsdon's man, had built the Theatre – first of London's theatres – in the fields by Holywell Priory out beyond Bishopsgate, where Shakespeare lodged later. Here in the melancholy vale were gibbets where hangings took place. All very neighbourly and recognisable to the audience which saw the play there. Oddly enough, the Abbess, who turns out to be Egeon's long-lost wife, is called Aemilia, the spelling which Shakespeare's Dark Lady affected for herself in publishing her poems years later.

The style corroborates what we may call the school character of the play – so much of it is built up on the regular usages in the teaching of rhetoric. Much use is made of *inventio*, i.e. the logical elaboration of an idea, or a conceit, step by step into the structure; and of stichomythia, i.e. dialogue alternating fixedly line by line. We encounter the endless punning, which the Elizabethans could not have enough of – and we easily too much. Shakespeare was a dab at this, an adept at word-play like no other – as he describes himself, in *Love's Labour's Lost*, 'conceit's expositor'. Difficult to put into modern English, this means that he was a virtuoso at word-play, at expressing ideas, notions, conceits. The play exhibits much rhyme, as in all the early plays: it came easily to him.

Sisson comments that 'the play is more difficult to follow in the study than on the stage, where conventional differences of costume help greatly. Shakespeare is not content with the adequate complexity of the original plot of his source, but exercised ingenuity in doubling the confusions of persons. The play is in fact a remarkable *tour de force* of construction, and a show piece.' It is highly artificial – in the Elizabethan sense of the word (an artifact) as well as the modern. It shows off well with a cast of young actors, as at Stratford – a piece of bravura: how like him, thus early!

Still more is the original touch of placing the farce in a serious setting, with Egeon's life in question, through no fault of his own, to arouse our sympathy at the outset.

The text is a good one, from the First Folio in 1623, fairly certainly from a manuscript of the author, for the speech-prefixes prefer descriptive characters to personal names. This tendency of Shakespeare's points to his thinking in terms of characters as they fitted his available cast.

The Taming of the Shrew

1591-2

In Elizabethan times the word 'shrew' was pronounced 'shrow', as we still do in Shrewsbury, and as the rhymes make clear in the play – there is a good deal of rhyme in it. It follows upon the heels of *The Comedy of Errors*; once Shakespeare got going he was a very rapid worker, as everything shows and Ben Jonson tells us.

The *Shrew* goes straight forward to its target, with one direct impulse, high spirits, and complete assurance of technique. It is a gleeful play, on a subject highly popular with the Elizabethans and, dealing with 'the war between the sexes', has an archetypal situation to make play with. Hence its undying appeal. That it appealed much to Shakespeare and released his genius we can tell from its memorable characters: Kate the reformed shrew ('Kiss me, Kate'), her wooer Petruchio, and Christopher Sly, the Warwickshireman from Shakespeare's home-ground, who provides the framework for the play and watches the fun from up above in the gallery. These are the first of his unforgettable comic creations, along with Launce.

At the same time there is plenty that brings this original play into close association with the *The Comedy of Errors* and *The Two Gentlemen*. The suitors gain access to the younger daughter, Bianca, under the guise of schooling her in books and music. We have several Latin tags from Ovid and Terence, the latter through the medium of Lyly's grammar, used in all schools. The names Tranio and Grumio come from Plautus. Classical references come easily and naturally in all the early plays, since Shakespeare was close to his schooling. Lucrece was in his mind – many references to her occur all through his work, as 'Venus and Adonis' is close too:

> Adonis painted by a running brook
> And Cytherea all in sedges hid.

Even more Italian phrases occur, which would come from his association with Florio, who was half-Italian, as was also the Dark Lady, Emilia Lanier. Her father was Baptista Bassano, and a leading character is a Baptista, father of Kate and Bianca.

A reference to Rheims reminds us of Marlowe, who had been sent there to report on the activities of the Catholic exiles. Lucentio 'hath been long studying at Rheims' – there is no reason why he should have studied there if Marlowe had not been close by. The *Shrew* was originally a Pembroke's play, a troupe for which Marlowe was also writing. The two writers obviously knew each other well. The play was so popular that it was almost immediately pirated; it has remained popular ever since, to conquer new audiences through film and television.

The subject was ready to hand, but use was made of Gascoigne's *Supposes*, itself an adaptation from Ariosto. To this there is a direct reference in the last scene: Bianca marries the right lover, after the confusion made

> While counterfeit supposes bleared thine eyne.

Once more the young men are travelling abroad

> To seek their fortunes farther than at home,
> Where small experience grows.

Once more a trade-embargo is made use of, as in *The Comedy of Errors*:

> Your ships are stayed at Venice, and the Duke –
> For private quarrel 'twixt your Duke and him
> Hath published and proclaimed it openly.

Again the utmost use is made of disguising to forward the intrigue of the plot. Shakespeare repeats himself, like any other writer – only more frequently, from the exigencies of the theatre, each time improving as he goes.

—— oOo ——

The most original thing about the *Shrew* is the Induction, for which Shakespeare drew upon his Stratford background and his own early experience with a travelling troupe of players. Christopher Sly the tinker, for whose benefit the play is performed in the hall below, is old Sly's son of Barton-on-the-Heath – where Shakespeare's uncle and aunt, the Lamberts, lived. 'Ask Marian Hacket, the fat ale-wife of Wincot', a hamlet just south of Stratford. There were Hackets around Stratford, as we know from the parish registers; and we have 'old John Naps of Greet', not far away (it was misprinted as Greece, and editors have mostly been too timorous to correct it). Sly was a Stratford name, as even E.K. Chambers recognised.

A travelling troupe of players, heralded by their trumpet, are themselves introduced – as later in *Hamlet*. A boy-actor is dressed up to play the part of a lady and appear as Sly's wife grieving for his long delusion (he has fallen asleep drunk); if the boy can't readily produce tears,

> An onion will well do for such a shift,
> Which in a napkin being close conveyed
> Shall in despite enforce a watery eye.

The players are to stay the night, and meanwhile are taken into the buttery for a meal – exactly as used to happen and Shakespeare had often experienced.

The drunken sleeper is to be carried up into the great chamber of the lordly country-house, hung round with wanton pictures, his head bathed in warm distilled water, and attendants are to 'burn sweet wood to make the lodging sweet.' When he awakes,

> Let one attend him with a silver basin
> Full of rose-water and bestrewed with flowers,
> Another bear the ewer, the third a diaper . . .

just as in an aristocratic mansion. When Sly awakes to look down on the play below, it is just as the 'quality' would have looked from the usual gallery upon the goings-on in the great hall beneath. In fact the Elizabethan proscenium in the theatre recapitulated the end of a hall, with its doors to buttery and kitchen, as we see in a college hall or historic house still.

—— oOo ——

We hear more than ever about hunting in this play; in the first scene a lord returns from hunting with huntsmen and train, and there follows a lot of knowledgeable talk about the qualities of individual hounds. In Act IV an expert passage about hawking describes how Kate is gradually to be subdued, broken in and trained like a falcon, kept hungry and without sleep,

> To make her come and know her keeper's call;

all to be done gently and with the best intentions:

> This is a way to kill a wife with kindness.

The out-of-doors countryman knew about hawking, as about deer-hunting and coursing the hare – perhaps about keeping a wife in order too: Anne Shakespeare never raises her voice, though we know that the clever daughter Susanna ran the household later: she took after her father. He favoured bowls too, another gentlemanly sport (in those days):

> Well, forward, forward! Thus the bowl should run,
> And not unluckily against the bias.

Naturally the writer was not less well acquainted with the usages of printing and publishing. Lucentio is bidden to make sure of Bianca, 'cum privilegio ad imprimendum solum', as with the privilege of the sole right in printing: the copyright formula at the time. And we may catch a reference to contemporary writing in the references to 'cony-catching' – the arts of confidence-tricksters on which Robert Greene was writing his popular tracts. Something happened between Shakespeare and Greene which has been, alas, lost.[1]

The theme of the play was much to the fore in that age and the moral driven home was in keeping with it. Shakespeare's moral outlook, as a normal family man, was always conservative and conformist, unlike Marlowe's. It is important – in our day of revolution in the status of women, Women's Lib., and the rest of it – to get this right and not be anachronistic about it.

Shakespeare's view is the normal Elizabethan one. It is not in the least that he was unsympathetic to the rights and claims, or the duties, of women. So far from that, as a woman critic points out: 'Shakespeare's sympathy with and almost uncanny understanding of women characters is one of the distinguishing features of his comedy, as opposed to that of most of his contemporaries.' (Marlowe had no interest in women: he preferred boys.) The Elizabethan position was the traditional one of the Christian church, as laid down by St. Paul: 'Let women be subject to their husbands, as to the Lord; for the husband is the head of the woman, as Christ is the head of the Church.'

What is more original in Shakespeare's play is that the man subdues the unbroken-in, coltish jade that Kate is by comic means, outwardly roughly, but inwardly by love. He really loves Kate, and the psychological subtlety – which only Shakespeare would have been capable of – is that Kate has fallen for her man too, though she is too proud and obstinate to confess it. She is reduced by firmness plus unmitigated love; and she likes that: her man is a completely masculine type, as William Shakespeare was.

Petruchio never once lays hands on her, even though she slaps him. So that it is utterly crude and psychologically wrong to bring Petruchio on the stage beating, or ever even smacking, Kate: she is to be treated comically, and her uncouthness brought home to her humorously with love. It is no less anachronistic and out of keeping to treat what Shakespeare wrote as if it were ironical and he did not mean it when he said:

> Thy husband is thy lord, thy life, thy keeper,
> Thy head, thy sovereign; one that cares for thee
> And for thy maintenance; commits his body
> To painful labour both by sea and land,

> To watch the night in storms, the day in cold,
> Whilst thou liest warm at home, secure and safe.

Though a bit poetically emphatic, it is simply what William Shakespeare meant and all Elizabethans thought. And fair enough: menfolk were exposed to all the hazards of life by sea and land; women were secure at home, their chief hazard came from childbirth.

Everybody in his proper place, according to order – the natural and social order. There is no evidence that matrimonial relations were any more unhappy in his day than in ours; actually they were far more stable and harmonious. Though women's place was a secondary one in the struggles of the outer world – their kingdom was house and home – one cannot but allow that women were much to the fore in the Renaissance world. Such eminent rulers as Elizabeth I and Catherine de Medici, the successive women Regents of the Netherlands who made a better job of it than the menfolk did, are in the forefront; women could make remarkable careers for themselves, if along the royal road of matrimony – witness the famous Bess of Hardwick, ancestress of three dukedoms. Women had a foremost part in culture and as patrons of literature and the arts.

The whole play is an expression of, and in keeping with, the age. It was thought hardly proper for a younger sister, like Bianca, to be married off before the elder, such as Kate. We recall that the scrupulous Sir Thomas More passed over a younger sister, whom he would have preferred, to marry a shrewish eldest sister whom he did not wish to humiliate. Baptista will not bestow his younger daughter,

> Before I have a husband for the elder.

This sets the action in train. When disappointed in his suit, Hortensio declares:

> I will be married to a wealthy widow
> Ere three days pass, which hath as long loved me
> As I have loved this proud disdainful haggard.

This beckoning road was as open in Elizabethan society as in America today. Widows had by right one-third of their husbands' estate: this gave them a great advantage in the marriage market: witness the matrimonial careers of Lettice Knollys, Frances Walsingham, Frances Howard – each of them married four times, the first two to become countesses, the third a royal duchess, Duchess of Richmond and Lennox.[2] So great was the financial attraction of marrying a widow that a Bill in Parliament was preferred to discourage it on demographic grounds.

Further to its contemporary relevance, the continuing success of the play should bring home that it has a deeper, more universal appeal and probes to levels in human nature beyond the contemporary, the topical and controversial. William Shakespeare speaks home to the truth about human nature and society.

In this play we catch him here, there, and everywhere: in the virtuosity of his knowledge of horse-flesh; in the refinement of the senses in his increasing acquaintance with aristocratic life; in the endless punning and verbal play. Oddly enough, we are given less bawdy in this play, though there is a naughty suggestiveness in Sly's approach to the boy, acting the part of a wife, to go to bed with him – this never fails to raise a laugh; while the 'standing' joke is repeated from *The Two Gentlemen:*

> PAGE: I hope this reason stands for my excuse.
> SLY: Ay, it stands so that I may hardly tarry so long.

The text of the play as it has come down to us from the First Folio is a fairly good one, probably from Shakespeare's working draft for performance. Written for Pembroke's early company, which ended in 1593, he would have carried it along with him to the Lord Chamberlain's when it was formed the following year. It quotes a number of catches and has snatches of song. The use of the Induction to put the play in its charming Stratford setting was not unprecedented – in production the opportunity should be taken to evoke Shakespeare's Warwickshire.

---

1. *v.* my *Shakespeare the Man*, pages 59-61 (Macmillan, London, and Harper & Row, New York, 1973)
2. *v.* my *Simon Forman: Sex and Society in Shakespeare's Age*, chapter X (Weidenfeld & Nicolson, London, 1974); American title *Sex and Society in Shakespeare's Age: Simon Forman the Astrologer* (Scribner, New York, 1975)

The Two Gentlemen of Verona

1592

The fascinating thing about this play is that it is entirely autobiographical in inspiration and subject – no wonder pedants have never found a 'source' for it – and that this has only recently been realised. Everyone has treated it as an academic exemplar of the literary debate between friendship and love, and that in fact is its theme. The two friends, Proteus and Valentine, are in love with the same girl, Silvia. Proteus betrays friendship and his friend; and yet, because he repents his offence, Valentine receives him back again and resigns his girl to the offender:

> Who by repentance is not satisfied
> Is nor of heaven nor earth; for these are pleased.
> By penitence th'Eternal's wrath's appeased.
> And, that my love may appear plain and free,
> All that was mine in Silvia I give thee.

Everyone has been affronted by this upshot, and regarded it as unconvincing and improbable – without noticing that it was precisely what happened between Shakespeare and young Southampton over Emilia. The situation is clearly described in the parallel Sonnets 33-35 concurrently:

> Though thou repent, yet I have still the loss:
> Th'offender's sorrow lends but weak relief
> To him that bears the strong offence's cross.

The situation between them is made perfectly clear in the very first scene of the play. Proteus says:

> Yet writers say, as in the sweetest bud
> The eating canker dwells, so eating love
> Inhabits in the finest wits of all.

To which Valentine:

> And writers say, as the most forward bud
> Is eaten by the canker ere it blow,
> Even so by love the young and tender wit

Is turned to folly – blasting in the bud,
Losing his verdure even in the prime,
And all the fair effects of future hopes.

Who are 'the writers' who say just that? – Shakespeare is referring to himself. The related Sonnet makes clear:

No more be grieved at that which thou hast done . . .
Clouds and eclipses stain both moon and sun,
And loathsome canker lives in sweetest bud.

The Sonnets of just that time describe the cloud that the affair had brought upon the relationship:

Full many a glorious morning have I seen . . .
But out, alack, he was but one hour mine,
The region cloud hath masked him from me now . . .
Why didst thou promise such a beauteous day . . .
To let base clouds o'ertake me in my way?

The situation between the friends is described again in these words at the end of the first Act:

O how this spring of love resembleth
The uncertain glory of an April day,
Which now shows all the beauty of the sun,
And by and by a cloud takes all away.

From this the play proceeds, and this is what it is about – the date, 1592, concurrently with those related Sonnets. It was completely characteristic of William Shakespeare to put *everything* of his experience into his work – needs must, with his limited beginnings, if he were to make a living with his pen. We can observe this throughout his work, if we have the wit to perceive it. The very words –

so eating love
Inhabits in the finest wits of all –

show what he thought of himself; as the next words confirm the hopes entertained of the young patron in the Sonnets, with the fear that an affair with the experienced (and promiscuous) Emilia might make a fool of him and moreover blast

all the effects of future hopes.

The hopes naturally entertained of the young earl are again politely, and recognisably, referred to:

> if he make this good,
> He is as worthy for an Empress' love
> As meet to be an emperor's counsellor.

(In the event Southampton never achieved the Queen's approval, and nearly lost his life for Essex; not until James I came to the throne did he become a counsellor.)

The play starts with a send-off of a young gentleman, Valentine, by his friend Proteus, on a tour abroad which was the regular thing for a young gentleman to undertake:

> To see the wonders of the world abroad;

his friend bids him to look out for

> Some rare noteworthy object in thy travel.

This was especially a time when young men set out–

> Some to the wars to try their fortunes there,
> Some to discover islands far away –

(like Sir Walter Ralegh and Sir Richard Grenville)

> Some to the studious universities.

Proteus later follows his friend; his man Launce is late in getting aboard ship; a fellow-servant hurries him up:

> Thy master is shipped, and thou art to post after with oars.
> You'll lose the tide if you tarry any longer.

It is, of course, the tidal Thames, where it was important to catch the tide if one was to 'shoot' London Bridge – to go down river to ship for a sea-voyage. It does not matter that Shakespeare leaves the places somewhat mixed up in the play – too busy to bother about details of that sort.

—— oOo ——

There are two specific references to the theme of Hero and Leander. The subject would be to the fore in Shakespeare's mind in 1592, when Marlowe was writing his *Hero and Leander* in rivalry with *Venus and Adonis* for the favour of Southampton.

The women come out best in the play – and that again is characteristic. It is not very *chic* of Valentine to hand over his girl, while Proteus comes out badly; his name describes but does not excuse him, in the battledore and shuttlecock between them to which the ladies are subjected. A woman critic notes of this, Shakespeare's first romantic comedy: 'his tendency to hand over most of the initiative and just judgment to the women in his cast of characters was already marked.'

We may add that Julia, in assuming the guise of a page to follow Proteus, provides a first example of what the practising actor-dramatist was to employ so much later. Since women's parts were played by boys, it was practical to invent a plot in which the women had to disguise themselves as boys.

We have a recognisable reminiscence from Shakespeare's own boyhood, when Julia says:

> at Pentecost,
> When all our pageants of delight were played,
> Our youth got me to play the woman's part,
> And I was trimmed in Madam Julia's gown.

It reminds one of the Whitsun pastorals which were performed at Stratford and in so many places all over the country in that dramatising age. The part she played was a classical one, Ariadne lamenting Theseus's perjury and flight – to remind us that the dramatist's schooling was in the classics.

—— oOo ——

Most appealing to us today are the scenes that bring the life of the time realistically before us. Notably in the characters of Launce, and no less his dog Crab, and his fellow-servant Speed: they are drawn authentically from life below stairs, and have their just comment to offer on their betters and what goes on above. In the talk between these two we have Shakespeare's sharp ear for the speech and idiom of the people – like Scott or Hardy; and absolute virtuosity in Launce addressing his dog, which never fails to bring the house down:

> He thrusts me himself into the company of three or four gentleman-like dogs under the Duke's table. He had not been there – bless the mark – a pissing-while but all the chamber smelt him. 'Out with the dog,' says one. 'What cur is that?', says another. 'Whip him out,' says the third. 'Hang him up,' says the Duke. I, having been acquainted with the smell before, knew it was Crab, and goes me to the fellow that whips the dogs. 'Friend,' quoth I, 'you mean to whip the dog?' 'Ay, marry, do I,' quoth he. 'You do him the more wrong,' quoth I, ''twas I did the thing you wot of.' He makes me no more ado, but whips me out of the chamber. How many masters would do this for his servant?

Anyone who knows the strict regulations governing great households of the time, conduct in hall, cleanliness in courtyards, etc. will appreciate the authentic note of this. And then, a final reproach: 'Nay, I remember the trick you served me when I took my leave of Madam Silvia. Did not I bid thee still mark me and do as I do? When didst thou see me heave up my leg and make water against a gentlewoman's farthingale? Didst thou ever see me do such a trick?'

There are the usual bawdy exchanges between these good fellows – on the love-affairs of the gentry, for example:

> SPEED: Why, then, how stands the matter with them?
> LAUNCE: Marry, thus: when it stands well with him, it stands well with her.

There follows a good deal of bawdy talk and punning about standing: the same joke as Shakespeare applies to himself in regard to his mistress, 'rising at thy name', in Sonnet 151.

Sisson notes how from this time on Shakespeare delights in Italian settings, Italian stories and names. And no wonder, when we realise that this play, reflecting the conflicting claims of friendship between men and love of a woman, paralleled the triangular relationship at the time of Shakespeare, Southampton and Emilia. Nor is it surprising that Shakespeare for the first time imports song into this play:

> Who is Silvia? what is she
> That all our swains commend her? . . .
>
> Is she kind as she is fair?
> For beauty lives with kindness.
> Love doth to her eyes repair,
> To help him of his blindness.

It is the language of the Sonnets. No doubt it was an element in the subjugation of this most musical of writers that the half-Italian Emilia Bassano (Mrs Lanier) was musical too.

—— oOo ——

The text which we have is a good one, from the First Folio, probably from the Company's prompt-book based on Shakespeare's manuscript.

Love's Labour's Lost
1593

Love's Labour's Lost follows close upon the heels of the *The Two Gentlemen*, and is hardly less autobiographical in inspiration. Professor C.J. Sisson says, with some naiveté, 'the plot of *Love's Labour's Lost* appears to have been of Shakespeare's own devising.' But, of course, it is a skit on what we may call the Southampton theme: the young patron's well-known refusal to respond to women – the subject of the first section of the Sonnets – or at least to be 'roped and tied' (in the American phrase) by the bond of marriage.

The play starts with the young king of Navarre (Southampton) pledging himself and his friends to abstain from the company of women for a period, to give themselves up to their studies. Berowne thinks this to be nonsense:

> But love first learnèd in a lady's eyes . . .
> Courses as swift as thought in every power,
> And gives to every power a double power,
> Above their functions and their offices.

He concludes then:

> From women's eyes this doctrine I derive.
> They sparkle still [ever] the right Promethean fire:
> They are the books, the arts, the academes,
> That show contain and nourish all the world.

Everyone has recognised that Berowne expresses Shakespeare's point of view, but no one had recognised that Shakespeare is portraying himself in this skit on the Southampton circle by its poet-actor-dramatist.

When we come to the lady with whom Berowne pairs off in the play, she is described in almost precisely the language in which Emilia is described in the Sonnets:

> O, if in black my lady's brows be decked,
> It mourns that painting and usurping hair
> Should ravish doters with a false aspect:
> And therefore is she born to make black fair.

Berowne goes on like this, and in rhyming sonnet form.

So, when his dark lady in the play turns round and describes Berowne, it is William Shakespeare laughing at himself:

> a merrier man –
> Within the limit of becoming mirth –

(in itself a joke, for we know how much he was given to bawdy)

> I never spent an hour's talk withal.
> His eye begets occasion for his wit,
> For every object that the one doth catch,
> The other turns to a mirth-moving jest.
> Which his fair tongue, conceit's [fancy's] expositor,
> Delivers in such apt and gracious words
> That agèd ears play truant at his tales,
> And younger hearings are quite ravishèd,
> So sweet and voluble is his discourse.

Joking – but, all the same, we see that William Shakespeare had a good conceit of himself, as Robert Greene had seen, and what a formidable competitor he would be to the university wits.

Thus the scene is set, the action of the play foreshadowed by Shakespeare as Berowne:

> Then fools you were these women to forswear;
> Or, keeping what is sworn, you will prove fools.

The women in question prove to be the Princess of France and her ladies, and all is very topical. It was quite natural – as well as polite and complimentary – that the young patron should figure as the king of Navarre, very popular in England, especially with Essex and Southampton. Essex had led the expedition to Normandy to Navarre's aid in 1591, and Southampton had broken away and gone across the Channel, without permission, to serve under him.

By 1593 there was already some fear that Navarre would convert to Catholicism – he was already under instruction – hence the issue of oath-breaking is glanced at in the play. (Next year he did break his word, to win Paris – 'Paris is worth a Mass.') The names given to the characters are those to the fore at the time: Longaville (Longueville), Dumain (Mayenne), Berowne (Biron). They in fact appear in the pamphlets that Richard Field, Shakespeare's fellow townsman from Stratford, was printing contemporaneously in Blackfriars, along with *Venus and Adonis*, 1593, and *The Rape of Lucrece*, 1594.

It is obvious that the play was originally written for private performance in the young patron's select circle, and it used to be thought of as an enigma to which the key had been lost. We now have the key and know what the answer is. The play is naturally full of allusions, most of which can now be interpreted, and private jokes, some of which are lost – no great loss (one of them, a poor Latin pun I interpreted years ago). Everyone can see that the play is an acutely personal one, Shakespeare himself stamped in every line, his high spirits and sheer delight in verbal dexterity – endless puns and innuendos – which sometimes carried him away and makes some difficulties for us four hundred years later.

All the more important, indeed necessary, to know what was going on at the time, and who was who.

—— oOo ——

One important character in the play is immediately identifiable: Don Adriano de Armado, 'a fantastical Spaniard' (he was in fact identified years ago by the historian, Martin Hume) with his immense conceit, his airs and graces, his inflated and flattering rhetoric. Philip II's ex-Secretary of State, Antonio Pèrez, was in England from April 1593 to July 1595, until he outwore his welcome and fatigued his sponsors, Essex and his secretary Anthony Bacon. Essex – Southampton's admired leader and friend – gave Don Antonio Pèrez an apartment at Essex House. So we have:

> Our Court, you know, is haunted
> With a refinèd traveller of Spain;
> A man in all the world's new fashion planted,
> That hath a mint of phrases in his brain;
> One who the music of his own vain tongue
> Doth ravish like enchanting harmony;
> A man of compliments . . .
> From tawny Spain . . .

Pèrez was a professional rhetorician, and his inflated language is made fun of throughout. He was a homosexual, and a great snob, so that to make him fall in love with Jacquenetta, 'a base wench', a country girl, was an obvious hit.

So too with Holofernes, 'a schoolmaster', with his fantastic use of rare and odd words, which is ridiculed. John Florio was during these years Italian tutor to Southampton, living in his household. He later dedicated his Dictionary, *A World of Words*, to Southampton; but already, a couple of years before our play, in his *Second Fruits* of 1591, he had expressed a low view of English plays as 'neither right comedies nor right tragedies', but 'mere representations of histories, without any decorum.' This was fair enough comment on the three parts of *Henry VI*, which had won Shakespeare such popularity, and which had very probably gained him Southampton's attention.

Here was Shakespeare's come-back. That Florio was partly in mind we see from the proverb Shakespeare quotes from Florio's *First Fruits*:

> Venetia, Venetia,
> Chi non ti vede, non ti pretia.

'Venice, he who doth not see thee, doth not value thee.' There are a number of parallel passages between Shakespeare and Florio; Italian phrases he could always have got from the tutor in Southampton's household, where the play probably had its first performance. That the play had its special relation to the Earl and his circle is corroborated by the fact that he had it produced again specially for James I at Southampton House in 1605.

Sisson made the perceptive point that 'the Italian language, for Shakespeare as for Holofernes, was perhaps more familiar in sound than in writing.'[1] How apt this comment was, with Florio and Emilia Bassano close by just at this time! Again Henry of Navarre had, in historical fact, received just such missions from the French royal ladies as that which is featured in the play; and, moreover, he became a patron of just such an Academy.

On the literary side, the contemporary pamphlet-war between the Cambridge intellectuals – Gabriel Harvey on one side, Robert Greene and Thomas Nashe on the other – is made use of to extract fun. The incorrigible young Nashe's pen was wickedly inspired whenever he thought of Harvey, conceited don as he was. In the play Nashe features as 'tender Juvenal', by which he was referred to by Greene and others. He tried to bounce himself into Southampton's patronage with an unsolicited dedication, but this post was already pre-empted. Subsequently he gained the notice of Sir George Carey, Lord Chamberlain Hunsdon's son, who succeeded him as patron of Shakespeare's company. He lived in Blackfriars, where the Lord Chamberlain also had a house, as Richard Field his press. We see how definite and closely associated this circle was in just these years.

—— oOo ——

We must always remember, in reading, that a play is a play is a play, and the actor-dramatist thought and composed in scenes. The King and courtiers, the Princess and her ladies, speak in verse: their part, with its teasing love-interest, is romantic comedy. And at this period when the Sonnets were being written several sonnets appear in the play. The Armado and Holofernes scenes, and the yokels all in prose, are pure farce and should be played as such. The country clowns' presentation of the Nine Worthies ridicules the regular doggerel familiar on such Elizabethan occasions – though Shakespeare interposes a kind-hearted realistic touch when one of them breaks down:

'There, an't please you: a foolish mild man; an honest man, look you, and soon dashed! He is a marvellous good neighbour, faith, and a very good bowler; but, for Alisander – alas! you see how 'tis – a little o'er-parted.' (i.e. the part is too much for him).

The masque of Muscovites which the courtiers present masked reflects the marked interest of the Elizabethans in Russia, since they were the first to open up direct Russian contact with the West through the voyages to Archangel. These were written up in Hakluyt's *Navigations*, the first edition of which had appeared a few years before, in 1589 – and we know that Shakespeare, a keen and rapid reader, read Hakluyt. Embassies were exchanged, and Russian ambassadors were presented to the Queen. A pageant of Russians at the Gray's Inn Revels at Christmas time 1594 does not upset our dating of the play, for it was obviously revised, with additions, for public performance in 1597. As a professional to his finger-tips Shakespeare would naturally touch up a play written for a private occasion and a special audience when it came before the public.

Everything bespeaks the specialised appeal to the aristocratic audience for which it was written – notably the sophisticated wit of an intellectual kind; Elizabethans enjoyed this kind of sparring, which much attracted Shakespeare – though less today. Caroline Spurgeon, in her book on his imagery, noticed how his senses became more refined with his entry into this aristocratic circle; and, sure enough, the 'base vulgar' have their strong smell – true enough to Elizabethan conditions.

—— oOo ——

We encounter many personal touches. The schoolmasterly clichés – *pauca verba* (few words), *haud credo* (I don't think) – remind us of his schooldays and the information from an early source that, for a time, he was a young usher in a country school. The passage at arms, with Dull misunderstanding the schoolmaster's *haud credo*, is based on a pun: Dull protests that it was not a *haud credo* (au'd grey doe) but a pricket, i.e. a young buck. This again reminds us of Shakespeare's perfect fixation on hunting the deer in his early days. The Latin tag the schoolmaster quotes from Mantuan, the Renaissance poet popular in schools, goes back to them: 'Old Mantuan! who understands thee not loves thee not.' There is more about Elizabethan schooling and schoolmasters in Shakespeare than in any other dramatist of the time.

We are reminded of the university in the line,

Proceeded well, to stop all good proceeding!

for it was the regular term at Oxford for proceeding to one's M.A. He was acquainted with Oxford from passing through it on his way to and from

London; actually, it is more than likely that the poet was present with his young patron, when Southampton, a Cambridge man, proceeded M.A. at Oxford in 1592.

From first to last, in spite of the disillusionment he suffered from his dark mistress (the Rosaline of the play, the notorious lady of the Sonnets), Shakespeare had a romantic conception of the love of men and women – unlike Marlowe or Francis Bacon or Ben Jonson. This has always been a basic element in his world-wide appeal. *Love's Labour's Lost* – the very title may have come from Florio's *First Fruits*, 'it were labour lost to speak of Love' – is a manifesto in favour of love and life, nature and natural feeling, against intellectualism, pedantry and affectation. Here we have Shakespeare – an edge is added to it by the fact that we have a naturally clever man, himself an intellectual, tilting against various absurd forms of intellectualism.

The play ends in parting, not the usual consummation of romantic love, and this is in keeping with the actual situation behind the play, which sparked it off and which it reflects: Southampton would not and did not marry for some years yet. Berowne (Shakespeare) has the last word and points to the exception that it is:

> Our wooing doth not end like an old play:
> Jack hath not Jill: these ladies' courtesy
> Might well have made our sport a comedy.

We may be sure that Shakespeare played the part of Berowne in the original performance; it would be a proper idea to present Berowne as William Shakespeare in producing the play today.

He makes further use of song in this play – understandably in its ambience, dismissing his characters from the stage with two magical evocations. They still evoke Stratford for us: in Spring –

> When daisies pied, and violets blue,
>   And lady-smocks all silver-white,
> And cuckoo-buds of yellow hue,
>   Do paint the meadows with delight . . .

And then in Winter –

> When icicles hang by the wall,
>   And Dick the shepherd blows his nail,
> And Tom bears logs into the hall,
>   And milk comes frozen home in pail.

> When all aloud the wind doth blow,
>   And coughing drowns the parson's saw,
> And birds sit brooding in the snow,

And Marian's nose looks red and raw,
When roasted crabs hiss in the bowl,
Then nightly sings the staring owl.
                              Tu-whit,
Tu-who, a merry note,
While greasy Joan doth keel the pot.

—— oOo ——

Cuthbert Burby printed the play in 1598, 'as it was presented before her Highness this last Christmas. Newly corrected and augmented.' Evidently the play had been revised for public performance. The editors of the First Folio in 1623 reprinted the play from the 1598 copy, with some checking from their prompt-book. The revision and the transmission account for a certain number of misprints, textual confusions, and changes. These need not, however, detain us. Shakespeare had more urgent things to do, busy as he was, than to tie up loose ends to present a smooth surface, nor was he much concerned in the printing of his plays. He naturally changed his mind, from one draft to another, as any writer does; and Dr. Johnson, with his own experience of writing as a professional – as pedants are not – observed that the dramatist sometimes scamped the ending of a play in a hurry, for the next was being called for.

The play in production is the thing, and an admirable producer, Granville Barker, concludes that 'style' must be the keynote of any satisfactory production answering to Shakespeare's ideas. That is in keeping with our conception of the stylishness of the young Southampton's circle, of which the actor-dramatist was the poet. Then, for all the fun and frolics, the posturing and caricaturing, at the end the shadow of reality falls upon the scene, with the messenger announcing the death of the Princess's father. She must withdraw and away: dramatically effective, it raises the end to a higher level, with a touch of emotion and reality to conclude the light-hearted matter.

1. Sisson, Charles Jasper *New Readings in Shakespeare*, vol. I page 112 (Cambridge University Press, Cambridge, 1956). This was the more perceptive because Sisson was writing before my identification of the Dark Lady.

A Midsummer Night's Dream

1594

The play was written, or adapted, for a wedding celebration. We know from Sonnet 106 that, in 1593, Shakespeare was reading Chaucer, from whose 'antique pen' had come the 'Knight's Tale', which provides the framework for the play; and we may infer from Sonnet 98 that he was thinking of a 'summer's story'. When we come to the close of the play, however, we find that it is Maytime, and the young lovers return from observing Mayday to grace the marriage of the elderly, stately couple, Duke Theseus and his betrothed Hippolyta.

Thus was the play adapted for the wedding of the elderly Privy Councillor and Vice-Chamberlain to the Queen, Sir Thomas Heneage, and Southampton's mother, the Countess, on 2 May 1594. Moreover, this wedding was a private occasion, certainly not graced by the presence of the Queen, who did not favour it – we know independently that Heneage was out of favour with her that spring. For one thing, he was old – why should he want to marry? – and, for another, the Countess was a Catholic. From her point of view, it was a good protective move, for the Vice-Chamberlain was a staunch Protestant; her family needed protection, for her son had offended Lord Treasurer Burghley by breaking his promise to marry his grand-daughter and the Queen never favoured Southampton, for his wayward adolescent ways.

Nor is it probable that the actor-dramatist – who was all gentlemanly courtesy and tact – would confront the Virgin Queen on a first performance with –

> To live a barren sister all your life,
> Chanting faint hymns to the cold fruitless moon.

(Elizabeth was all too frequently hailed as Cynthia, the cold goddess of the moon, 'the mortal moon', etc.)

> But earthlier happy is the rose distilled
> Than that which, withering on the virgin thorn,
> Grows, lives and dies in single blessedness.

This is an image with which Shakespeare had chosen to address his young patron in the Sonnets, urging him to marry; in it we recognise the Southampton theme.

So the marriage of the elderly couple was a private one, which the Queen did not attend – that is why little is known about it; we do not know where it took place, except in a private house, probably Southampton House in Holborn, its gardens running down Chancery Lane (we can still trace the shape of the site).

—— oOo ——

The plot of the play – the double-plot of the elderly match and the complications of the young lovers at cross-purposes – is hardly important, though it provides the framework. What the world remembers are the twin elements of the fairy-tale and the performance of the 'rude mechanicals', the characters of Titania and Oberon, above all Puck; of Bottom the weaver and his crew of joiner, carpenter, bellows-mender, tinker and tailor, above all Bottom.

Though the fairy-tale is a primitive, archetypal form of literature, and there are other examples in the Elizabethan age, we may regard *A Midsummer Night's Dream* as a perennial inspiration and a fountain-source of fairy-tale literature ever after, up to our own day with Kipling's 'Puck of Pook's Hill'. The play was a favourite with those elect spirits, Milton and Keats, as well as with the world in general. Even in Shakespeare's own day, his fellow Warwickshire man Drayton's charming 'Nymphidia' was greatly influenced by it, perhaps inspired by it.

How perceptive Quiller-Couch was in writing about Puck and Robin Goodfellow: rather than from books, 'it is even more likely that he brought all this fairy-stuff up to London in his own head, packed with nursery legends of his native Warwickshire. When will criticism learn to allow for the enormous drafts made by creative artists such as Shakespeare and Dickens upon their childhood?' Q. was himself a creative writer, and he knew.

The historian too can appreciate that Shakespeare never lost touch with his native Stratford. The mechanics are straight out of the streets and occupations of the country market-town we know so much about – after all, his father was a glover (as Drayton's was a butcher), Richard Field's a tanner, further down in Henley Street was blacksmith Hornby. It is like this clever man, always ready for a joke, that the names of the artisans (Elizabethans called them 'mechanics') pun upon their occupations – a 'bottom' is the skein upon which the weaver winds his yarn, and so on. As for their performance, Shakespeare is caricaturing what he, the professional, had often seen in country plays and provincial performances. Once more, after they have been laughed off the stage, there is a kind-hearted comment that bespeaks the author: 'the best in this kind are but shadows, and the worst are no worse, if imagination amend them.' There he is, speaking directly to our hearts.

Such are the elements that go to the making of this play: marriage and married love, love crossed and brought together again, the competing claims of love and friendship – so much to the fore in these years, in *The Two Gentlemen of Verona* as more powerfully in *The Merchant of Venice*. This theme is the very crux of the Sonnets, and what gives them their dramatic tension, almost like another play.

Scholars have traced the mingled elements out of which the play was blended. There is Chaucer, along with Shakespeare's favourite poet, Ovid. We know that he read the *Metamorphoses* in the original – and Beeston of the Globe Company told John Aubrey that 'he understood Latin pretty well, for he had been in his younger years a schoolmaster in the country.' Nevertheless, for a busy player and playwright, it was handier and more convenient to reach down Golding's translation, which he used more often. The chief contemporaries who influenced Shakespeare, apart from Marlowe, were Sidney and Spenser – from the latter comes Oberon. Bottom's woeful Pyramus and Thisbe play was suggested from Ovid.

—— oOo ——

Various touches serve to give us the contemporary background and make the play more real to us.

> The thrice three Muses mourning for the death
> Of learning, late deceased in beggary –

refers to the death of Robert Greene in penury and want some eighteen months earlier. Greene, a Cambridge man, always asserted his M.A. from both universities; and Shakespeare, who respected learning, several times pays tribute to his rival, Marlowe, in the Sonnets for his greater learning, as a university man: 'his well-refined pen', that 'worthier pen' and 'able spirit', whose favour from the young patron adds 'feathers to the learned's wing'. The reference continues:

> That is some satire, keen and critical,
> Not sorting with a nuptial ceremony –

which is appropriate enough to Greene's sharp and realistic cony-catching pamphlets and descriptions of low life, which were more successful than his plays; or even to the envious attack on Shakespeare from his death-bed in 1592.

In the summer of that year the Queen had paid a visit to Oxford, when Southampton was made an M.A. That Shakespeare was in attendance we may well infer from the authentic note of the Duke's speech:

> Where I have come, great clerks have purposèd

> To greet me with premeditated welcomes;
> Where I have seen them shiver and look pale,
> Make periods in the midst of sentences,
> Throttle their practised accent in their fears,
> And in conclusion dumbly have broke off.

Upon occasion this was precisely what had happened to scared academics confronting Queen Elizabeth I.

The description of the disastrously wet summer of 1594 does not disturb our dating, for this play, too, being a private one in origin, would have been revised and expanded for public performance. It is a countryman who writes (and Shakespeare was a countryman, unlike Marlowe and Ben Jonson, who were townees):

> the green corn
> Hath rotted ere his youth attained a beard.
> The fold stands empty in the drownèd field,
> And crows are fatted with the murrain flock,
> The nine men's morris is filled up with mud,
> And the quaint mazes in the wanton green
> For lack of tread are undistinguishable.

We are reminded that it was in the Cotswolds, on the threshold of Stratford, that morris dancing never died out, and from there was revived in this century.

The play is full of country lore, country activities and observations. We have yet again Shakespeare's early passion for hunting:

> My love shall hear the music of my hounds.
> Uncouple in the western valley, let them go . . .

> their heads are hung
> With ears that sweep away the morning dew,
> Crook-kneed, and dewlapped like Thessalian bulls;
> Slow in pursuit; but matched in mouth like bells,
> Each under each. A cry more tuneable
> Was never holla'ed to, nor cheered with horn.

This is a hunting man's enthusiasm – nothing like it in other Elizabethan dramatists. We note the sportsman's eye for birds:

> As wild geese that the creeping fowler eye,
> Or russet-patèd choughs, many in sort,
> Rising and cawing at the gun's report,
> Sever themselves, and madly sweep the sky.

Or sounds:

> More tuneable than lark to shepherd's ear,
> When wheat is green, when hawthorn buds appear.

Country beliefs and superstitions, traditional lore, are woven into the texture of the play, which is largely fabricated out of them. Life is electrified by ghosts, who visit us by night; with dawn,

> At whose approach, ghosts, wandering here and there,
> Troop home to churchyards: damnèd spirits all,
> That in crossways and floods have burial.

At cross-roads suicides were buried.

> Now it is the time of night
> That the graves, all gaping wide,
> Every one lets forth his sprite,
> In the churchway paths to glide.

In the ghost-haunted churchway path at Stratford there was a charnel-house in his time.

Even the unimaginative E.K. Chambers saw that Puck, or Robin Goodfellow, was the most characteristic creation of *A Midsummer Night's Dream*, the symbol of what he calls a 'dramatic fantasy'. Puck comes straight out of folklore:

> are you not he
> That frights the maidens of the villagery,
> Skim milk, and sometimes labour in the quern,
> And bootless make the breathless housewife churn,
> And sometimes make the drink to bear no barm,
> Mislead night-wanderers, laughing at their harm?

All this added a dimension to the simple lives of country folk, and lapped it round with poetry. Puck boasts of his feats:

> And sometimes lurk I in a gossip's bowl,
> In very likeness of a roasted crab,
> And when she drinks against her lips I bob,
> And on her withered dewlap pour the ale.
> The wisest aunt, telling the saddest tale,
> Sometimes for three-foot stool mistaketh me:
> Then slip I from her bum, down topples she,
> And 'tailor' cries, and falls into a cough.

> And then the whole choir hold their lips and laugh,
> And waxen in their mirth, and neeze, and swear
> A merrier hour was never wasted there.

Much of this play is in rhyme, and rhyme comes easily and naturally to a born poet – not to those who are not. The most moving poetry occurs in these evocative passages from country life and lore, for this is what was at heart with Shakespeare. He was an historically-minded, backward-looking man, inspired by the past and the life of the past, like Scott and Hardy – not a forward-looking, more superficial kind of writer, like Shaw or H.G. Wells. As an inspired painter, Samuel Palmer, wrote: 'The Past for poets', and he added, 'the Present for pigs.'

One gesture to the contemporary world is vouchsafed by the poet, a salute to the Queen – there are not many in Shakespeare (as against Spenser, for example), for he was aligned through Southampton with Essex, who moved into dangerous opposition. (Shakespeare's disenchantment with Essex can be traced in the Plays.) It is thought that the following may refer back to the splendid Entertainments Leicester laid on for her at Kenilworth in 1575 – which Shakespeare could have seen as a boy of eleven; for this was Leicester's last attempt to capture the Queen in marriage. Cupid aims

> At a fair Vestal, thronèd by the west . . .
> But I might see young Cupid's fiery shaft
> Quenched in the chaste beams of the wat'ry moon.
> And the imperial Votaress passed on
> In maiden meditation, fancy-free.

We see Shakespeare's early genius at its most authentic in the comic transcripts from real life; as Dr. Johnson saw, his initial gift was for comedy – in keeping with his nature.

—— oOo ——

The text of this play has come down to us in very good state, probably from Shakespeare's own revised draft, and presents few problems. There are signs of alternative endings to the play – a masque for private performance (appropriate to the wedding), an epilogue for public performance. It was not in the interest of the Company, or the author, to publish their plays: the theatre was their first and last concern, and they wanted to keep their property for theatrical performances. So great was Shakespeare's appeal that his plays were often pirated, got by memory – perhaps with the connivance of lesser actors – and printed in reported versions (the Bad Quartos).

This play was printed in a good quarto in 1600, 'as it hath been sundry times publicly acted by the Right Honourable the Lord Chamberlain's servants.' It was reprinted by Jaggard in 1619, and from this again in the First Folio of 1623, the great collection of all Shakespeare's work for the theatre, brought together by his fellows, Hemming and Condell, in his honour. It was compared with the Company's own copy, as we know from a charming touch that has crept into the final Interlude, which is annotated:

> Tawyer, with a trumpet before them.

Tawyer was Hemming's servant, who was buried in St. Saviour's, Southwark (the present cathedral) a couple of years later, in 1625. It brings the performers of this magical play home to us.

The Merchant
of Venice
1596

The alert dramatist with his ear to the ground for what would appeal – what we would call box-office returns – ever since he began successfully with the *Henry VI* plays, found a topical subject to hand for *The Merchant of Venice*. For, at the time and for long afterwards, the play was often referred to as 'The Jew of Venice'. Shylock was the dominant character, the one who remains above all the rest in the mind, and the play relates to the theme that has had so terrible a resonance in our time: the Jew in Europe and the evil phenomenon of anti-Semitism. It is necessary to confront it directly and simply, without flinching.

Europe has had a shocking record in regard to the Jews, reaching its evil climax in our demotic days with Auschwitz, Belsen, Dachau, and all the rest. The 16th century record was nothing like so bad, and Jewish characteristics, the addiction to money and usury, etc. were regarded as matter for comedy – as were other national characteristics, Scotch, Irish, Dutch, German, French, or Spanish, as in *The Two Gentlemen of Verona* and again in this play, good for a laugh. It must be realised that, to the Elizabethans, Shylock was a comic character, though we may think of him as more tragic.

He derives directly from Barabas, the leading figure in Marlowe's savage, farcical play, *The Jew of Malta*. With the popular excitement over the Lopez affair running high in 1594, Marlowe's play was revived by the Admiral's company and given some fifteen performances later that year. The Chamberlain's men saw their chance to go one better, as their actor-dramatist certainly did with the play he wrote for them. Marlowe's play was the chief influence upon his mind, though Shakespeare placed the action once more in the setting of a familiar Italian story, from the collection called *Il Pecorone*, contemporary with Boccaccio. He fused these two main elements into a play which has been always successful – particularly, we note, perhaps significantly, in Germany.

Dr. Lopez, the Queen's physician, we repeat, had been shockingly handled in England. He had been too successful for some people's taste – and that had somewhat gone to his head; he dabbled dangerously in political intelligence and he had made aspersions against Essex's sexual health. It was Essex who ran him down, made it a point of 'honour' to bring him down. The humane Queen never believed that Lopez intended to poison her, but could not hold up for ever the popular clamour against him. We must remember (a), Shakespeare's indirect affiliation to Essex through Southampton; (b), his usual conformity with popular opinion.

Considering that, it is rather wonderful what he made out of the play, though we today may feel sensitive about it – far more than the Victorians, with whom it was very popular.

On the other hand it provides an illuminating contrast with Marlowe's play: the contrasting genius of the two men stands out sharply. Marlowe's Barabas is a comic villain, savagely belaboured and brought to book for the delight of the spectators. Shakespeare begins with the popular representation of Shylock as a Jew to be despised, but his humanity cannot help breaking in. Shylock *has* been wronged, and 'hath not a Jew eyes? hath not a Jew hands, organs, dimensions, senses, affections, passions? fed with the same food, hurt with the same weapons, subject to the same diseases, healed by the same means, warmed and cooled by the same winter and summer, as a Christian is?' Here is the real Shakespeare: a very different soul from Marlowe, for all that he owed to him.

We find virtual quotations from Marlowe, besides phrases and other touches – Shakespeare's infallible ear picked up and registered everything usable. An Elizabethan audience found it funny when the Jew's daughter ran away to marry a Christian – though we may not. Shylock's outburst is as follows:

> My daughter! O my ducats! O my daughter!
> Fled with a Christian! O my Christian ducats!

The words are practically the same as Marlowe's, the situation repeated from his play. The Elizabethans laughed at the absconding Jessica playing fast and loose with his money: 'Your daughter spent in Genoa, as I heard, one night, fourscore ducats.' I do not find that funny. One critic says reasonably that, in this disturbing play, Shakespeare 'tries to have it both ways.'

In fact, though he does try to even up the scales, they are tipped against Shylock: one cannot say that he receives justice. So no wonder he lingers in everybody's mind, no comic figure but an ambivalent one, hovering between comedy and tragedy. From the beginning one sympathises with him at the ill-treatment he has received from Antonio:

> Fair sir, you spat on me on Wednesday last,
> You spurned me such a day, another time
> You called me dog: and for these courtesies
> I'll lend you thus much money?

When he demands his pound of flesh, however, the audience would recognise the reference to Lopez, *lupus*, the wolf:

> thy currish spirit
> Governed a wolf, who hanged for human slaughter . . .

> . . . thy desires
> Are wolvish, bloody, starved and ravenous.

The idea of exacting a pound of flesh is to us melodramatic and uncon-vincing, yet it comes with the story and the very phrase has entered into common usage. The medievals, infantile as they were, believed even worse of the Jews. One cannot think that Shylock receives any kind of justice when Antonio generously remits one half of his goods, to claim the other half – provided he becomes a Christian and leaves everything to his absconding daughter and her husband. The Elizabethans evidently thought that that was good enough for him.

—— oOo ——

The theme of friendship between men is continued here from *The Two Gentlemen of Verona*, in more emotional tones, in that between Antonio and Bassanio. Sisson noted, with his usual awareness of how much of the life of the time went into the plays, 'the name Bassanio could well have come from a London family of Italians.'[1] The name of the numerous family of royal musicians, Bassano, was usually rendered by the English Bassany, and it is likely that, like Florio, they were Italian Jews. Dr. Lopez was a Portuguese Jew.

This brings the Italian-Jewish theme of *The Merchant of Venice* more closely home to Shakespeare, for it is more than likely that Emilia Bassano, Mrs. Lanier, was half-Jewish. William Shakespeare knew what he was writing about – as Dr. Johnson thought was the case, if only we knew more about his time and circumstances. And now we do know much more about these than the 18th century did.

Everything bespeaks the time, and there is no difficulty about dating.

> . . . my wealthy *Andrew* docked in sand,
> Vailing her high top lower than her ribs
> To kiss her burial –

refers to the Spanish galleon, the *St. Andrew*, which ran aground and was taken at the capture of Cadiz in the summer of 1596. She nearly ran aground again when being brought up-Channel. In the play Antonio's ship is reported wrecked in the Narrow Seas, on the Goodwin Sands. The play belongs to that autumn.

> Plucking the grass to know where sits the wind,
> Prying in maps for ports, and piers and roads,

in the first scene, watching out for their argosies upon the high seas – this is precisely what one finds the merchants who were clients of Simon Forman doing at the time.[2]

The Queen herself was an accomplished orator, and there is every likelihood that the perambulating actor would have heard her perform:

> And there is such confusion in my powers
> As, after some oration fairly spoke
> By a belovèd prince, there doth appear
> Among the buzzing pleasèd multitude,
> Where every something being blent together,
> Turns to a wild of nothing, save of joy
> Expressed and not expressed.

Jokes against neighbour nations and their characteristics were common fare, then as now. Here again is the Scot: 'he hath a neighbourly charity in him, for he borrowed a box of the ear of the Englishman, and swore he would pay him again when he was able.' The Elizabethans thought drunkenness the notable vice of Germans. Portia, when asked how she liked her German suitor, replies: 'Very vilely in the morning when he is sober, and most vilely in the afternoon when he is drunk: when he is best, he is a little worse than a man, and when he is worst he is little better than a beast.' When Portia says to Antonio's friend, Bassanio:

> I fear you speak upon the rack
> Where men enforcèd do speak any thing,

we reflect that there the brutality of the age stands revealed, the rack in the background. But was it any worse than Europe four hundred years on?

—— oOo ——

We turn with relief from these barbs to make fools laugh to the personal touches that bring Shakespeare before us. Here is the love of sports and outdoor activities so obvious in the plays he wrote when younger:

> In my schooldays, when I had lost one shaft,
> I shot his fellow of the self-same flight
> The self-same way, with more advisèd watch
> To find the other forth, and by adventuring both
> I oft found both.

The archery-butts at Stratford were on the low-lying ground by the bridge – one often thinks of them, and the schoolboy, when passing over it. Had he a particular experience in mind when he wrote –

> All things that are
> Are with more spirit chasèd than enjoyed.

We hear the echo from the Sonnet:

> The expense of spirit in a waste of shame
> In lust in action . . .
> Enjoyed no sooner but despisèd straight.

Much has been made of the friendship theme, the intimate feeling by which Bassanio would sacrifice everything to save Antonio:

> But life itself, my wife, and all the world
> Are not with me esteemed above your life.
> I would lose all, ay, sacrifice them all
> Here to this devil, to deliver you.

On which the spirited Portia, something of a feminist, comments:

> Your wife would give you little thanks for that
> If she were by to hear you make the offer.

However, the friendship theme is subordinate to the far more powerful emotions aroused around Shylock. The love theme around Portia is cool and subdued, the choosing among suitors, with its dramatic appeal for a rather simple audience, is hardly moving to a modern one: it is a commonplace of the traditional story Shakespeare is adapting.

It may be worth observing the report of Portia:

> she doth stray about
> By holy crosses where she kneels and prays
> For happy wedlock hours.

Wayside crosses were a feature of Elizabethan England, and there were still old-fashioned people to pray at them. Of course the action of the play is in Italy; Shakespeare was a conforming member of the Church of England, but an old-fashioned one to whom the terms and habits of the old faith came naturally: priests are priests, people cross themselves, we hear of holy unction and holy bread; oaths are the old ones, 'Marry' and 'by our Lady', 'by the mass' and 'by God's wounds', the conservative Queen's customary oath.

The play is, as usual, fairly sprinkled with the classical allusions, figures and images, that welled up from both schooling and reading.[3] The last Act is different in character from the dramatic tensions of the previous Acts: it is intensely lyrical and magical, drenched in moonlight and music. (In our time it has inspired Vaughan Williams's 'Serenade to Music'.) But when the disparate images of Troilus and Cressida, along with Thisbe, occur we can see Shakespeare with his Chaucer open before him at the pages where they occur together. Those famous broken paragraphs of verse, each beginning, 'In such a night,' marvellously evoke moonlit Belmont:

> In such a night
> Stood Dido with a willow in her hand
> Upon the wild sea banks, and waft her love
> To come again to Carthage.

Perhaps he was thinking of Marlowe and his *Dido* – as certainly he was when he wrote that Portia's

> sunny locks
> Hang on her temples like a golden fleece,
> Which makes her seat of Belmont Colchos' strand.

So in the poem written in rivalry with *Venus and Adonis* had Marlowe described Southampton's:

> His dangling tresses that were never shorn,
> Had they been cut and unto Colchos borne,
> Would have allured the venturous youth of Greece
> To hazard more than for the golden fleece.

There is more music than ever in this play. We are given the charming song:

> Tell me where is Fancy bred,
> Or in the heart, or in the head?

Much of the last Act is performed to the sound of music, and we have Shakespeare's tribute to its power, which was evidently spoken from his heart:

> The man that hath no music in himself,
> Nor is not moved with concord of sweet sounds,
> Is fit for treasons, stratagems, and spoils,
> The motions of his spirit are dull as night,
> And his affections dark as Erebus.

The action is spun out by the intrigue about Portia's ring, which Bassanio gave away to procure the learned doctor (Portia in disguise) to plead Antonio's case and save his life. Thus, when all is resolved, the comedy is dismissed with Shakespeare's characteristic (and popular) bawdy: Gratiano, Bassanio's friend and Nerissa's suitor, says,

But were the day come, I should wish it dark
Till I were couching with the doctor's clerk.
Well, while I live, I'll fear no other thing
So sore, as keeping safe Nerissa's ring.

—— oOo ——

The text is a good one, a quarto published in 1600; E.K. Chambers 'saw no reason why the copy used for [it] should not have been in Shakespeare's hand.' It was reprinted in the First Folio, with a few additions of stage directions from the Company's prompt-book.

1. Sisson, Charles Jasper *New Readings in Shakespeare*, vol. I, page 135 (Cambridge University Press, Cambridge, 1956)
2. *v*. my *Simon Forman: Sex and Society in Shakespeare's Age*, chapter VIII (Weidenfeld & Nicolson, London, 1974); American title *Sex and Society in Shakespeare's Age: Simon Forman the Astrologer* (Scribner, New York, 1975)
3. cf. my *Shakespeare's Globe: His Moral and Intellectual Outlook*, chapters I and II (Weidenfeld & Nicolson, London, 1981); American title *What Shakespeare Read and Thought* (Coward, McCann and Geoghegan, New York, 1981)

As You Like It

1598

Many revealing touches combine to make this a particularly personal work of Shakespeare's, full of touches not only from the life of the time but from his own. In the first place, it was based upon Thomas Lodge's *Rosalind: Euphues' Golden Legacy*. This romance was not only one of the most popular in the 1590s but was dedicated to Lord Chamberlain Hunsdon 'as a patron of all martial men . . . wearing with Pallas both the lance and the bay.' Lodge was a friend of Hunsdon's sons, Edmund and Robert Carey, with whom he had been at Trinity College, Oxford, contemporaneously with the foppish but intelligent Edward Hoby. They all were familiars of the Court.

The theme of Lodge's novel, the dispute between an elder and a younger brother over their inheritance, came from his prolonged dispute with his elder brother, William, over theirs. Shakespeare made this the mainspring of his play, using situations and themes from the novel, to improve upon them both dramatically and in accordance with the actors available in the Company. He did not hesitate to use the name of Lodge's heroine, Rosalind, for his own or to seize upon a phrase in Lodge's Preface for his title, where it appears, 'If you like it, so.'

We see how this connects up with the Hunsdons' circle, while much else in the play reflects and illuminates Shakespeare's own background and acquaintance.

Early in 1598 the Admiral's Company came out with a couple of 'greenwood'-romantic Robin Hood plays by Munday and Chettle: the dramatist of the Chamberlain's Company would go one better. In the same year Lodge's romance had another edition, while the publication at last of Marlowe's *Hero and Leander* brought him vividly back to mind. We now know that Shakespeare's association with Marlowe – for all the contrast in their personalities – was closer than hitherto realised, and that Marlowe was writing *Hero and Leander* in rivalry with Shakespeare's *Venus and Adonis* for Southampton's patronage when he was killed in 1593.

That poignant memory came back with the touching reference, virtually by name, to the author of the famous line:

> Dead shepherd, now I find thy saw of might:
> 'Who ever loved that loved not at first sight?'

Much more too came now to the forefront of Shakespeare's mind to light up the association for us. He would have known perfectly well how the impulsive Marlowe came by his end: stupidity 'strikes a man more dead than a great reckoning in a little room.' The fatal quarrel in the little room in the Deptford tavern had been over the reckoning, according to the Inquest at the time.

As for Hero and Leander – he 'would have lived many a fair year though Hero had turned nun, if it had not been for a hot midsummer night. For, good youth, he went but forth to wash him in the Hellespont and, being taken with the cramp, was drowned – and the foolish chroniclers of that age found it was "Hero of Sestos".' Marlowe had begun his play, *Dido*, with Jove dandling his page Ganymede – and Rosalind is given that name in taking the guise of a youth.

Lodge, in dedicating his novel to Hunsdon, says that he wrote it during a voyage to the Canaries; since then he had gone, as far as the coast of Brazil, on Cavendish's voyage into the South Sea, i.e. the Pacific. In the play Rosalind thinks 'an inch of delay', in hearing about her lover, 'a South Sea of discovery.' Her affection 'hath an unknown bottom, like the Bay of Portugal' – so familiar to the seamen. So, too, with what the morose Jacques considered Touchstone's brain to be – 'as dry as the remainder biscuit after a voyage.'

The play was for the winter season of 1598. In 1600 publication was 'stayed', i.e. stopped – along with *Much Ado*, *Henry V*, and Jonson's success, *Every Man in his Humour* – obviously by the Company in the interest of their profitable stage production.

The time is otherwise brought home to us in many an authentic touch. 'Be it known unto all men by these presents' is the regular formula with which writs and bills began. Good old Adam, the faithful family retainer, who bore the exhausted Orlando on his shoulders – the tradition is that Shakespeare played the part of Adam – exemplified

> The constant service of the antique world,
> When service sweat for duty, not for meed [reward].
> Thou art not for the fashion of these times,
> When none will sweat but for promotiòn.

The usurping Duke pushes Orlando's brother out of doors, and orders his officers to

> Make an extent upon his house and lands –

the regular form when taking possession of property.

A 'why' is as 'plain as the way to parish church' – how that simple phrase brings the age before us! Rosalind describes Orlando and his love verses in these terms: 'O most gentle pulpiter! What tedious homily of love have you wearied your parishioners withal, and never cried "Have patience, good people!"' Obviously parsons in their pulpits often did – though the Book of Homilies read in church contains none on Love. Cynical Jacques's comment on Orlando's pretty love-speeches is this: 'have you not been acquainted with goldsmiths' wives and conned them out of their rings?' We hear of 'painted cloths' that hung in people's houses, of tilts and tilting that were a feature of Court life, and the executioner asking pardon on the scaffold before letting fall his axe. 'The howling of Irish wolves against the moon' is a phrase that might have occurred at any time; but Irish amenities were much to the fore in this critical year, that of the disaster to English arms at the Yellow Ford, which announced the opening of O'Neill's rebellion in Ulster.

—— oOo ——

A main theme of the play is the contrast between Court and Country. The good Duke has been banished and has taken to the forest with his faithful followers; other characters take refuge there from their troubles and trials – his daughter Rosalind is sent away from Court, and is accompanied by the bad Duke's daughter, Celia. Orlando takes refuge from the persecution of his brother. Before long everybody ends up in the forest, even the usurping Duke and the unkind brother are converted from their unkind ways.

All this provides a theme which recommends itself to Shakespeare's sceptical view of the world. Touchstone says, 'if thou never wast at Court thou never sawest good manners.' To which the countryman, Corin, replies: 'those that are good manners at the Court are as ridiculous in the country as the behaviour of the country is most mockable at the Court.' At Court people kiss hands, and courtiers' hands sweat as well as shepherds': the grease from handling sheep is as wholesome as the perfume courtiers use from civet, 'the very uncleanly flux of a cat.' Touchstone, the clown, claims to be a courtier: 'I have trod a measure [i.e. a dance]; I have flattered a lady; I have been politic [i.e. insincere] with my friend, smooth with mine enemy; I have undone three tailors; I have had four quarrels, and like to have fought one.'

This would have raised a good laugh at Court, and indeed with Shakespeare's upper-class audiences in general.

An underlying theme is that of faithfulness and simplicity against sophisticated selfishness and cruelty; for example, the elder brother's conduct to the younger – 'he lets me feed with his hinds, bars me the place of a brother and mines my gentility with my education.' Orlando reproaches his brother: 'my father charged you in his will to give me good education: you have trained me like a peasant, obscuring and hiding from me all gentleman-like qualities.' Shakespeare himself was very much set on being ranked as a gentleman and, unlike many denizens of the theatre, behaved like one.

We can catch something of him in personal reflections dropped in passing: it is Adam who says,

> Know you not, master, to some kind of men
> Their graces serve them but as enemies?

And again,

> . . . in my youth I never did apply
> Hot and rebellious liquors in my blood,
> Nor did not with unbashful forehead woo
> The means of weakness and debility.

Shakespeare speaks with a personal inflexion against drunkenness, as also markedly against ingratitude: the winter wind in the forest is not so unkind as man's ingratitude. Where the same sentiment is enforced again and again we may infer that it meant something special to the author. Here too we see the normal social man (so unlike Marlowe), accepting his place in society with its duties, obligations and pleasures:

> If ever you have looked on better days,
> If ever been where bells have knolled to church,
> If ever sat at any good man's feast,
> If ever from your eyelids wiped a tear
> And know what 'tis to pity and be pitied . . .

There we have Shakespeare the man, and we note phrases from church-service and the Bible, the Prodigal Son eating husks with hogs, etc.

—— oOo ——

It is vaguely suggested that the forest is the Ardennes, but everything shows that it is Arden, from which Shakespeare's parents came, the background of his own youth, that he has in mind, along with the shepherds and shepherdesses of the Cotswolds. A familiar enough sight at Stratford must have been

> . . . the whining schoolboy, with his satchel
> And shining morning face, creeping like snail
> Unwillingly to school.

We have the sheepcotes and bounds of feed (i.e. fences), the little cots, up in the Cotswold uplands. Twice we have the regular Elizabethan phrase an 'inland man' as indicating good manners, against the rough ways of the uplands, portrayed in the country folk, William and Audrey. A country vicar is made fun of in Sir Oliver Martext ('Sir' was the old fashioned appellation of a curate, one who was not a Master of Arts, and the recent Marprelate Tracts were much in people's minds. Shakespeare as usual demonstrates that he missed nothing.)

The description of the cottage:

> down in the neighbour bottom,
> The rank of osiers by the murmuring stream –

makes one think of the situation of the Hathaways' cottage. Even 'the acres of the rye', where in springtime 'these pretty folks would lie', applied well enough in his time to the way across the fields of rye to Shottery. William Shakespeare was a home-keeping man, so far as his profession allowed: he never lost touch with family and home, and was able to live there more in his last years, in the best house in the town from the proceeds of his life of hard work. Jacques, who has travelled abroad, to turn cynic, is thus addressed by Rosalind: 'look you lisp and wear strange suits, disable all the benefits of your own country . . . or I will scarce think you have swum in a gondola.'

In portraying Jacques Shakespeare was able to aim a hit at the contemporary cult of melancholy. Jacques asserts that he has 'neither the scholar's melancholy, which is emulation [i.e. competitiveness, envy – true enough]; nor the musician's, which is fantastical [compare Dowland's famous 'Lacrymae']; nor the courtier's, which is proud; nor the soldier's, which is ambitious; nor the lawyer's, which is politic.' All these shafts reach home, and we could give notorious illustrations of them from personages of the time.

The asides are more interesting than the love-talk, the baiting and banter, which we can take for granted: we all know that Rosalind was charming and Orlando a stout upstanding fellow. Their encounters are kept up with a good deal of versifying – the dramatist was a clever man to be able to keep it going.

The consciousness of his profession, the theatre itself, is ever-present as through all his work, in the Sonnets too. It finds expression in a famous oration of Jacques:

> All the world's a stage,
> And all the men and women merely players:
> They have their exits and their entrances,
> And one man in his time plays many parts.

Though this was a Renaissance commonplace, developed in terms of rhetoric, it is too real and vivid not to reflect personal observation: the whining schoolboy, the swearing, duelling soldier, the fat J.P. full of capon and wise saws, the lean and slippered pantaloon – old age, seen in terms of the stage.

We can envisage the boy-actors who took the parts of Rosalind and Celia for we are told: the former tall and fair, the other 'low and browner'. The play has, as often later, a masque-like ending with Hymen entering to marry up the couples. Once more, the sudden improbable changes that take place in the characters of the bad Duke and the wicked brother, would not have bothered Elizabethans. And there is a characteristically personal Epilogue, original for being spoken by a lady – Rosalind. 'I charge you, O women, for the love you bear to men, to like as much of this play as please you. And I charge you, O men, for the love you bear to women – as I perceive by your simpering, none of you hates them – that between you and the women the play may please.' How like Shakespeare! – polite and courteous, positively propitiating, the way to be popular; and how unlike Ben Jonson, whose attitude to the public was always, 'take it or leave it, as you please.' In this year the friendly, gentlemanly Shakespeare gave the rumbustious Ben his chance, by welcoming his play, *Every Man in his Humour*, to the Company and himself performing in it.

In this very personal play songs have a larger part than ever, and now they counterpoint the action: 'Under the greenwood tree', for example. So also with,

> Blow, blow, thou winter wind,
> Thou art not so unkind
>   As man's ingratitude . . .
>
> Freeze, freeze, thou bitter sky,
> That dost not bite so nigh
>   As benefits forgot . . .

In relating to the action these songs have a function, but one cannot but detect a personal inflexion in them too: they echo experiences otherwise recorded in the Sonnets. The folklore flavour of 'It was a lover and his lass', lying between the acres of the rye, is much in keeping with the greenwood, forest-of-Arden background. Acres of rye grew all around Stratford in those days. It all brings the Stratford countryside to mind: perhaps it was written at home there.

The text was first printed in the First Folio, Sisson thinks probably from a prompt-copy, and 'offers little difficulty.' (So why multiply minutiae, or, as Johnson said, display 'a rage for saying something when there is nothing to be said'?) The Company protected itself by having this play, along with three others, 'stayed' from publication in 1600. So there is no Quarto, and the play would have been lost to us if those good fellows, Hemming and Condell, had not specially gathered Shakespeare's plays together – an exceptional measure to do their exceptional fellow honour.

Much Ado About Nothing

1599

The comedy in *Much Ado* is set against a more serious, if rather melodramatic, story than its predecessor, and the love-combat of Beatrice and Benedick is an improvement on Rosalind and Orlando. It harks back in a way to Petruchio and Kate, but in wittier and more sophisticated fashion. Shakespeare found a promising story in Bandello's collection, which he knew both in Italian and in French. He tightened up the action and concentrated it for dramatic effect, at one point preferring Ariosto's version of the tale in Sir John Harington's recent translation of *Orlando Furioso* (1591), while some hints came from Spenser's *Faerie Queene* (1590), a prodigious influence for Elizabethan writers.

So there is little point in the pedantic hunt for remote and improbable 'sources' in studying Shakespeare: he took from what was ready to hand, often what was recent, that which seemed to him to offer the makings of a play, and then made it. He crossed it with a sub-plot, adding characters and inventions of his own, as a composer would take a musical theme and combine it with another to create further permutations. What we remember from *Much Ado* are the characters of Beatrice and Benedick, as Charles I noted in his copy of the Second Folio, and as Berlioz named his opera based on the play. Hardly less memorable are Dogberry and Verges, the constable and headborough, officers of the watch, who are convincing, if caricatured, transcripts from life. They are absurd but completely real.

It is arresting that Shakespeare should have chosen the name Hero for his heroine, upon whom a wicked trick is played to place her chastity under suspicion and her marriage in jeopardy: plenty of other names were available, but *Hero and Leander* (whose name also occurs) had recently appeared. The bastard brother of the Prince of Arragon was called Don John, and a familiar name to the Elizabethans was that of Philip II's bastard brother, Don John. In the play he is a despicable character, who wants to ruin Hero's marriage to Claudio out of pure malice – a forerunner of Iago in *Othello*. A good deal in the play verges on the tragic, reminding us of *Romeo and Juliet* or is to appear again in *The Winter's Tale* (as was the pastoral element of *As You Like It*). For Shakespeare constantly repeated situations and themes, re-using his basic elements, improving and refining upon his characters, while his experience was intensive and concentrated, not extensive and disparate.

—— oOo ——

The play belongs to 1599, and this is corroborated by various circumstances. There is a tell-tale reference–

>   like favourites,
>   Made proud by princes, that advance their pride
>   Against that power that bred it.

This exactly expressed what Essex was doing at that moment: advanced and favoured by the Queen, indeed spoiled by her, he was now challenging not only her popularity but her rule. Through his relationship to Southampton this was Shakespeare's affiliation, and he still had hopes of the gallant chivalrous figure that Essex was – Philip Sidney's heir – and expressed them. Here was the choice, the agonising crux, out of which *Troilus and Cressida* was to come. A reference to Troilus also comes in this play: Shakespeare's mind was full of echoes and reverberations, conscious and subconscious. Hence too the revealing images that spring up at any moment, almost involuntarily. No writer was ever more fortunate: on top of being a very clever man, his subconscious worked for him day and night, and he trusted it, gave scope to its promptings.

Owing to the publication of the play in 1600 from a theatre-copy we know that Dogberry was played by the Company's famous comedian, Will Kemp, who left the Chamberlain's men later this year. Verges was played by Richard Cowley, who had come on from Strange's, and lived in Shoreditch, as Shakespeare had at first, according to John Aubrey. Balthasar was played by the minstrel, Jack Wilson, who sang the lovely song:

>   Sigh no more, ladies, sigh no more,
>   Men were deceivers ever . . .

to counterpoint the theme.

Many touches bring the background to the fore. Beatrice begins by regarding Benedick as the plague: 'God help the noble Claudio, if he have caught the Benedick'. We must recall that *carduus benedictus* was a remedy for heart-disease. 'I charge thee on thy allegiance' was the regular form of an arrest, or warning before it. We have several references to writing in itself, with a ballad-maker's pen – even the news was sung in the form of ballads then – and to sonneteering. Some names 'run smoothly in the even road of a blank verse', but Benedick cannot express love in rhyme: 'I have tried: I can find out no rhyme to "lady" but "baby", an innocent rhyme; for "scorn", "horn", a hard rhyme; for "school", "fool", a babbling rhyme. Very ominous endings: no, I was not born under a rhyming planet.' Here we are permitted a glimpse of Shakespeare at his own work: himself *was* born under a rhyming planet, and rhymes came easily to him, though much of this play is in prose.

We note the usual hoary old jokes about horns, and cuckolding, of which heterosexual Elizabethans could never have enough – a whole song is devoted to it in *As You Like It*: to us boring, the appeal of the joke hardly intelligible. The literary background of one such joke –

In time the savage bull doth bear the yoke –

is more interesting, for it is a line from Kyd's immensely successful *The Spanish Tragedy* which the magpie memory of the actor has retained. Kyd's line comes from one of Watson's Sonnets, and both Kyd and Watson were close friends of Marlowe. *The Spanish Tragedy* was acted by Strange's men, with whom Shakespeare had some early association. Can he have acted in it?

A passing reference to the Duchess of Milan's gown suggests interesting possibilities. Hero's waiting woman says, 'I saw the Duchess of Milan's gown that they praise so.' To which Hero says, 'O, that exceeds, they say.' Margaret: 'By my troth, 'tis but a night-gown in respect of yours.' Holbein's famous portrait of Christina, Duchess of Milan, does indeed look like a night-gown, the long black gown of a young widow. Can Shakespeare have seen the picture? Zuccaro claimed to have seen it in the house of Henry, second Earl of Pembroke,[1] patron of the Company with which Shakespeare (and Marlowe) had brief associations. We must needs point out that this was *not* the son, William, third Earl – for the benefit of those who are confused and wrong about 'Mr. W.H.'.

To come down to earth, we hear of a Scotch jig – we did not know that there was such a splendid kind, 'hot and hasty, and full as fantastical.' Jokes about national idiosyncrasies never fail, in this like Shaw's rallying the English, which paid so well in our time. We have a hit at foreigners' clothing: 'like a German from the waist downward, all slops; and a Spaniard from the hip upwards, no doublet.' We may well see William Shakespeare in the reflection, 'what a pretty thing man is when he goes in his doublet and hose and leaves off his wit!' Or in, 'if a man do not erect in this age his own tomb ere he dies, he shall live no longer in monument than the bell rings and the widow weeps.' He was markedly aware of monuments, a notable expression of the art of the time.

We probably remember best today Shakespeare's transcripts from real life: out of the artificial comedy of *The Two Gentlemen of Verona*, Launce and his dog; from *A Midsummer Night's Dream*, Bottom the weaver and his rude mechanicals. This comic realism reaches an absurd height with the constable, Dogberry, and the headborough, Verges. These local officers of the watch provided regular farcical fare for the stage, but there is an extraordinary verisimilitude in Shakespeare's portrayal.

John Aubrey tells us that 'Ben Jonson and he did gather humours of men daily wherever they came' – no doubt: the proper way of writers at all times, observing human fooleries. The humour of the Constable, evidently Dogberry, 'he happened to take at Grendon in Bucks' – presumably, Long Crendon, along the road from London to Bicester, thence on to Oxford or Stratford.

The beast that bears me, tired with my woe,
Plods dully on, to bear that weight in me,
As if by some instinct the wretch did know
His rider loved not speed, being made from thee.

But those years were over now, in 1599.

Dogberry and Verges are delicious fools, better than all the professional jesters. Their language is perfectly convincing, for all that it is larded with malapropisms.

DOGBERRY: This is your charge: you shall comprehend [apprehend] all
vagrom [vagrant] men; you are to bid any man stand,
in the Prince's name.

SECOND WATCH: How if 'a will not stand?

DOGBERRY: Why then, take no note of him but let him go; and
presently call the rest of the watch together and thank
God you are rid of a knave.

VERGES: If he will not stand when he is bidden, he is none of the
Prince's subjects. [The usual bawdy joke, with gestures,
about standing.]

DOGBERRY: True, and they are to meddle with none but the Prince's
subjects. You shall also make no noise in the streets,
for, for the watch to babble and to talk is most tolerable
and not to be endured.'

The authenticity of this may be seen from a fascinating letter from the great Lord Burghley to Walsingham, the Queen's principal ministers, when the hue and cry was up for the Babington conspirators.

'Sir, As I came from London homeward in my coach, I saw at every town's end the number of ten or twelve standing with long staves, and until I came to Enfield I thought no other of them but that they had stayed for avoiding of the rain, or to drink at some alehouse, for so they did stand under pentices [penthouses] at alehouses. But at Enfield finding a dozen in a plump, when there was no rain, I bethought myself that they were appointed as watchmen, for the apprehending of such as are missing. And thereupon I called some of them to me apart, and asked them wherefore they stood there. And one of them answered, "To take three young men." And demanding how they should know the persons, one answered with these words, "Marry, my lord, by intelligence of their favour." "What mean you by that?", quoth I. "Marry," said they, "one of the parties hath a hooked nose." "And have you," quoth I, "no other mark?" "No," saith they. And then I asked who appointed them. And they answered one Banks, a head constable, whom I willed to be sent to me. Surely, sir, whosoever had the charge from you hath used the matter negligently. For these watchmen stand so openly in plumps as no suspected person will come near them; and if they be no better instructed but to find three persons by one of them having a hooked nose, they may miss thereof.'[2]

It is perfect Shakespearean dialogue, and just like the scene in *Much Ado*. It is pleasant to record that, all the same, the Babington conspirators were rounded up nearby at Harrow. Similarly, in the play, Dogberry and his fellows managed to get the truth out of Don John's villainous agent, Borachio, who bids 'Stand thee close then, under this pent-house, for it drizzles rain, and I will, like a true drunkard, utter all to thee.' He confesses to the trick by which Hero was accused wrongfully.

DOGBERRY: Flat burglary as ever was committed.
FIRST WATCH: And Count Claudio did mean, upon his words, to disgrace Hero before the whole assembly, and not marry her.
DOGBERRY: O villain! thou wilt be condemned into everlasting redemption [sc. perdition] for this.

We may well conclude that the intrigue, which provided occasion for this – the plot Shakespeare made use of from his 'sources' – is less important than these marvellous scenes from real life.

—— oOo ——

In the story Hero was at first framed by the odious Borachio enacting a love-scene at her chamber-window with her waiting-woman dressed up to resemble her. Claudio is taken in by this and disclaims her at the very wedding ceremony in church. Hero swoons at the disgrace, and is taken up for dead. Beatrice has more spirit. 'Is he not approved in the height a villain, that hath slandered, scorned, dishonoured my kinswoman? O that I were a man! What, bear her in hand until they come to take hands; and then, with public accusation, uncovered slander, unmitigated rancour – O God, that I were a man! I would eat his heart in the market-place.'

We see that Beatrice is a real woman, and her love-contests with Benedick are naturally more powerful and realistic than the romantic-pastoral of Rosalind and Orlando. However, we must let the play speak for itself. *Much Ado* was always popular; Leonard Digges, whose family were acquainted with Shakespeare, testified:

let but Beatrice
And Benedick be seen, lo, in a trice
The cockpit, galleries, boxes all are full.

A tribute of another kind is the fact that, a few years later, Heywood's *Fair Maid of the Exchange* (1607) has many borrowings from *Much Ado*.

For all that this comedy is given a setting of rather macabre melodrama – perhaps to set it off – it turns out a prime example of Shakespeare's comedy according to his specification: the ingredients – romance, the comedy of high life counterpointed by that of low life, courtly sophistication contrasted with rustic simplicity. The grandees were to be laughed with, the people to be laughed at. The dialogue of Beatrice and Benedick is indeed sparkling, as Sisson comments, 'giving us in fuller measure than is to be found in any other writer the image of conversation at its highest achievement in the witty, well-bred society of Shakespeare's day, which rejoiced in the play of intellect, and used language and thought as an instrument of skilled delight.'

It was indeed a far cry from early days at Stratford, and a contrast with demotic society at any time.

The text is a good one, from the first Quarto of 1600, in spite of the Company staying publication – and evidently from a theatre prompt-book, for in places it has the names of the actors, or descriptions of characters (e.g. 'Bastard' for Don John) instead of the names of the *dramatis personae*. Clearly not revised by Shakespeare for any publication, it was used in the First Folio, with a few corrections and misprints.

---

1. *v.* Strong, Roy *The English Icon: Elizabethan and Jacobean Portraiture*, page 347 (Routledge & Kegan Paul, Henley-on-Thames, 1969)
2. q. from the State Papers in my *The England of Elizabeth*, page 357 (Macmillan, London, and New York, 1951)

The Merry Wives
of Windsor
1599-1600

This bourgeois comedy, perennially successful, is the most purely amusing, from beginning to end, that Shakespeare ever wrote. It is a farce, though it has some continuity with the comic scenes in *Henry IV*, particularly in the characters of Falstaff and Mistress Quickly, who is given a larger part in the intrigue here; Justice Shallow appears again, with a different ninny for companion, his cousin Slender; Falstaff's followers, Bardolph and Nym, make a brief appearance, Pistol with his grandiloquent talk is retained. For the rest, there are as admirable comic creations as anywhere in Shakespeare: Mistress Ford and her jealous husband, whom Falstaff would cuckold, and the lively caricatures of Sir Hugh Evans, the Welsh curate and schoolmaster, and Dr. Caius, the French physician, each of whom 'makes fritters of English' in his own way. Shakespeare never wrote anything funnier – and the play has proved an inspiration to other artists in other fields, particularly music, with Nicolai's opera, Verdi's *Falstaff* and Vaughan Williams' *Sir John in Love*.

This last title gives the theme: Falstaff as the would-be seducer of a respectable citizen's wife of Windsor – his idea of making love (like his behaviour with Doll Tearsheet at the Boar's Head in East Cheap). It is the same old reprobate, with the same virtuosity of language in recounting his misadventures as that with which he had regaled Prince Henry.

It is evident that Shakespeare enjoyed writing this piece, such spirits and such merriment – the theme inspired him to these new comic creations, and to a superb piece of craftsmanship. (The poet Auden was silly enough to call it 'Shakespeare's worst play' – not much sense of humour there!) This is the more remarkable, and yet it demonstrates the complete mastery he had achieved, in that the work was obviously the answer to a royal command, and written at speed. An old tradition has it that the Queen expressed a wish to see Sir John in love – that was true to her, by the way: the language that surrounded her was that of love, demanded by the ageing maiden lady. And why should not she have been as disappointed as other people were at the absence of Falstaff from *Henry V*, when they had been promised more of him?

The play was put together rapidly, leaving various unimportant loose ends, and almost wholly in prose. It has, however, a more ceremonial ending in verse, evidently suited, or adapted, for a Garter Feast, probably at Windsor, with which Shakespeare was well acquainted from performances there. It is not known precisely which Garter Feast – the practical dramatist was always ready to tailor his piece for the occasion – nor does it greatly matter. The play's the thing.

Nor again do 'sources', beloved of pedants, matter. The Italian *novelle* familiar to Shakespeare are full of seducers of other men's wives – and Shakespeare himself was sufficiently experienced in the subject without book; the theme of the jealous husband, which admirably counterpoints Falstaff's attempts to board the wife – 'Boarding call you it? I'll be sure to keep him above deck' – owes something to Ben Jonson's jealous husband in *Every Man in his Humour*, in which Shakespeare acted in 1598. He did not act in Jonson's *Every Man out of his Humour* next year; but the considerable play that is made of, and at the expense of, 'humours' reflects Shakespeare's recent experience. *The Merry Wives* evidently follows these, and common sense indicates it comes after *Henry IV* and *Henry V*.

There had been some trouble over names in these plays, which has some contemporary point and calls attention to the real historical background, as opposed to literary conjecturing without solid foundation. Falstaff was originally called Sir John Oldcastle, from the famous Lollard of Henry V's reign. But Oldcastle was a collateral ancestor of Lord Cobham. William Brooke, 7th Lord Cobham, was the father-in-law of Sir Robert Cecil, opposed to Essex and his party, which was Shakespeare's grouping. The Brookes objected to Oldcastle being portrayed as the profligate Sir John on the stage, and 'Falstaff' had to be substituted.

When the first Lord Chamberlain Hunsdon died, in July 1596, he was succeeded as Chamberlain by Lord Cobham. This Cobham died in April 1597, when the second Lord Hunsdon succeeded him as Lord Chamberlain, and of course as patron of Shakespeare's Company. Again it was understandable that Lord Cobham should object to the family name of Brooke being made ridiculous as that under which the jealous husband solicits Falstaff's attentions to test his wife's fidelity. Shakespeare had to change the name Brooke to Broome. Now these people, both Hunsdon and Cobham, lived in Blackfriars, with which Shakespeare had long associations. So these shafts went home more closely than people have realised, though there is further evidence that Falstaff jokes had private references now lost to us, but laughed at in the Southampton circle.[1] Actually, Cobham was made a Knight of the Garter in 1599 and entertained the Queen in Blackfriars in 1600; if *The Merry Wives* was performed on either of those occasions there would be all the more reason to change the name of Brooke.

—— oOo ——

Windsor provides the stage-set, as it were: the Castle in the background, the Castle ditch where Page, Shallow and Slender 'couch till we see the light of our fairies', who are to torment Falstaff at Herne's Oak, of medieval folklore, in the Great Park. We hear of the Pettyward and the

Park-ward, and the way to Frogmore; Slender expected to marry Ann Page at Eton, Dr. Caius likewise at the deanery by St. George's Chapel; while Falstaff is tumbled from the dirty-linen basket into the Thames at Datchet Mead.

Shakespeare has drawn upon his experience of small-town life at Stratford for his *bourgeois* farce. Blank verse, the language of romance, and music are for Court and courtiers; none of this in *The Merry Wives* until we come to the fairies and the compliment to the Queen and the Order of the Garter at the end. Otherwise the characters are mainly drawn from middle-class citizenry, and speak prose. The Fords and Pages are respectable townsfolk. So is the Welsh cleric-schoolmaster, Evans; Shakespeare's school had had a Jenkins for schoolmaster in his time. Dr. Caius speaks French and broken English. The scenes between Henry V and his French princess Catherine, in *Henry V*, are mostly in French; and we know that Shakespeare was lodging in the French household of the Montjoys in Silver Street around 1600. Falstaff claims that Page's wife had examined his parts 'with most judicious *oeillades*'. Now where did Shakespeare get that surprising French word from?

The whole scene in which young William is put through his Latin accidence by Sir Hugh Evans is straight out of Shakespeare's schooling – while Mistress Quickly's ear is alert to the bawdy suggestions she suspects in declining such words as 'horum, harum, horum'. Though she is now Dr. Caius' respectable housekeeper her inclinations are to be as much of a bawd as ever – she has not changed her spots from the Boar's Head. Justice Shallow is still the old wag of his Gloucestershire garden, interested in the form of the greyhounds racing on the Cotswolds. We hear of Banbury cheese and an even more familiar memory in the glover's great round paring-knife, which Shakespeare would have handled himself in his youth. The joke about luces in Shallow's coat-of-arms may go back to the Lucys of Charlecote, whom Shakespeare had reason to know; Sir Thomas Lucy died about this time, in 1600.

Contemporary London is evoked in Falstaff's dismissive image of 'the lisping hawthorn buds that come like women in men's apparel and smell like Bucklersbury in simple-time' – sissies evidently, who smelt better than ordinary Elizabethans. Sackerson is mentioned, the bear that performed at Paris Garden, near the Globe on the South Bank, so famous as to be a character in his own right. Sir John denies to Mistress Ford that he has also been making up to her friend, Mistress Page: 'thou mightest as well say I love to walk by the Counter-gate, which is as hateful to me as the reek of a lime-kiln' – the Counter being the prison for debtors.

Oddly enough – though not oddly for the reading man Shakespeare was[2] – literary references are as much present in this play as sport and frolics. Sir John – his being a knight is his one claim to any respect – pays his attentions to the *bourgeoise* Mistress Ford in the inflated Court-language of love caricatured, with a line from Sidney's *Astrophel and Stella*:

Have I caught thee, my heavenly jewel?

Marlowe's famous poem, 'Come live with me and be my love', is garbled by Evans:

> To shallow rivers to whose falls
> Melodious birds sing madrigals;
> There will we make our peds of roses
> And a thousand fragrant posies.

The Company would seem to have had a Welsh actor, man or boy, in its cast at the time – and this beautifully constructed play had a good part for almost everybody. Marlowe's Dr. Faustus and Mephistopheles are not forgotten.

A couple of references show that Shakespeare had been reading Ralegh's *Discovery . . . of Guiana*, which came out in 1596. Falstaff assures Pistol and Nym that Mistress Page 'did so course o'er my exteriors with such a greedy intention that the appetite of her eye did seem to scorch me up like a burning-glass. She bears the purse too; she is a region in Guiana, all gold and bounty. I will be 'cheator [punning on escheator and cheater] to them both, and they shall be exchequers to me. They shall be my East and West Indies, and I will trade to them both.' It was in Ralegh that Shakespeare had been reading about the man-eaters, the Anthropophagi, and formed his own word out of it by analogy with Carthaginian. When Simple inquires for Falstaff at the Garter Inn the Host says, 'there's his chamber, his house, his castle [did Shakespeare still think of him as Oldcastle?], his standing-bed and truckle-bed. Go, knock and call. He'll speak like an Anthropophaginian unto thee.' The room was new-painted with the story of the Prodigal, by the way – as the White Swan at Stratford still has a room painted with that of Tobit and the Angel.

A phrase from the Prayer Book appears, quoted by Evans. 'What phrase is this, "He hears with ear"? Why, it is affectations.' It evidently struck Shakespeare's ear at church as odd, as it used to mine. Mistress Ford considered that Falstaff's disposition and his words 'do no more adhere and keep place together than the Hundredth Psalm to the tune of "Greensleeves".' William Shakespeare evidently attended church, like a good townsman, at Stratford. But what did he do in London? Southampton House was a nest of Catholics, a refuge for priests – and 'priest' and 'by the mass' are the words that come readily to Shakespeare. On Falstaff's second attempt on Mistress Ford's virtue he has to be smuggled out of the house as the fat Witch of Brentford, and beaten as such.

MRS. FORD: Nay, by the mass . . . he [her husband] beat him most unpitifully, methought.
MRS. PAGE: I'll have the cudgel hallowed and hung o'er the altar – it hath done meritorious service.

William Shakespeare was familiar not only with the traditional terms of the old faith but was on terms with Catholic usages, which were to the fore in the Southampton household and entourage.

The ninny Slender, whom his friends put up to marry Ann Page, sighs, 'I had rather than forty shillings I had my Book of Songs and Sonnets here': that is Tottel's Miscellany, the best known anthology of Shakespeare's youth, which would have provided Slender with some love-talk, in which he was wanting.

—— oOo ——

The play is firmly related to the Order of the Garter and must have been produced at one or other of its feasts – possibly even Cobham's in 1600, the name Brooke having been removed. The Quarto version of the play (1602), which has the original Brooke instead of Broome, also has a tell-tale 'cozen-Garmombles', altered later to 'Cozen-Germans'. In 1592 Count Mompelgart had visited England and, though anxious to be made a Knight of the Garter, went away without paying his debts. Evans reports that 'there is three cozen-garmombles [Germans] that has cozened all the hosts of Readins, of Maidenhead, of Colebrook, of horses and money.' The Count continued to pester the Queen for the Order; as Duke of Württemberg he got it in 1597, though she did not bother to send him the insignia.

To end all the jolly rough and tumble various characters disguise themselves as fairies to scare the timorous Falstaff at Herne's Oak.

> Elves, list your names; silence, you airy toys!
> Cricket, to Windsor chimneys shalt thou leap:
> Where fires thou find'st unraked and hearths unswept,
> There pinch the maids as blue as bilberry:
> Our radiant Queen hates sluts and sluttery.

The credulous Falstaff is terrified: he knows that to speak to the fairies is death.

> Search Windsor Castle, elves, within and out,
> Strew good luck, ouphs, on every sacred room,
> That it may stand till the perpetual doom,
> In state as wholesome as in state 'tis fit,
> Worthy the owner and the owner it.

As for the Order of the Garter:

> The several chairs of Order look you scour
> With juice of balm and every precious flower –

> Each fair instalment, coat, and several crest
> With loyal blazon, evermore be blest . . .

And

> *Honi soit qui mal y pense* write

– it is nice to note that the poet respected the mute 'e' in the manner of French verse –

> In emerald tufts, flowers purple, blue, and white . . .
> Buckled below fair knighthood's bending knee.

The authoritative text is that of the First Folio, from the Company's prompt-book as copied from Shakespeare's manuscript by the regular scribe, Ralph Crane. In the process some gaps occurred, which an earlier Quarto of the play, of 1602, has helped to fill – as, for instance, in the admirable text of our leading textual scholar, Fredson Bowers, in the (American) Pelican Shakespeare.

---

1. cf. my *Shakespeare the Man*, page 162 (Macmillan, London, and Harper & Row, New York, 1973)
2. cf. my *Shakespeare's Globe: His Moral and Intellectual Outlook* (Weidenfeld & Nicolson, London, 1981); American title *What Shakespeare Read and Thought* (Coward, McCann and Geoghegan, New York, 1981)

Twelfth Night
1601

Twelfth Night or What You Will is the last of Shakespeare's romantic comedies; it and *As You Like It* are twin peaks in that vein. John Manningham, a young barrister of Middle Temple, saw it performed on Candlemas day in their splendid hall, which has survived the barbarity of our time. 2 February 1601-2: 'at our feast we had a play called *Twelfth Night, or What You Will*, much like the *Comedy of Errors* or *Menaechmi* in Plautus, but most like and near to that in Italian called *Inganni*. A good practice in it to make the Steward believe his Lady was in love with him, by counterfeiting a letter as from his Lady in general terms, telling him what she liked best in him, and prescribing his gesture in smiling, his apparel, etc; and then, when he came to practice, making him believe they took him to be mad.'

We see from this what Elizabethans most appreciated in a play: some piece of sharp practice, some notable act of cozening at which they all shouted out, as well as the love-scenes which similarly stimulated them to acts of love, produced assignations, sent them hurrying home to their wives or, as we are told, to the stews along the South Bank. (The City Fathers were right in thinking that the theatres were hardly schools of morals.)

—— oOo ——

It is significant that the unappealing character of Malvolio should so dominate people's impression of the play: once more it is Shakespeare's own invention that stands out. That appreciative reader, Charles I, a cultivated connoisseur of the arts – unlike the iconoclastic Puritans – registered as much by noting 'Malvolio' beside the play in his copy of the Second Folio. There is the originality of the character: Malvolio is in love with himself, and that is something new and different. His mistress, the Countess Olivia, diagnoses what is wrong with him: 'you are sick of self-love, Malvolio, and taste with a distempered appetite.' There follows a sharp psychological observation: 'to be generous, guiltless and of free disposition is to take those things for bird-bolts that you deem cannon-bullets.' That is, Malvolio took things too seriously (Ben Jonson was like that, the good-humoured Shakespeare the opposite).

Though we must not take Malvolio for a Puritan, he is somewhat puritanical: the minx Maria says only that 'sometimes he is a kind of puritan'. He takes his job as the Countess's steward seriously and much objects to the caterwauling her ruffianly uncle, Sir Toby Belch, keeps up with boon companions in the hall below (Sir Toby is also engaged in heavily fleecing the simpleton, Sir Andrew Aguecheek). So far we can only sympathise with Malvolio, trying in vain to keep order in the nursery.

His self-love and conceit, his perfectly honest pride in his job, are his undoing: they lay him open to the trick that is played upon him, of making him believe that the Countess is in love with him. He has no sense of humour, always a preservative. Maria then thinks up another trick, of having him confined in a dark hole of the house, while the Clown dresses up as a minister, Sir Topas, to exorcise the evil spirit from him. All this is very Elizabethan, though the nonsense of exorcising is still with us today.

Perhaps it is not so surprising, after all, that this unattractive character has attracted most attention, and even sympathy, out of the play. Shakespeare may have got the name, and one or two others, from a couple of Italian plays he looked at – Manningham noticed one of them; but the story was suggested by one of those in a recent book of Barnaby Rich. Shakespeare would seem to be conveying by the name the ill-will the Steward felt for the crew of roisterers and drunks below stairs. From the first his was the part that drew the crowd:

> The cockpit, galleries, boxes are all full
> To hear Malvolio, that cross-gartered gull.

It is to be feared that hearty Elizabethans – no sensitive Victorians – much enjoyed his persecution and treatment.

The characters of the main plot are less interesting. The love-sick Duke goes on mooning about the Countess Olivia, who cannot respond to him, and is hardly sympathetic. The Countess herself is much more so; she at any rate is a personality and has a will of her own, though she throws herself at the head of Viola disguised as an attractive youth. The romantic love-talk is as usual in verse; when it comes to Olivia's declaration of love in form it is in rhyme.

More original and memorable are the lesser characters. Maria is a very well-depicted minx. Sir Toby Belch is authentic caricature, the kind of old ruffian grandees had to put up with in their great houses, for he was a poor relation. Sir Andrew Aguecheek belongs to the tribe of Shakespeare's simple-minded country gentlemen, who exist to be taken in and laughed at, like Slender in *The Merry Wives* or even Justice Shallow. Feste the Clown has quite an important part to play, but it is the Elizabethan jesting, the role of the licensed jester – like the wit-combats of the earlier comedies – that has become dated. Verbal wit is such diaphanous stuff – William Shakespeare, clever man that he was, had a great weakness for it. In his time it had much appeal.

With Feste an important new personality entered the cast of the Company. Will Kemp had departed, a boisterous, extrovert personality in the line of the famous clown, Tarleton, and his place was taken by Robert Armin. Armin was a subtler personality, introvert and temperamental, which made him right for the touching part of the Fool in *King Lear*, written for him, touched with poetry and melancholy, like so many clowns of genius. He was a writer himself, but again discontinuous. The lovely songs of this play are sung by him.

—— oOo ——

This is the most musical of all the plays – not only in songs and catches but in the whole atmosphere, which is drenched in music, like the Belmont Act of *The Merchant of Venice*. It begins, as it ends, with music:

> If music be the food of love, play on;

of course music *is* the food of love, and it is the accompaniment to the romantic love-talk. Then there are the songs:

> O, mistress mine, where are you roaming?
> O, stay and hear: your true love's coming . . .

One's heart turns over at the music to it, possibly Morley's:

> What is love? 'tis not hereafter;
> Present mirth hath present laughter;
>   What's to come is still unsure.

It is the Duke again who asks for an old song:

> The spinsters and the knitters in the sun
> And the free maids that weave their thread with bones
> Do use to chant it.

The age was intensely musical, and people made their own music: they did not get it canned. So Feste sings a song that goes to the heart of this play, suffused as it is with the music of melancholy:

> Come away, come away, death,
>   And in sad cypress let me be laid.

The play ends with a folksong, placing it in the perspective of time:

> When that I was and a little tiny boy,
>   With hey, ho, the wind and the rain . . .

There are, too, Sir Toby's roaring catches and snatches. 'Hold thy peace, thou knave', 'Three merry men be we', 'There dwelt a man in Babylon, lady, lady!' 'O, the twelfth day of December'.

Then there are the dances. 'Why dost not thou go to church in a galliard and come home in a coranto? My very walk should be a jig.' Sir Toby's 'passy measures pavin' would be a rather slow pavan. And at a time when people had to make their own entertainments there were numerous games – here we have tray-trip and cherry-pit. Bear-baiting was a familiar spectacle in the towns: Viola, disguised as a youth, is terrified at the thought of a duel with the timid Aguecheek: Cesario (Viola) 'pants and looks pale, as if a bear were at his heels.' A typical piece of Shakespeare bawdy follows: 'a little thing would make me tell them how much I lack of a man.'

—— oOo ——

Some reflections point as usual to the man writing.

> O spirit of love! how quick and fresh art thou,
> That, notwithstanding thy capacity
> Deceiveth as the sea . . .

we remember the 'capacious' image applied to the Dark Lady in the Sonnets, and then –

> nought enters there . . .
> But falls into abatement and low price,
> Even in a minute.

It is 'the expense of spirit' again, no sooner had but despisèd straight. The Duke thinks that a woman should take an older than herself (though Shakespeare had taken a woman to wife who was much his senior):

> So wears she to him,
> So sways she level in her husband's heart;

for men's

> fancies are more giddy and unfirm,
> More longing, wavering, sooner lost and worn
> Than women's are.

No doubt that spoke for William Shakespeare. On the other hand, there were women who could not take the beating of too strong a passion:

> no woman's heart
> So big, to hold so much: they lack retention.

That had certainly been true of Emilia Lanier:

> Alas, their love may be called appetite . . .
> That suffer surfeit, cloyment and revolt.

He had experienced both.

As usual many touches bespeak the time, give us a picture of it, and help us to place the play in its perspective. There are no Italian phrases now as in the days of Florio, but there are French phrases, as noticeably in *The Merry Wives*. These would be the years when Shakespeare was lodging with the French Montjoys. The Countess Olivia betrothed herself to Sebastian (twin brother of Viola-Cesario) by 'mutual joinder' of hands, 'strengthened by interchangement of your rings.' Handfasting, betrothal with a ring before witnesses made a legal contract of marriage in those days. And this is precisely what 'Master Shakespeare' himself effected in 1602 at Madame Montjoy's motion for the daughter of the house and Stephen Bellot, the apprentice at tire- and wig-making. (There is a passage about different sorts and fashions of 'tires' contemporaneously in *The Merry Wives*.)

The songs help us to date the play. A version of 'O mistress mine' appeared in 1599, 'Farewell, dear heart, since I must needs be gone' in 1600. 'The new map with the augmentation to the Indies' refers to Mollineux's map of the world, on a new projection, of 1599. Fabian ticks off Sir Toby with 'you are now sailed into the North of my lady's opinion, where you will hang like an icicle on a Dutchman's beard.' The Dutchman was William Barentz, of the Bering Straits, and his recent Arctic voyage of 1596-7. A couple of references to the Sophy (or Shah) of Persia relate to the account of the Shirley brothers' journey and treatment there, recently published in 1600. Everything shows Shakespeare with attentive ear to the ground picking up everything going on at the time.

Orsino, Duke of Bracchiano, paid a visit to the Queen in January 1601; Shakespeare used his name for his Duke. That is all we can say. From his constant performances at Court he *may* have picked up a hint for Malvolio from Sir William Knollys, Comptroller of the Household, who was a bit of a sourpuss – the Knollyses were puritanically inclined – though he made a fool of himself over Mary Fitton.[1] 'Policy I hate: I had as lief be a Brownist as a politician.' Both terms were derogatory at the time: by politics Elizabethans meant unscrupulous party intrigue, faction-fighting; politicians meant not the estimable, unself-interested figures of today, but more like Machiavellian intriguers or self-seekers. And to be a Brownist was ludicrous sectarianism: William Browne gave the church-authorities a lot of trouble (besides beating his wife) by starting a separatist Puritan sect; he ultimately suffered a relapse into conformity and sense.

—— oOo ——

The text presents few difficulties; first printed, probably from the Company's prompt book, it is a good text, with the usual misprints.

---

1. cf. 'The True Story of Mary Fitton' in my *Discoveries and Reviews from Renaissance to Restoration* (Macmillan, London, and Barnes & Noble, New York, 1975)

Troilus and Cressida

1602

The years 1600-1602 were critical years, both in politics and in the theatre. To understand *Troilus and Cressida* we have to set it in the contemporary perspective: without a knowledge of that people have not known how to take it, and critics have been more than usually off the point and in disagreement. In Shakespeare's own profession these years were marked by the notorious War of the Theatres. This was sparked off by Ben Jonson's explosive temper, in a quarrel with Marston, for whom Dekker too entered the fray and took up the cudgels. The parties wrote against each other, produced their plays caricaturing each other, and this involved the Chamberlain's Company, since the men's companies were aligned against the revived boys' companies, whose shrill voices suited the satires, the invective and personal abuse that flew to and fro.

Shakespeare characteristically kept out of the quarrel personally, though his company and he were affected by it, and traces remain in both *Hamlet* and *Troilus and Cressida*. The upshot of the War of the Theatres was important: Comedy was never the same again. It ended the reign of romantic comedy which had prevailed through the 1590's, of which Shakespeare's last example was *Twelfth Night*. Henceforth the future of comedy was with Ben Jonson's satiric comedy, which was not congenial to Shakespeare's spirit.

Nevertheless he provided his own example of it in *Troilus and Cressida* – a more scathing, brilliant and memorable example than anybody else's. It is almost as if Jonathan Swift had taken to writing a play. *Troilus and Cressida* is one of the most remarkable plays that Shakespeare ever wrote, but it has always been 'caviare to the general'. A play that goes so much to the heart of human folly, and exposes it in its most glaring manifestations – love, politics and war – can hardly be expected to be taken to the throbbing heart of the people. But it was not intended for them; it was intended for a private, sophisticated audience, probably at one of the Inns of Court.

This has led to much understandable uncertainty as to what kind of a play it is; though it defies categorisation, it should be thought of as a satirical comedy. Its reference to Ben Jonson and the controversy in the theatres is clear. In his *Poetaster* in 1601 Jonson had brought on his Prologue Armed 'in well erected confidence' against his detractors. That was typical of him. It was no less characteristic of Shakespeare next year to mark himself off from Ben, with a gentle reproof, by also bringing on a

Prologue armed, not in confidence of author's pen or actor's voice, but suited to the argument of the play. Shakespeare emphasises this point also in *Hamlet*. It is most significant.

—— oOo ——

The political events of those years are no less important than the literary and dramatic, for politics and war are equal themes of the play with love and its disillusionment. Politics in the last years of the Queen's reign were dominated by the bitter faction-fighting, dizzily led by Essex and Southampton, jostling for position to dominate the situation at Elizabeth's death and to control the accession of Scottish James. The situation was a critical one, people's tempers were on edge; the war with Spain was still going on and on, as it had done for nearly twenty years, pointlessly it seemed, as there appeared no end. The crisis burst openly with Essex's attempted *coup* to get possession of the Queen, in February 1601, his outbreak into the City, hoping for support, the fiasco for which he paid with his life on the scaffold, and his leading supporter, Southampton, with a suspended death-sentence.

It was heart-breaking for the Queen; and it must have affected Shakespeare intimately, watching from the side. For he had owed so much to Southampton, and this association shaped his alignment. The governmental side in the lacerating faction-fighting was led by the Cecils (backed by the Queen), and Shakespeare expressed what his friends felt about old Lord Burghley in old Polonius. While Shakespeare's affections and sympathies were with Essex and Southampton (as many literary folks' were), his mind was always with government and authority. He saw that the Queen and her government were right, his friends irresponsible and wrong.

Nothing is more sickening than to see one's friends steering straight for disaster. Observing it all – as Shakespeare did from close at hand, his mind and heart divided, his sympathies torn in two – accounts in part for the searing disillusionment of the play, its acuity and excruciating psychological incisiveness. It is, after all, not very funny, it is much more satire than comedy. 'Fools on both sides' is the reflection of the disillusioned author, so much disturbed that he never wrote more brilliantly. And the play contains some of his deepest reflections on politics.

—— oOo ——

The atmosphere is of that queasy time, when people's nerves were on edge – the people resented the death of Essex, always popular, though he had made it inevitable. There is a phrase in the play that expresses it:

> There is no help –
> The bitter disposition of the time
> Will have it so.

We note recognisable touches of Essex and his situation:

> He is so plaguey-proud that the death-tokens of it
> Cry 'No recovery'.

That was exactly like him: he never would make submission, so that the situation got beyond repair. Upon his fall:

> What the declined is
> He shall as soon read in the eyes of others
> As feel in his own fall; for men, like butterflies,
> Show not their mealy wings but to the summer;
> And not a man, for being simply man,
> Hath any honour but honour for those honours
> That are without him – as place, riches, and favour . . .

And so it goes on, as Shakespeare had observed from nearby, frequently performing (and watching) at Court.

An Elizabethan audience knew what to expect from the story of Troilus – no romantic illusions about love, but the disillusionment of a fool, who has fallen for a faithless young creature, who is Cressida. They are brought together, in a sense sold to each other, by the archetypal Pandarus, one of the most vivid creations. Even more striking is the cynic Thersites, who plays the part of jester and chorus together, commenting on and railing against the various sorts of idiocy incarnate – the blockhead Ajax, the arrogant Achilles, his boy-friend Patroclus, the empty-headed Helen, not much better than Cressida – and all in the most astonishing virtuosity of invective. Against all these are arrayed a few decent characters in contrast: Agamemnon is noble, Nestor respect-worthy, an experienced old man; lastly, Ulysses through whom Shakespeare expresses his profound political understanding.

The war goes on and on – and all because the beautiful Helen had been carried off from her Greek husband by Paris to Troy: (Marlowe's) Helen of Troy. Could it conceivably have been worth it? The issue is discussed between Hector and his brother Paris (both of whom were to die for her). Hector argues:

> Let Helen go.
> Since the first sword was drawn about this question,
> Every tithe-soul 'mongst many thousand dismes
> Hath been as dear as Helen – I mean, of ours.
> If we have lost so many tenths of ours
> To guard a thing not ours, nor worth to us –
> Had it our name – the value of one ten,

why not give her up? The only reply Paris can give is:

> But I would have the soil of her fair rape
> Wiped off in honourable keeping her –

a foolish argument. After arguing against it, Hector ends up by proposing to keep her:

> For 'tis a cause that hath no mean dependence
> Upon our joint and several dignities.

The anti-climax is laughable, in flagrant contradiction to his argument. On the Greek side Diomedes, who is to cuckold Troilus with Cressida, agrees as to Helen:

> She's bitter to her country. Hear me, Paris:
> For every false drop in her bawdy veins
> A Grecian's life hath sunk; for every scruple
> Of her contaminated carrion weight
> A Trojan hath been slain; since she could speak
> She hath not given so many good words breath
> As for her Greeks and Trojans suffered death.

An intelligent audience of young lawyers would enjoy the to-and-fro of the debate, and the railing contests, like wit-combats, that go on around Thersites. This ragged and scurrilous cynic has the last word on the issue:

> After this, the vengeance on the whole camp! or, rather the
> Neapolitan bone-ache [i.e. syphilis]. For that, methinks, is the
> curse dependent on those that war for a placket [i.e. a whore].

(The long-continuing war had introduced a good deal of syphilis into England.) The Trojan war would continue to the destruction of Troy.

—— oOo ——

The image of the destruction of Troy was what had always impressed Shakespeare's imagination, not the chivalric fighting fools. We know what Falstaff thought about the Elizabethan code of 'honour', and the un-numbered asses of young men who got killed fighting duels (William Shakespeare never involved himself in this nonsense, as Marlowe and Ben Jonson did). Hector argued sensibly,

> these moral laws
> Of nature and of nations speak aloud
> To have her back returned –

and then goes on to allow 'honour' (emotional preference) to overrule his reason:

> Mine honour keeps the weather of my fate.
> Life every man holds dear; but the dear man
> Holds honour far more precious-dear than life.

So, of course, he is killed by the great Achilles. But Achilles would not come out of his tent, until moved by passion at Hector's killing his boy-friend, Patroclus. And Achilles kills Hector when he is unarmed – one sees how much honour Shakespeare thought there was in that!

Nor was there much but contempt – the excitement of sex, of course – in his rendering of Troilus' passion for Cressida, and his portrayal of the two characters, the one light-headed with love, the other light-hearted. In this he was in keeping with the traditional medieval view, which he derived from Caxton. But his portrayal of the characters was his own; something of his own earlier experience went into the rendering. When Cressida breaks her plighted word to Troilus to go with a Greek, her excuse is:

> The error of our eye directs the mind . . .
> Minds swayed by eyes are full of turpitude.

Troilus can hardly believe the evidence of his own eyes, her assignation with another; his heart wishes him to believe contrary to the evidence: an obstinate hope

> That doth invert th'attest of eyes and ears,

as if they were the deceivers. This is precisely the experience expressed in the Sonnets:

> Thou blind fool, love, what dost thou to mine eyes
> That they behold and see not what they see? . .
> If eyes corrupt by over-partial looks,
> Be anchored in the bay where all men ride,
> Who of eyes' falsehood hast thou forgèd hooks
> Whereto the judgment of my heart is tied?
> Why should my heart think that a several plot
> Which my heart knows the wide world's common place?
> Or mine eyes seeing this, say this is not . . .

Troilus is in the situation William Shakespeare had known from experience.

The disillusionment with love is less interesting intellectually than the reflections of wise Ulysses on the facts of politics and society. In this century we have come to appreciate better Shakespeare's mature and responsible thought in this sphere. A normal man, a family man, grafted into society, his thinking here is so much more responsible than that of intellectuals like Marlowe and Jonson, odd men out. Precisely because Shakespeare was a more sensitive man, who hated cruelty and suffering, he realised how, if the order of society is shaken, it only leads to yet more suffering – as we have seen in the revolutions of our time. So his reflections on these matters are as relevant today as when they were written. He knew, as Burke and Dr. Johnson did, that

> There is a mystery, in whom relation
> Durst never meddle, in the soul of state,
> Which hath an operation more divine
> Than breath or pen can give expressure to.

It follows that there must be order in human society, as in the universe:

> How could communities,
> Degrees in schools, and brotherhoods in cities,
> Peaceful commerce from dividable shores,
> Prerogative of age, crowns, sceptres, laurels,
> But by degree, stand in authentic place?

When order is broken down in society, Shakespeare well understood that it is reduced to a power struggle:

> Then everything includes itself in power,
> Power into will, will into appetite;
> And appetite, an universal wolf . . .
> Must make perforce an universal prey,
> And last eat up itself.

How exactly we have seen that borne out in the revolutions of our time, when impartial authority and just government have handed over to military dictatorships in African states, preying on neighbours or within themselves. Or in the spawn of revolution eating each other up – nine members of Lenin's Politburo liquidated by their fellow, Stalin; or Hitler's murders of his former comrades; or Mussolini's of his son-in-law, and rivals. Shakespeare knew far better what to expect of humans than those who entertain liberal illusions about them.

Ulysses says a great deal more on this head: on faction-fighting, for example, the party and personal envies that impede common purpose:

> The general's disdained
> By him one step below, he by the next,
> That next by him beneath; so every step
> Exampled by the first pace that is sick
> Of his superior, grows to an envious fever
> Of pale and bloodless emulation.

This was the contemporary case, as everyone would recognise in 1602.

At the end of Elizabeth's reign the opposing factions of Essex and Ralegh were both war-minded, all for action and going on fighting. Ulysses, who speaks for political judgment, condemns them:

> They tax our policy and call it cowardice,
> Count wisdom as no member of the war,
> Forestall prescience, and esteem no act
> But that of hand.

They disparaged and discounted

> the still and mental parts
> That do contrive how many hands shall strike,

and calculate the nation's resources, what it could afford, and what was 'the enemy's weight.'

Shakespeare, as always, shared the view of authority and sympathised with the difficulties of government, rather than the simple (often personal) resentments of opposition. He had by now taken Essex's measure:

> Things small as nothing, for request's sake only,
> He makes important . . .

This is exactly as Essex had behaved with the Queen, always pressing her for jobs for his own followers, such as Bacon. It was intolerable. When he could not get his way, he would retire from Court and sulk in his tent, with Southampton, just like Achilles with Patroclus. (We need not suppose that the relations of Essex and Southampton were the same.)

It is given to the wise Ulysses (as it might be clever Robert Cecil) to flatter the foolish Ajax to the top of his bent, and to Thersites to express what is thought of the fighting fools – in terms of contemporary bull-baiting:

> The cuckold and the cuckold-maker are at it. Now, bull! now, dog!
> 'Loo, Paris, 'loo! now my doubled-horned Spartan! 'loo, Paris, loo!
> The bull has the game. Ware horns, ho!

The stage itself, as always with the actor-dramatist, provides images. To amuse Achilles his minion Patroclus mimics the other Greek leaders,

> . . . like a strutting player whose conceit
> Lies in his hamstring, and doth think it rich
> To hear the wooden dialogue and sound
> Twixt his stretched footing and the scaffoldage.

Shakespeare himself must have often observed how

> . . . Time is like a fashionable host
> That slightly shakes his parting guest by the hand
> And, with his arms outstretched as he would fly,
> Grasps in the comer.

Again we see the man well grafted into society in the thought

> That no man is the lord of anything,
> Though in and of him there be much consisting,
> Till he communicate his parts to others;
> Nor doth he of himself know them for aught
> Till he behold them formed in th'applause
> Where they're extended; who, like an arch reverberate
> The voice again.

There speaks the dramatist, and it is signally revealing: he had not found his full powers until the theatre reverberated them back to him.

—— oOo ——

The play was first mentioned in a blocking entry in the Stationers' Register in February 1603. In 1609 (the year in which the *Sonnets* were published by Thomas Thorp, who had got hold of the manuscript from their only possessor) a Quarto of this play was published, a good text apparently from a draft of Shakespeare's own manuscript. The Folio text followed this, with a few changes. But the Quarto has an interesting Preface, calling it 'a new play, never staled by the stage, never clapper-clawed with the palms of the vulgar.' This implies that it had been written for private production. It continues with praise of comedies, 'especially this author's comedies, that are so framed to the life that they serve for the most common commentaries of all the actions of our lives.' It proceeds to boost Shakespeare: 'And believe this, that, when he is gone and his comedies out of sale, you will scramble for them.' In fact they never have gone out of sale or ceased to hold the stage. Even this, the most barbed, brilliant and rebarbative of the comedies, has received a marked revival in our time, to which it is highly relevant and for which it holds a message.

All's Well That Ends Well

1603

It is usual to refer to *All's Well* and *Measure for Measure*, which go together, as problem plays; they are certainly not comedies in the usual sense of the term, except that at the end all's well and they have happy endings. They are both serious plays; *Measure for Measure* borders on tragedy. *All's Well* has much intellectual interest, though its particular concern for Shakespeare has not been realised. Perhaps he stood too closely to what he put into it, so that it gives the impression of being thought out, not distanced so as to fire the imagination. Also it was experimental, he was trying something new, under the influence of his junior, Ben Jonson. He was getting older; a conflict between the older and younger generation is one theme, and the time was unpropitious. The verse is bare, sometimes congested with thought. In part he was filling in, as a writer does, by drawing on what he had known personally: it adds greatly to the interest of the work when we recognise how much.

He drew on a familiar story that goes back to Boccaccio, then changed details, as usual, to make a play out of it, and filled it out with his own inventions – particularly the character of Parolles, the braggadocio soldier, whom Charles I thought the most striking. Bernard Shaw considered the Countess's 'the most beautiful old woman's part ever written', and certainly the women win all round; the men show up poorly, except for the ailing King of France, who retains regal authority for all the pathos of his situation. The Countess has a son, Count Bertram, fatherless, light-headed, a delayed adolescent. Helena, daughter of a famous doctor, who is dead, is in love with him; but he is beyond her reach, far out of her class, and will not marry. (Where have we met this young man before? In the Sonnets of course.)

The King is sick of an incurable disease. Helena cures him by the art learned from her father, and procures as her reward the King's command upon the young Count to marry her. Thus enforced, he refuses to consummate the marriage and goes off to the wars in Italy, attended by the braggart Parolles. In the fighting he acquits himself bravely; Parolles is an arrant coward, a man of words – a lesser Falstaff without the merriment.

The Count, who will not recognise his wife, plans to seduce a chaste Florentine girl, appropriately called Diana (a 'Capilet', observe). Helena follows him to Italy and defeats him by the 'bed-trick', beloved of Elizabethans, substituting herself for the girl. Rings are exchanged, by which the consummation is proved and the Count is rounded up by the women.

The good old Countess has stood by Helena all along, willing to receive her as her daughter, in preference to the son who has fallen down on his duty, and earned the King's disfavour. In the end the Count is caught and makes his submission – needs must – and all is well.

Where have we met all this before? As a good editor of the play remarks, one must realise 'the creative interplay between author and environment, the fact that the feelings of the author are a creative part of the climate of opinion in which he lives.'[1] Of course – as with any creative writer.

—— oOo ——

Early in 1603 the Queen entered her last illness and died. People were struck numb; the theatre folk affected, for the theatres were closed. Also it was a year of severe plague; sickness and death were all around. The King's sickness dominates the first part of the play, and this sets the action going. We are supposed to see this in terms of folk-tale, and it has some anthropological significance. But it is also contemporary. The King has been given up by the learned doctors of 'the congregated College', and he could not 'prostitute our past-cure malady to empirics.' The Royal College of Physicians contained the learned doctors and they persecuted empirics, who sometimes effected surprising cures.[2] The professional physicians adhered to the traditional authority of Galen, empirics were apt to follow the new teaching of Paracelsus. Helena effects the King's cure, the courtiers are amazed: 'to be relinquished of the artists – both of Galen and of Paracelsus – of all the learned Fellows . . . that gave him out incurable!'

There had been no curing the old Queen: Elizabeth I died in March 1603, and a new world opened up: the Jacobean age. Older people did not like it: Shakespeare's fellow-Warwickshireman, Drayton, detested it and the new generation that disconsidered him. The old King says of his young lords:

> but they may jest
> Till their own scorn return to them unnoted
> Ere they can hide their levity in honour.

The King agrees with the young Count's father:

> 'Let me not live', quoth he,
> 'After my flame lacks oil, to be the snuff
> Of younger spirits, whose apprehensive senses
> All but new things disdain; whose judgments are
> Mere fathers of their garments; whose constancies
> Expire before their fashions.'

Did this speak for William Shakespeare too, in the new age opening before them?

It was a crass and vulgar world, without the dignity which the historic figure of Elizabeth I had given, and James and his Queen were incapable of emulating. Parolles is a figure of the new society, with its opportunism and its false values: 'Simply the thing I am shall make me live', he declares after his exposure. In a world of fools such a type as Parolles can

> by foolery thrive:
> There's place and means for every man alive.

—— oOo ——

In an unstable society the issue of Class becomes uncomfortably sharpened; in an older, traditional world people know their place and act in accord. Shakespeare had already touched on the theme of gentility, about which he had reason to be conscious, in *As You Like It*. The issue of Class is to the fore in *All's Well*, for Helena's love for the Count is an 'ambitious love' as she recognises, and a doctor's daughter is disqualified from marrying a nobleman – except for the miraculous cure she has effected.

As to the miracle Shakespeare puts something significant into the mouth of an old lord. 'They say miracles are past, and we have our philosophical persons to make modern and familiar things supernatural and causeless. Hence it is that we make trifles of terrors, ensconcing ourselves into seeming knowledge, when we should submit ourselves to an unknown fear.' Evidently Shakespeare was no superficial rationalist: he had an old-time view of the mystery of things, closer to the old faith.

The Countess is firm in these values; she respects the 'honesty' (i.e. honourableness, in Elizabethan meaning) of Helena's lower-class origin, but sets more store by the 'goodness' she achieves. 'I have those hopes of her good that her education promises; her dispositions she inherits – which makes her fair gifts fairer.' The son scorns Helena for her origin:

> She had her breeding at my father's charge –
> A poor physician's daughter my wife! Disdain
> Rather corrupt me ever!

The King replies in a long speech which gives the message of the play.

> Strange is it that our bloods –
> Of colour, weight, and heat poured all together
> Would quite confound distinction – yet stands off
> In differences so mighty.

In disdaining a physician's daughter the Count overlooks innate quality for the name. (We may recall that a king could afford to ignore such distinctions – as Henry VIII did.) Shakespeare draws the moral in rhymed couplets some people have found uncongenial – but he uses them, as Elizabethans did, to enforce moral lessons, for didactic sentences and apothegms:

> From lowest place when virtuous things proceed,
> The place is dignified by the doer's deed . . .

>   Honours thrive
> When rather from our acts we them derive
> Than our foregoers. The mere word's a slave,
> Debauched on every tomb, on every grave,
> A lying trophy, and as oft is dumb,
> Where dust and damned oblivion is the tomb
> Of honoured bones indeed.

That is a pretty trenchant statement for an age which set such store by raising magnificent family monuments, with their trophies and epitaphs, in the churches where altars, shrines and images of the saints had stood. And it shows that, for all his proper respect for degree and gentility, Shakespeare had no illusions, no falsification of values underneath. Himself had certainly earned his place in society from his acts, his quality and achievement: *Non sans droit.*

The King is angered by the Count, who has dishonoured him by his disrespect – 'My honour's at the stake' – and makes him obey, contracting him to Helena with 'Proud, scornful boy'. One must remember that 'Boy!' was a term of insult with Elizabethans; the Count is several times thus described: he is an adolescent. His values are false: he attaches more importance to a ring that is a family heirloom:

> It is an honour 'longing to our house,

(a verbal echo from Marlowe, by the way)

> Bequeathed down from many ancestors,
> Which were the greatest obloquy i'th'world
> In me to lose.

Diana prizes her chastity no less.

After his enforced marriage the Count compounds his misconduct by stealing away from Court to the war in Italy, to cheat Helena of her marital rights. This earns the 'everlasting displeasure of the King, who had even tuned his bounty to sing happiness to him.' His mother pleads for him that it was

> Natural rebellion done i' th'blade of youth.

(This was the burden of the Countess of Southampton's plea for her son after his rebellion with Essex – and everybody accepted the plea of his youth, though he was old enough to know better.) When the Count is rounded up by the women and all is forgiven, the King is gracious:

> I am not a day of season,
> For thou may'st see a sunshine and a hail
> In me at once. But to the brightest beams
> Distracted clouds give way. So stand thou forth;
> The time is fair again.

This was precisely what was said of Elizabeth I, and how she kept order in the nursery by alternating storm and sunshine: after an overcast sky, what bliss when all was clear in the firmament again!

Helena also excuses the Count's stealing away, regarding herself as responsible for his being driven from 'the sportive Court, where thou wast shot at by fair eyes.' In the war abroad he served, bravely, as General of Horse (as Southampton had done in Ireland). On the rumour of his wife's presumed death a companion comments, 'the great dignity that his valour hath here acquired for him shall at home be encountered with a shame as ample' – for he would be held responsible for her death. His real fault was the light-headed irresponsibility of a spoiled aristocrat (just like Southampton), the refusal to face the responsibilities of adult life.

This is the theme of the Sonnets: the young lord who will not do his duty by his family, marry and carry it on – and yet allows himself to betray his friend with his friend's mistress. Ironically enough, the Count uses Shakespeare's argument with his young Lord against the Florentine girl's chastity:

> You are no maiden but a monument . . .
> And now you should be as your mother was
> When your sweet self was got.

Diana replies with an image which, for all its being a commonplace, is from the Sonnets:

> when you have our roses,
> You barely leave our thorns to prick ourselves.

Helena's comment is the forceful one:

> But, O strange men!
> That can such sweet use make of what they hate,
> When saucy trusting of the cozened thoughts
> Defiles the pitchy night; so lust doth play
> With what it loathes for that which is away.

155

Here is 'the expense of spirit in a waste of shame is lust in action' again – Shakespeare's complex about sex, which was to be expressed shortly in *King Lear*.

For the moment, we may take it that his attitude is that of the sceptical relativism he usually enforces: 'How mightily sometimes we make us comforts of our losses! And how mightily some other times we drown our gain in tears!' And the conclusion? –

> 'The web of our life is of a mingled yarn, good and ill together; our virtues would be proud if our faults whipped them not, and our crimes would despair if they were not cherished by our virtues.'

This is Shakespeare's signature-tune. It is as well that he ends his comedy with,

> Mine eyes smell onions; I shall weep anon.
> Good Tom Drum, lend me a handkercher –

we should hardly know it for a comedy else.

—— oOo ——

Two references to the sack of Troy, and to Cressida, indicate that the recent *Troilus and Cressida* was still in mind. Though the satire is less biting than in that play, there are satirical reflections on the code of honour, on Court affectations, and on the war, still not yet brought to an end: 'the muster-file, rotten and sound, upon my life, amounts not to fifteen thousand poll; half of the which dare not shake the snow from off their cassocks lest they shake themselves to pieces.' Parolles regards Captain Dumaine (note the name from *Love's Labour's Lost* – Southampton was in mind) as good enough to instruct the doubling of files at Mile-End, where the musters were trained – and where Justice Shallow had watched 'a little quiver fellow' manage his piece.

Shakespeare's reading in the Voyages has a reflection:

> Thus, Indian-like,
> Religious in mine error, I adore
> The sun that looks upon his worshipper.

Contemporary religious controversy receives a hit from the Clown: 'If men could be contented to be what they are, there were no fear in marriage; for young Charbon the Puritan and old Poysam, the Papist, howsomever their hearts are severed in religion, their heads are both one; they may jowl horns together like any deer i'th'herd.' Here is the hoary old joke about horns and cuckolding again. We may note that the Clown's patter is suggestive rather than outright bawdy, though there is some of that. For the rest, the Clown's wit dates more than anything else. The funniest episode is the uncasing of Parolles. The cult of melancholy is glanced at: 'I know a man that had this trick of melancholy sold a goodly manor for a song.'

The bed-trick – the trick that is played upon the young Count to get him to bed with his own wife – was popular with Elizabethans, if hardly congenial to our mind. Any notable act of cozenage gave them pleasure in the theatre, and Count Bertram was fair game. Diana puts the point as it appeared, and appealed, to them:

> Only, in this disguise, I think't no sin
> To cozen him that would unjustly win.

It is to be observed once more how Shakespeare tips the balance in favour of his women.

—— oOo ——

Professor Hunter comments that 'Shakespeare had some knowledge of French, and the atmosphere of the play is decidedly French; the names . . . seem to indicate a mind at work strongly imbued with a consciousness of French meanings'. But, of course, Shakespeare was lodging with the Montjoys in Silver Street in these years.

And what are we to make of the close parallels between the young Count and the young Earl Shakespeare had known so closely? Everything shows that Southampton's mother, the Countess, was a charming woman, who never lost the good will of the Queen for all her son's escapades. He, too, was fatherless and irresponsible; he had dishonoured the great Lord Treasurer by breaking his word to marry his granddaughter and, rather than do it, had stolen off from Court to France. Later on, from France again he meant to go further, into Italy, but was brought back by Essex to marry his cousin ('shot at with fair eyes'), one of the Queen's Court ladies, Elizabeth Vernon, at the last moment of her pregnancy. Again and again he earned the Queen's disfavour. Essex made him General of Horse abroad in Ireland (like the young Count in Italy), where he acquitted himself bravely. The Queen cashiered him. In the end, when he followed Essex into rebellion, the only plea for him was his youth and immaturity.

Southampton, too, had his Parolles – a braggadocio Captain Piers Edmonds, whom the Earl made his corporal-general when he was General of the Horse: 'he ate and drank at his table and lay in his tent. The Earl of Southampton would cull and hug him in his arms and play wantonly with him.'[3] Essex would take this professional soldier for coach-rides with him. Did Shakespeare know the fellow? It is not unlikely, and the type is certainly a familiar one.

Dr. Johnson felt sure that Parolles was the character Shakespeare took most delight in drawing – his exposure provides rollicking fun. But the great man could not 'reconcile his heart' to Bertram. Nor can we.

The text, from the First Folio, is a fair one and offers few difficulties. These, however, appear to indicate a copy from the author's own manuscript. For, as in *Much Ado*, *Romeo and Juliet*, and *2 Henry IV*, the name occasionally given is that of the rôle and not that of the character. Professor Hunter concludes, 'it looks as if Shakespeare was finding out, in the course of composition, what to call these characters; if this inference is correct then the manuscript behind the Folio must represent a stage at which the play was still being composed.'

1. Hunter, G.K. *Arden Shakespeare* edition, page iiii (Methuen, London, 1959)
2. cf. *Simon Forman: Sex and Society in Shakespeare's Age*, chapter III (Weidenfeld & Nicolson, London, 1974); American title *Sex and Society in Shakespeare's Age: Simon Forman the Astrologer* (Scribner, New York, 1975)
3. Historical MSS Commission *Salisbury (Cecil) Manuscripts Preserved at Hatfield House, Herts.*, vol XI (1601) nos. 94 and 108 (H.M.S.O., London, 1906)

Measure for Measure
1604

Measure for Measure is an inspired play, where *All's Well* is an excogitated one. With the former coming shortly upon the heels of the latter, *All's Well* gives something of an impression of a trial-run. The situation upon which the plot hangs, the intrigue, is similar. The villain of this piece, Angelo – Count Bertram was not a villain – is caught similarly by the bed-trick, his betrothed substituted for the woman he fancies. The light-weight lying courtier Lucio is shown up and exposed as the lying and cowardly Parolles was. And yet, in spite of similarity of plot and its unravelling, how different these two plays are, which are often thought of as twins!

The ailing King in *All's Well* is totally different from the mysterious Duke – who disguises himself as a Friar, to observe the proceedings of government in his absence. Isabella is a more appealing character than Helena, when all is said; the villainous, tormented Angelo a more powerful creation than the adolescent Count Bertram. Parolles is not rivalled, but the low-life and prison scenes of *Measure for Measure* are more gripping than the army-life around Bertram which, after all, Shakespeare did not know. Moreover, the atmosphere is different from that of its predecessor.

It all goes to show the extraordinary variety of his invention, and what little importance he attached to plot, 'sources' and that kind of thing. He took a story he could turn into a play, then let his playwright's expertise and his poetic imagination play upon it. In this case he looked over various versions of the story he had it in mind to dramatise: a closet-drama by George Whetstone and the prose-version in his *Heptameron*, but also Cinthio's collection of Italian stories, *Ecatommiti*. With that he set to work, this time both heart and mind were kindled, the play makes a homogeneous integrated impact. We know that the dramatist thought in terms of scenes, and this play provides several of great power.

—— oOo ——

A main theme is government, the mystery of state, its workings, whether satisfactory or not. We now appreciate, in this century better than before, how much Shakespeare's mind reflected upon the problems of society, of government and order. They were naturally much in mind at this moment of the take-over by James I from Elizabeth, the coming of a new dynasty. The first words of this play are

Of government the properties to unfold . . .

The Duke, withdrawing to observe and test the rule of his Deputy,

Angelo, has been too permissive and let slip

> The needful bits and curbs to headstrong weeds . . .
> Sith 'twas my fault to give the people scope,
> 'Twould be my tyranny to strike and gall them
> For what I bid them do: for we bid this be done
> When evil deeds have their permissive pass
> And not the punishment.

The Deputy is a precise, stern, cold-seeming man – when he makes water, his urine is congealed ice, says Lucio – and he puts the law against fornication into effect, thus catching Claudio, who has got his girl with child before marriage. This is disagreeably harsh; but the uncivilised Puritans under the Commonwealth brought in the death-penalty against adultery, though it remained a dead letter through the common sense of the country. The Duke knows well that his Deputy is 'precise, and scarce confesses that his blood flows.' – Now

> shall we see,
> If power change purpose, what our seemers be.

Power is apt to corrupt and, now that he has the chance, the Deputy is determined to enforce the death-penalty on the offending Claudio. He is prevented only by himself falling from grace, by arranging an assignation with Claudio's chaste sister, Isabella – as he thinks, but for whom his own betrothed, whom he had deserted for insufficiency of dowry, is substituted. Such is the plot, and it borders all the way along on tragedy, until the Duke reveals himself and puts things right. Shakespeare was also writing *Othello* this year; we may regard *Measure for Measure* as a tragi-comedy.

Various comments of the author by the way illuminate what those in authority have to put up with:

> No might nor greatness in mortality
> Can censure 'scape; back-wounding calumny
> The whitest virtue strikes. What king so strong
> Can tie the gall up in the slanderous tongue?

We see again the contemporary use of rhymed couplets for moral *sententiae* – no point in depreciating such verse, it shows an anachronistic lack of understanding on the part of critics. Again:

> O place and greatness, millions of false eyes
> Are stuck upon thee. Volumes of report
> Run with these false and most contrarious guests
> Upon thy doings, thousand escapes of wit

> Make thee the father of their idle dream,
> And rack thee in their fancies.

This was the kind of thing that Queen Elizabeth, unmarried as she was, had to put up with all her life. There is no end to the nonsense people will say and believe about persons in high place. William Shakespeare was a governmental man; government never had any reason to fear his tongue or pen – he understood too well the mystery of state, the pressures and strains upon those who rule.

James I was now king. A clever, kind, well-educated man, he was more of a don than a monarch; with no sense of dignity and not much of an appearance, he did not care for the public shows in which the great actress, his predecessor, cut such a figure. The Duke is in accord:

> I love the people,
> But do not like to stage me to their eyes;
> Though it do well, I do not relish well
> Their loud applause and aves vehement.

He adds a reflection of Essex which Shakespeare noted several times:

> Nor do I think the man of safe discretion
> That does affect it –

i.e. that cultivates popularity, as Essex (who gave hints for Bolingbroke) had done. James I positively disliked the people thronging around him:

>   even so
> The general [populace], subject to a well-wished king,
> Quit their own part, and in obsequious fondness
> Crowd to his presence, where their untaught love
> Must needs appear offence.

James had been besieged by crowds all his way down from the North to take possession of his new kingdom. Unfortunately his first year coincided with a severe outbreak of plague. Mistress Overdone, the bawd – another Mistress Quickly – sums up the times: 'Thus, what with the war, what with the sweat, what with the gallows, and what with poverty, I am custom-shrunk.' The war was not ended till next year, 1604. Meanwhile the gallows claimed some notable exhibits: George Brooke, Lord Cobham's brother, and Father Watson; while Lord Cobham, the great Sir Walter Ralegh and Sir Griffin Markham were condemned to the gallows, but their sentences left suspended over their heads.

It was a queasy, uneasy time. We have an unsurpassed picture of contemporary low life, which so embarrassed Victorian commentators. It is obvious that William Shakespeare was acquainted with this as with the Court – a man of the theatre would be with both. *Measure for Measure* has a full gallery of bawds, pimps, gaolbirds, a provost, a constable, an executioner thrown in – all completely authentic and convincing, a realistic portrayal if to be taken and played comically. The drunken gaolbird, Barnardine, for example, does not care whether his head is chopped off. Foreign observers noted that the English cared little for death and took a death-sentence nonchalantly; they objected more to the foreign sentence of breaking on the wheel, leaving men maimed for life.

Elbow, the constable, is another Dogberry, his malapropisms as amusing and to the point. Shakespeare is quite at ease with all this, the bawdy fuller and more flowing than ever – no point in being embarrassed by the facts of life. Even the lofty Deputy, the great Angelo, makes his assignation in a 'garden-house', which was a favourite *locale* for such encounters, as we know from Forman. These creatures' dialogue flows more easily than that of the camp in *All's Well*, except for Parolles with his virtuosity of vituper-ation. There is a Dickensian inventiveness in the very names of the company in prison:

> 'First, here's young Master Rash. He's in for a commodity of brown paper and old ginger, nine-score and seventeen pounds, of which he made five marks ready money. Marry, then ginger was not much in request, or the old women were all dead. Then there is here one Master Caper, at the suit of Master Threepile the mercer, for some four suits of peach-coloured satin, which now peaches him a beggar. Then have we here young Dizzy, and young Master Deepvow, and Master Copperspur, and Master Starve-lackey, the rapier and dagger man, and young Dropheir that killed lusty Pudding, and Master Forthright the tilter, and brave Master Shoe-tie the great traveller, and wild Half-Can that stabbed pots, and I think forty more – all great doers in our trade and are now "for the Lord's sake".'

With what gusto Shakespeare wrote that passage!

—— oOo ——

One catches sight of him, for a moment forgetting himself, when he makes the Duke say suddenly in the surroundings of prison: 'Look, th'unfolding star calls up the shepherd' – as if he were out on the Cotswolds once more. (Perhaps he was writing at home in Stratford.)

Many famous passages give us his reflections on life:

> but man, proud man,
> Dressed in a little brief authority,
> Most ignorant of what he's most assured,

> His glassy essence, like an angry ape,
> Plays such fantastic tricks before high heaven
> As make the angels weep . . .

Man – an angry ape . . . The Duke, in a tremendous formal oration, presents a disenchanted view of life:

> If I do lose thee, I do lose a thing
> That none but fools would keep; a breath thou art,
> Servile to all the skyey influences
> That dost this habitation where thou keep'st
> Hourly afflict.

This is an old man speaking. On the other hand, Claudio, who is young:

> Ay, but to die, and go we know not where,
> To lie in cold obstruction and to rot;
> This sensible warm motion to become
> A kneaded clod; and the delighted spirit
> To bathe in fiery floods, or to reside
> In thrilling region of thick-ribbèd ice,
> To be imprisoned in the viewless winds
> And blown with restless violence round about
> The pendent world –

that was one Elizabethan view of what happened after death.
 We are given a revealing reflection from Isabella, the virtuous:

> Women, help heaven! Men their creation mar
> In profiting by them.

Did that speak for William Shakespeare? Isabella has been universally admired, especially perhaps by maiden ladies in universities, for her adamant refusal to sacrifice her chastity to save her brother's life:

> I had rather give my body than my soul.

This moral absolute is less highly regarded today; a modern audience might well think she attached an exaggerated importance to it. But then, there has supervened the most universal of revolutions – that in the position and status of women. To make her situation more poignant, her refusal to exchange her virginity for her brother's life, she is made a quasi-nun. In Shakespeare's 'source' she makes the sacrifice; in his play, she will not. This is significant of his dramatic art: he always pushes the situation to extremes – particularly in the tragedies – both for dramatic effect and for the deeper revelation of character. Here he does it in a 'comedy' which borders on tragedy.

Pervasive and more permanent, perhaps, are the themes of justice and of truth against seeming, of what is a man's nature as against what it appears, either to others or even to himself. Angelo's is a convincing progress of discovery of himself: he is not so cold and unimpassioned as he thought himself to be – he is seduced by 'modesty' where he never would be by 'lightness' – and his ignorance of his true self fractures his sense of justice.

One reflection bespeaks Shakespeare the social man, as always:

> Heaven doth with us as we with torches do,
> Not light them for themselves; for if our virtues
> Did not go forth of us, 'twere all alike
> As if we had them not.

This play has been well-nigh buried under a mountain of moralising – quite superfluously, since all along Shakespeare draws the morals himself:

> That we were all, as some would seem to be,
> Free from our faults, as faults from seeming free.
> He who the sword of heaven will bear
> Should be as holy as severe . . . etc.

And by the lips of Isabella Shakespeare pronounces the ultimate moral statement that guided him: forgiveness, charity, mercy:

> Why, all the souls that were were forfeit once,
> And He that might the vantage best have took
> Found out the remedy. How would you be,
> If He, which is the top of judgment, should
> But judge you as you are? O think on that . . .

We are already in the atmosphere of the great tragedies.

—— oOo ——

The text, first printed in the First Folio, is thought to have been printed from a transcript of an autograph manuscript, prepared by the Company's scribe, Ralph Crane. The triple process of transmission led to a number of confusions and mislineations. For example, the Duke's line quoted above, 'Look, th'unfolding star calls up the shepherd', printed as prose, is obviously a blank verse line. These things are not important; the undue attention given to them by academic commentators – a veritable Shakespeare industry – buries the plays under a mountain of commentary and notes. Better, for our time, to modernise linguistic usage as we already do spelling and punctuation from superseded Elizabethan.

SHAKESPEARE'S
TRAGEDIES

Each age flatters itself that it understands the past better than its predecessors have done. But I am sure that we in our time do understand the Elizabethan age better than the Victorians did, for not the best of reasons. The Victorians enjoyed a blissful period of security, exceptional in human history, such as the Elizabethans did not have and we can never hope to enjoy. Our insecurity, the sense of contingency upon which all life hangs, the clouds hanging over humanity in our time, the nuclear threat to life on the planet, give us better – or, rather, worse – reasons for understanding the tragic depiction of life in Shakespeare's greatest works.

For it is as a tragic dramatist that he is most highly estimated – or at least, since he shines equally in comedy, history and romance, it is the great tragedies that are his highest achievement.

It is all the more remarkable since his natural gift had been for comedy – a euphoric spirit. His earliest attempt at tragedy, *Titus Andronicus*, was visibly not natural to him and went against the grain. The author was not involved by its blood-curdling horrors – he was merely engaged in going one better than his model, Thomas Kyd. And yet, as with all the early work, one glimpses the elastic potentialities of finer things to come.

Experience deepened, and certainly darkened, his view of life and the character of mankind, until we reach the despairing depiction of *King Lear* and the disillusionment of *Timon of Athens*. From the time of *Julius Caesar* and *Hamlet* there are no illusions; after *Timon* there was nothing for it but to turn to the consoling world of fantasy and romance.

We come to a more specific reason for our understanding his tragedies better. With our remarkable advances in modern psychology – though experience could have told us – we no longer expect consistency or much reason from human beings. Shakespeare has often been criticised for improbability or inconsistency – and Bradley, in a celebrated monument to Victorian rationalism, struggled in vain, like a good man struggling with sin, to reduce Shakespearean tragedy to a system of ethics.

Let us be quite clear: there is a firm moral background to Shakespeare's thought, but it is that of the Elizabethans, not the Victorians.[1] And he was not one to challenge the accepted code, the norms and beliefs, of the age – unlike Marlowe, who died young. Shakespeare was a maturer spirit, with a vein of scepticism, like Montaigne, who also conformed. It is the subtler spirit who is apt to conform.

On the superficial question of probability or improbability, of course it is true that the Elizabethans did not go to the theatre to see what was probable: they preferred the improbable, the exciting and sensational, the truly dramatic. There *are*, however, murderers, like Richard III or Macbeth; psychotics like Leontes; evil men like Iago, who hate others' happiness; or foolish old men like Lear, who give away all they have and then expect gratitude. There are even such women as Goneril and Regan. Oddly enough, a case of their kind happened about the time of the play. Sir William Harvey married Cordelia, the youngest daughter of Brian Annesley, an old servitor of Queen Elizabeth. His two elder daughters had sought to have him 'agnominated' a lunatic to get his property.[2]

We must dig deeper, for Shakespeare moves along deeper levels of the human spirit in his tragedies.

He strains his situations to the utmost limit, not only for the purpose of achieving sensation in the theatre – though that was one motive – nor could anything be more exciting than the ominous developments of *Macbeth*, *Othello*, or *Hamlet*. We derive a clue from the observation of a short-story writer of genius, Flannery O'Connor, that it is at moments of emergency, of extreme tension, that people reveal their true character. Thus it is that we recognise in the theatre, and carry away from it, the essential *truth* of the characters – that this is the way Macbeth or Othello would have behaved, when Shakespeare has heightened the tension beyond the historical fact or even what was necessary to account for it.

Robert Bridges perceived that: 'his success depends on the power and skill with which this character is chosen and enforced upon the audience; for it is when their minds are preoccupied with his personality that the actions follow as unquestionable realities and, in *Macbeth*, even preordained and prophesied.' Bridges, as a Victorian, was shocked by the lengths to which Shakespeare would go.

For Shakespeare, with his unparalleled observation of human nature, intuited the workings of the subconscious and unconscious, and is closely corroborated by the findings of modern psychology. He prefigures these in his dramatic art, above all in the tragedies. People have been accustomed till recently to think that moral character was all of a piece, simple and integrated. 'But in life, as we know, perhaps every personality is in some degree dissociated; and this fact of universal significance, which is given gross expression in certain pathological states, often finds a species of covert (and perhaps obscurely cathartic or therapeutic) release in art.'[3]

In everyone there are these recesses, these dark forces, ready to spring out, given the circumstances. A time which has witnessed the horrors of Belsen and Auschwitz, the mass-murders of Communist Russia or China, let alone of darkest Africa, need have no difficulty in recognising the truth of Shakespeare's revelation of what lurks beneath the surface, smiling or unsmiling. A Jewish critic observes perceptively that we all have a touch of paranoia in us. We are all (or almost all) capable of anything, when the bonds of customary civilised behaviour are broken. Iago is not at all incredible, as so many good people have said. Othello already has the grounds of suspicion in him, as he himself owns pathetically: he is a Moor, declined in the vale of years, and had made a marriage which was contrary to the mores of Venice. Macbeth already had murder in him: the evil spirits corroborated and confirmed his unconscious desire.

Most of these characters are unaware of the workings of their unconscious; certainly Othello and, pitifully, King Lear. Interestingly, Iago may very well have been self-aware – he was of the stuff of which such are made: a reason for his closing up at the end, with

> From this time forth I never will speak word.

Hamlet too was extremely self-aware: another reason why he speaks to us today more than any of Shakespeare's tragic heroes, or above any other of his characters. He is almost a symbol of modern man caught in his tragic fate and in his awareness of it.

Similarly Shakespeare reached down to profound archetypal situations: Hamlet's sexual revulsion from his mother's marriage to his uncle so soon after his father's death; Leontes' sexual jealousy of his wife; Othello's killer-reaction to suspected infidelity. And the dramatist reaped the rewards of trusting to his intuition. When Desdemona receives the shock of learning what Othello suspects, and answers Emilia's inquiry, 'Faith, half asleep', it is not insensibility but the numbness a woman feels from shock. When Coriolanus wants to fire the beloved city that has rejected him, his reaction is well known to contemporary psycho-analysis.

Hence the universality of the appeal: the world bears witness to the truth to human nature of these depictions by the writer who observed its operations with most understanding. The setting and the trappings may be realistic enough, for his declared object was to hold the mirror up to nature; then he went further and deeper, always ready to follow his intuitions and clothe them with the splendour and terrors of his imagination.

As to the effect, there is no shadow of doubt. It reaches so deeply into such depths of our conscience, our sense of regret and remorse, guilt and grief, that sometimes one can hardly bear to look or hear the searching words that are being spoken. The tender heart of the great bully, Dr. Johnson, could not bear to think of the last scene of *Lear* with the old man carrying the dead body of Cordelia. Here we see the *ne plus ultra* of Shakespeare: other versions end happily; it was out of the rigour of his imaginative understanding that he saw it could end only thus.

This is why he has meant so much to the world. And has no equal.

---

1. cf. my *Shakespeare's Globe: His Moral and Intellectual Outlook* (Weidenfeld & Nicolson, London, 1981); American title *What Shakespeare Read and Thought* (Coward, McCann and Geoghegan, New York, 1981)
2. cf. my *Shakespeare's Southampton*, pages 209-10 (Macmillan, London, 1965)
3. Stewart, J.I.M. *Character and Motive in Shakespeare*, page 90 (Longmans, 1949)

Titus Andronicus
1590-1

This play is Shakespeare's first historical tragedy, tethered to his reading of Ovid and Seneca, filled with classical references and Latin tags, to show that, though not a university wit, he was as good as they were. It is already strongly marked by Shakespearean characteristics: the effective plotting, the use of rare impressive words – accite, affy, palliament; the vigorous attack, the rhetoric; in particular, the mingling of classical oratory with numerous country images. It is a countryman writing. The horrors, in which the newcomer strove to outdo Kyd – and succeeded – themselves come from classical sources: the story of Tereus and Philomela, the fearful banquet served up from Seneca's *Thyestes*. These things make the play repellent to modern taste, though it much appealed to Elizabethan. Shakespeare wrote them up from a distance, himself not engaged emotionally. But, after all, they are not much removed from the horrors of Belsen and Auschwitz in our own enlightened time. We must however view the play in its proper Elizabethan perspective.

It belongs to the early Elizabethan stage, which was dominated by Marlowe's *Tamburlaine* and *The Jew of Malta*, and by Kyd's *Jeronimo, or the Spanish Tragedy*, with the last two of which *Titus* has strong affinities. The most striking character in the piece, the villain Aaron the Moor, is suggested by Marlowe's Barabas. It is significant that, where Barabas has no love-interest, Shakespeare's Aaron is the lover of the Empress Tamora, who has a base black child by him. (The play has even a topical racialist interest today.) The feigned madness of Titus was suggested by Kyd's Jeronimo, which Shakespeare succeeded in equalling in popularity, to Ben Jonson's grumpy disapprobation from the superior vantage-ground of a quarter of a century later.

The play was good theatre – if to us horrid, with its murders on stage, the chaste Lavinia raped, tongue torn out and hands cut off so that she could neither tell nor write her tale; let alone the cannibal banquet *pour comble de tout*. The public wanted to read the play too: three quartos were printed in Shakespeare's lifetime – the first discovered only in ours. (So that we need not be struck dumb at one's discovering something new about Shakespeare.) From these imprints we learn that the play had been performed by the following Companies – Pembroke's (which was broken by the plague in 1593), Derby's (active between September 1593 and April 1594, though earlier as Lord Strange's); Sussex's, and the Lord Chamberlain's from the formation in the summer of 1594. This gives us some idea of the Companies Shakespeare was connected with, or writing for, before he betook himself and his plays to his permanent partnership with the Chamberlain's men.

Among the plays which were originally Pembroke's were *2* and *3 Henry VI*, which chime with *Titus*: there are verbal echoes, and both the Third Part of *Henry VI* and *Titus* are Revenge plays. In the last the wicked Empress Tamora – the Queen of the Goths whom the gulled Emperor Saturninus had married – appears disguised as Revenge, with her sons as Rape and Murder on either side. Shakespeare seems to have picked up the story from some chapbook, which got it from Italy, though the outlines were familiar enough. He garnished it from his classical schoolbooks, naïvely citing them and their tags on the stage:

> TITUS: Lucius, what book is that she tosseth so?
> BOY: Grandsire, 'tis Ovid's Metamorphoses.

Again:

> DEMETRIUS: What's here? a scroll, and written round about,
> Let's see:
> Integer vitae, scelerisque purus,
> Non eget Mauri iaculis, nec arcu.
> CHIRON: O, 'tis a verse in Horace; I know it well:
> I read it in the Grammar long ago.

This is very much early Shakespeare – school was not far away as usher. There are many such classical clichés all the way through – no play has so many. Several times situations in the action remind us of Coriolanus: the election by the Romans of Titus, their general, for his good service against the Goths; he makes way for Saturninus as Emperor. Then, for all the wrongs put upon him, he goes over to the Goths against Rome:

> Who threats in course of his revenge, to do
> As much as ever Coriolanus did.

In fact, this play of a novice already foreshadows so much: Titus is a kind of Coriolanus; Aaron, the villain who is pure evil incarnate, looks forward to Iago; the racial theme to *The Merchant of Venice*; the ruthless Tamora to Lady Macbeth. And, if the stage ends up littered with dead bodies, so it does in *Hamlet*. The difference is that the tragedy in *Hamlet*, as in all the great tragedies, is *innerlich* and is borne home deeply to the emotions, where the impact of *Titus* is external. We may, however, suffer from shock: when performed in London, not long after the war and the revelations of Belsen, people went out sick. On the continent of Europe the production had marked success.

On his classical ground-work and the pseudo-classical basis of the story the actor-dramatist worked in his own Gothic enrichment, his recognisable imagery, phrasing and background. An unlikely feature of the play, considering its nature, is the depiction of countryside, country sports and aspects it contains. Had it been written at Stratford and brought up in the playing-fardel Greene gibed at? Tamora, somewhat improbably, waxes eloquent about countryside:

> The birds chant melody on every bush,
> The snake lies rollèd in the cheerful sun,
> The green leaves quiver with the cooling wind,
> And make a chequered shadow on the ground.

Nothing like that in Marlowe. And it is a prelude to a fond description of a deer-hunt, on which the countryman had a perfect fixation in all his early work. Nothing of that in the urban (but not urbane) Marlowe either.

> The hunt is up, the morn is bright and grey,
> The fields are fragrant and the woods are green.
> Uncouple here and let us make a bay.

Not only is the country everywhere in the background of this play, but the countryman turned author betrays himself:

> What, hast thou not full often struck a doe,
> And borne her cleanly by the keeper's nose?

He seems to be on familiar terms with the operation. He also knows, what we do not, things about country lore – that a surfeit of clover can be fatal to sheep. Red clover was known as 'honeysuckle' in Warwickshire, and we find that feeding 'honey-stalks' to sheep could end in their being 'rotted with delicious feed.' Or, rustic enmities could

> Make poor men's cattle break their necks;
> Set fire on barns and haystacks in the night.

Not much bawdy appears – in which he was to become so prolific (London life!); but Lavinia does hail Tamora:

> Under your patience, gentle empress,
> 'Tis thought you have a goodly gift in horning,
> And to be doubted that the Moor and you
> Are singled forth to try experiments.
> Jove shield your husband from his hounds today!
> 'Tis pity they should take him for a stag –

i.e. with cuckold's horns. This was indeed to ask for trouble at Tamora's hands, though the come-uppance Lavinia received proved rather severe.

—— oOo ——

Some touches of contemporary life appear in this play loaded down with the classics. When Tamora's dreadful sons 'enter braving', Aaron cries,

> Clubs, clubs! these lovers will not keep the peace.

This was the regular cry at a street-brawl of the time to call the watch. And he reproaches them:

> So near the emperor's palace dare ye draw,
> And maintain such a quarrel openly!

It was a special offence to quarrel and draw swords within what was known as the verge of the Court. The base black child of Tamora and the Moor is incongruously thus found by a Goth:

> Renownèd Lucius, from our troops I strayed
> To gaze upon a ruinous monastery . . .

Shakespeare must have seen many such as he toured the post-Dissolution countryside, with its wreckage – 'bare ruined choirs'; he had an eye for such things, overthrown monuments and ripped-up brasses, 'slave to mortal rage'.

—— oOo ——

The text of the play offers no problems, even that of the quartos. The stage-directions are full and 'suggest an author's hand', according to E.K. Chambers. The Folio printing was set up from the latest quarto of 1611, with the addition of a whole scene.

The first illustration of a Shakespeare play is of a scene from this one, in which Tamora kneels to Titus to spare her sons from execution, with speeches reproduced beneath. It is signed and dated by Henry Peacham, 1594 or 5. 'Who this Peacham was,' says the Arden editor, 'we do not know.' On the contrary, he was the well-known author of a standard book, *The Compleat Gentleman*, and is the subject of a full biography in the *Dictionary of National Biography*. In addition to writing much, 'he could paint, draw, and engrave portraits and landscapes', and he wrote a treatise on pen-drawing and limning in watercolours, published during Shakespeare's career, in 1606. There is no reason whatever why the depiction of the scene should not be authentic: misplaced scepticism is as absurd as superfluous conjectures.

Romeo and Juliet
1594-5

With *Romeo and Juliet* we come to the most ever-popular of the plays, along with *Hamlet* and *Richard III*, and it has been a never-ending source of inspiration for the sister arts of painting and music. In our time it has been the direct source of inspiration for a remarkable musical, *West Side Story*, with a score by Leonard Bernstein, which may be regarded as a modern version of the play in American idiom.

The play visibly belongs to the period of the late Sonnets, of which it has several echoes; no less than three sonnets are incorporated in the play, and there is a good deal of rhyme – one whole scene being in rhyme, as in *Richard II*, to which it is also close. Both are lyrical tragedies, with Shakespeare's characteristic mixture of artificial – or, as Elizabethans would say, 'conceited' – language, along with simple. Indeed, he gives us a pointer to his use of 'conceits':

> Conceit, more rich in matter than in words,
> Brags of his substance, not of ornament –

i.e. the idea behind it is more important than the expression, it is not mere decoration. And that goes largely too for the verbal play, the punning, to which he was so much given.

The plague of 1592 and 1593, that had such decisive effects on his career, is in the immediate background. Friar John and a brother friar were visiting the sick, when

> the searchers of the town,
> Suspecting that we both were in a house
> Where the infectious pestilence did reign,
> Sealed up the doors, and would not let us forth.

This was the regulation in plague-time. Juliet's Nurse, a marvellous down-to-earth old crone, gives us a corroboration of date:

> On Lammas-eve at night shall she be fourteen . . .
> 'Tis since the earthquake now eleven years.

This would be 31 July, and in the summer of 1583 there had been an earthquake in the county of Dorset which opened a large cavity in the vale of Blackmore, according to Camden.

The story is one of young love, 'star-crossed' by the deadly feud between the families of Montagu and Capulet: Romeo is a Montagu, Juliet is a Capulet. They are victims of the feud; so are Romeo's friend, Mercutio, and Juliet's cousin, Tybalt. Her mother, Lady Capulet, drives forward her revenge for her nephew against Romeo. The love-story is placed against the background of feuding and duelling. Though a modern mind may find it adolescent – the main characters are adolescents – it was utterly true to the age. Marlowe was involved in several such affrays, and had recently been stabbed to death in a tavern-brawl; Ben Jonson killed the quarrelsome actor, Gabriel Spencer. Marlowe's friend, the poet and musician, Thomas Watson, came to Marlowe's aid in his affray with William Bradley and killed him.

Mercutio says of his friend Benvolio, 'an there were two such, we should have none shortly, for one would kill the other. Thou! why, thou wilt quarrel with a man that hath a hair more, or a hair less in his beard, than thou hast.' Actually, Mercutio is describing himself, much quicker on the draw. He describes Tybalt, the leading Capulet swordsman: 'he fights as you sing prick-song, keeps time, distance, and proportion, rests me his minim rest, one, two, and the third in your bosom; the very butcher of a silk button, a duellist, a duellist.' Tybalt kills Mercutio; then Romeo kills Tybalt: this is fatal to his love for Juliet, for the Capulets, egged on by Lady Capulet, are determined on revenge.

One theatre-person who never involved himself in this kind of thing was the prudent dramatist. What suggested to his mind the placing of his next love-story in the backgound of fatal family-feuding? The suggestion came from close at hand.

Down at Titchfield Southampton was close friends with his Wiltshire neighbours, two swordsmen, Sir Charles and Henry Danvers. The Danvers family were engaged in a bitter feud with another county family, the Longs of Wraxall. Sir John Danvers, the father, was a quiet man, but his wife, Lady Danvers, drove her sons on. John Aubrey, who knew them, describes her as 'Italian' – he means in temperament; for he goes on, 'a great politician [i.e. schemer], great wit and spirit, but revengeful.'

On 4 October 1593 the two Danvers brothers with their following broke into the house at Corsham where the Long party were, and Henry Danvers – Southampton's bosom friend – killed Henry Long, son and heir of his house. The brothers fled and took refuge in a lodge in Southampton's park at Titchfield, where he fed them and enabled them to make their get-away across the Channel to Henri IV. When the sheriff was leading the hue-and-cry after them over Itchen Ferry, a couple of the Earl's servants threatened to throw him overboard: one of them was 'Signor Florio, an Italian'.

The two young swordsmen remained in the service of the former Henry of Navarre. Their scheming mother procured their return; Aubrey tells us how. The father was 'of mild and peaceable nature [just like old Capulet in the play], and his sons' sad accident brake his heart.' Thereupon, his spirited widow 'to obtain pardon for her sons married Sir Edmund Carey, cousin-german to Queen Elizabeth.' This is correct: Carey was a son of Lord Chamberlain Hunsdon and a friend of Thomas Lodge from whose *Rosalind* Shakespeare took the subject for *As You Like It*. We see these things come together – when we know enough about them in detail to interpret them.

—— oOo ——

We have already seen that it was Shakespeare's way to take a suggestion from some immediate circumstance or event, and he found what he wanted to ignite his play ready to hand in the story of Romeo and Juliet, and the feuding of Montagus and Capulets. He read it up in Arthur Brooke's poem, *The Tragical History of Romeus and Juliet*, and in the prose story in Painter's *Palace of Pleasure*. He adhered fairly closely to the poem, speeding it up and telescoping events; the play moves at tremendous speed, making all the more impact – we are swept off our feet, as Romeo and Juliet were, by the inspired upthrust and onrush of the play, as if composed at high pressure in one musical movement.

His chief addition is the character of Mercutio, Romeo's devoted friend. We may well see flecks of Marlowe in the quarrelling, poetic Mercutio, given to fantasy and friendship. The love of women is not for Mercutio (any more than it was for Marlowe); he rallies Romeo on it and goes in for a gay combat of wits with him. And, 'is not this better now than groaning for love? Now art thou sociable; now art thou Romeo. Now art thou what thou art, by art as well as by nature.' When Romeo goes off wenching, 'stabbed with a white wench's black eye,' Mercutio takes to his single 'truckle-bed'. But he is given the most magical poetry in the play, the wonderful evocation of Queen Mab – which looks as if it has been left over from *A Midsummer Night's Dream*. These dreams

> . . . are the children of an idle brain,
> Begot of nothing but vain fantasy,
> Which is as thin of substance as the air,
> And more inconstant than the wind.

Is 'Mercutio' intended to suggest 'mercurial'? We remember Drayton's tribute to Marlowe: 'his raptures were all air and fire.'

It is Lady Capulet who drives forward revenge upon Romeo for Tybalt's death: she would send to one in Mantua to give him a dram that would make him soon keep Tybalt company.

The citation of Petrarch – the only one in Shakespeare – he could easily have got from the company of Florio, of whom he would have seen a good deal in Southampton's household at this time. Mercutio says of Romeo in love: 'Now is he for the numbers Petrarch flowed in. Laura, to his lady, was but a kitchen-wench – marry, she had a better love to be-rhyme her; Dido a dowdy, Cleopatra a gipsy, Helen and Hero hildings [sluts] and harlots, Thisbe a grey eye or so, but not the purpose. Signor Romeo, *bon jour*.' This passage has many reverberations: all of these ladies were celebrated one way or another, either by Marlowe or by Shakespeare.

Juliet's excited speech beginning,

> Gallop apace, you fiery-footed steeds,
> Towards Phoebus' lodging –

echoes a speech from Marlowe's *Edward II*, as Lady Capulet's lament over Juliet, when she thinks her dead, is an echo from Kyd. No work of Shakespeare is without a reference to his profession: on the young Montagus entering masked for the party at the Capulets, we find Benvolio saying,

> We'll have no Cupid hoodwinked with a scarf,
> Bearing a Tartar's painted bow of lath . . .
> Nor no without-book prologue, faintly spoke
> After the prompter, for our entrance.

—— oOo ——

We note Shakespeare's personal idiom in the phrase to 'groan' for love, which occurs contemporaneously in the Sonnets:

> Thy face hath not the power to make love groan.

And we observe his increased familiarity with the *train-de-vie* of a great house: he would know Southampton's house in Holborn, and Titchfield in the country. Here we have the serving-men preparing the Capulets' banquet:

> SAMPSON: You are looked for and called for, asked for, and sought
> for, in the great chamber.

That would be the great presence-chamber, upstairs, as at Hardwick or Hatfield. And Potpan replies:

> We cannot be here and there too.

How authentic! how often one has heard that in the days when there were servants. Lady Capulet herself keeps the keys of the spice-cupboard, and

They call for dates and quinces in the pastry –

i.e. the pastry-kitchen.

Shakespeare reveals himself in his knowledge of cheveril, the first of several times he mentions it: the glover's son knew the softest doeskin, of which gloves were made. Rather than marry Count Paris Juliet says:

> Or hide me nightly in a charnel-house,
> O'er-covered quite with dead men's rattling bones,
> With reeky shanks, and yellow, chapless skulls.

In Shakespeare's day there was such a charnel-house along the churchyard path to the parish church at Stratford. The little page who accompanies Paris to the Capulets' monument, treading the hollow churchyard path, says charmingly:

> I am almost afraid to stand alone
> Here in the churchyard; yet I will venture.

Folk customs and beliefs appear; for example, in 'did'st thou not fall out with a tailor for wearing his new doublet before Easter?' Again, in:

> Some say the lark and loathèd toad change eyes.

And in the belief that mandrakes – a forked earth-plant with two hairy roots – shriek when torn out of the earth and 'living mortals, hearing them, run mad.' Evidently, a piece of sympathetic magic.

—— oOo ——

Romeo and Juliet is notable for much greater use of music and references to music, contemporary songs and ballads, than any play so far. Several occasions are made for music, of which indications remain in one or other of the quartos. When Juliet sees Romeo down from her window at dawn, after the night they had spent together, and questioning whether they would meet again, she speaks words that echo a haunting Elizabethan air, 'Fortune, my foe', and may have sung a verse of it to herself after he has gone. A whole scene is given to the musicians who had been engaged for her wedding-feast to Count Paris. Peter the Clown bids them play the famous tune 'Heart's ease, Heart's ease', while his own heart plays 'My heart is full of woe'. In the end he sings the early Elizabethan song, 'When griping grief the heart doth wound', written by Richard Edwards, Master of the Children of the Chapel and producer of their plays.

Why is there a marked increase of musical interest in this play?

We have noticed something of the immense amount Shakespeare

learned from the prolonged association with Southampton, the introduction into a cultivated aristocratic circle with sophisticated taste in painting, etc. We need not think that he learned nothing from his exposure to the charms of the musical dark lady, daughter and wife of royal musicians, one of whose spells was the touch of her fingers upon the virginals. A tell-tale reference in a later play may reflect back: 'Not so young, sir, to love a woman for her singing?'

Perhaps we should also notice a marked increase of bawdy and suggestive talk.

The text is a fair one. An unauthorised quarto of so popular a play was put out in 1597, a reported version, which was also cut, though it preserves some useful readings which do not appear in the authorised quarto of 1599, as 'newly corrected, augmented, and amended'. The first quarto had some descriptive notes as to stage-business evidently from some actors; the second quarto also contains errors, but was printed from the author's manuscript, whose stage-directions reveal him when he says at one point, 'Enter Will Kemp' for 'Enter Peter'. Peter, the Clown, is not a large part for a star; I dare say he doubled it with another part. The Folio text was based on a reprint in 1609 of the 1599 quarto. Editors have had fun conflating and supplementing to arrive at a sufficiently satisfactory text.

Julius Caesar

1599

Julius Caesar is, along with *Coriolanus*, the most classic of Shakespeare's plays, as if to show the world – and in particular Ben Jonson, who was at this time writing for the Chamberlain's Men – that he knew quite well what classic decorum demanded, though it was not in keeping with his richer, romantic nature. Paradoxically, Dr. Johnson preferred Shakespeare's characteristic mixture, the more coloured texture, the richer variousness – and perhaps this betrays a latent romanticism in the soul of the great Augustan.

Nothing of this impeded the success of the play in the dramatist's own age, more catholic in its tastes. John Weever tells us:

> The many-headed multitude were drawn
> By Brutus' speech that Caesar was ambitious:
> When eloquent Mark Antony had shown
> His virtues, who but Brutus then was vicious?

Years later Leonard Digges testified to the response of the audience:

> So have I seen when Caesar would appear,
> And on the stage at half-sword parley were
> Brutus and Cassius – O how the audience
> Were ravished! with what wonder they went thence!

This is contrasted with the failure of Ben Jonson's 'tedious, though well-laboured' classic plays. Shakespeare's sense of the theatre was infallible, whether tragedy or comedy, romantic (though even those plays are full of classical allusions, from his education) or even classic in the more specialised sense of the word.

Though classic work, the dramatic onrush is irresistible – as a gifted producer, Granville-Barker, emphasises, and as all audiences find. The play is short, swift and stream-lined, with little decoration; no sub-plot, hardly a comic touch or even a sentence that is bawdy (a rarity), but it is exciting, even haunting, full of famous lines that go on and on in the mind and have entered into the consciousness of all those who speak the English language.

The dramatist already had *Julius Caesar* in mind before finishing *Henry V*. In the Prologue to the last act of that he had described the city's expectation of a welcome to Essex on his return from Ireland. Now in the very first scene of *Julius Caesar* we find:

> Many a time and oft
> Have you climbed up to walls and battlements,
> To towers and windows, yea, to chimney-tops,
> Your infants in your arms, and there have sat
> The live-long day with patient expectation
> To see great Pompey pass the streets of Rome;
> And when you saw his chariot but appear,
> Have you not made an universal shout . . .

Windows and chimney-tops . . . this is not ancient Rome, but the London mob giving Essex the send-off from which he returned so abortively. We see how quickly Shakespeare worked. In this same year the young Swiss tourist, Thomas Platter, reports 'after dinner on 21 September, about 2 o'clock, I went with my companions across the water, and in the straw-thatched house saw the tragedy of the first emperor, Julius Caesar, excellently performed by some fifteen persons.' The play has a much larger number of characters, so some parts were, as usual, doubled. It was followed by a jig, danced by two actors as men and two as women.

—— oOo ——

Much as Shakespeare had depended upon Hall and Holinshed for his English history, he had even more congenial reading for his classical plays in Sir Thomas North's translation of Plutarch. Plutarch's interest in character was as lively as his own, while North was a cultivated aristocrat who wrote the language like a gentleman. Whole passages of fine prose could be rendered in as fine, or finer, blank verse with ease. (Much of Elizabethan prose communication goes readily into blank verse – as indeed is the case with the speeches of Abraham Lincoln, whose style was formed by the Bible and Shakespeare.)[1]

The quick reading man wrote with North's Plutarch open beside him; he also read Sir John Davies' philosophic poem, *Nosce Teipsum*, and the congenial Daniel's *Musophilus* contemporaneously. At the assassination of Caesar, Cassius says,

> How many ages hence
> Shall this our lofty scene be acted over
> In states unborn and accents yet unknown!

Shakespeare had been struck by the fine passage of Daniel:

> And who in time knows whither we may vent
> The treasure of our tongue, to what strange shores
> This gain of our best glory shall be sent,
> To enrich unknowing nations with our stores?

> What worlds in the yet unformèd Occident
> May come refined with th'accents that are ours?

But, observe, where Daniel is reflective, Shakespeare instinctively turns the lines into theatre, 'our lofty scene . . . acted over'.

The criticism that the play falls into two halves, with Caesar disappearing in the middle, is inapposite, for the subject is described, in so many words, as 'the spirit of Caesar': his spirit dominates the play as his assassination did the historical event. It might alternatively be described as the tragedy of Brutus, who has a far larger part and whose character is more fully delineated.

The dramatist wrote Caesar down in the interests of dramatic balance, and wrote Brutus up, better than he deserved. We are assured that Brutus was an honest, indeed the one honourable, man in the conspiracy against Caesar: he was the only one moved by what he considered to be the public interest, as against the others, who were moved by envy or personal resentment. In fact Brutus had personal reason to be grateful to Caesar, who was attached to him.

Shakespeare depicts Caesar as deaf, and gives Cassius a long speech enumerating Caesar's weaknesses, even timorousness which was quite untrue: he was a man of indomitable courage and resolution. He was also a supreme opportunist, very clear-sighted about the way things were going and ready to take advantage of them. Antiquated republican institutions were breaking down, and personal rule was inevitable, to take their place. Like Bolingbroke, who *had* to take the crown for sheer self-preservation, Caesar had to cross the Rubicon and march on Rome or his enemies would have destroyed him; then civil war would have broken out anyway. His assassination made civil war inevitable.

Once more Shakespeare shows his regular concern for social order, and the horror of its breakdown.

However, for the balance of his play, the dramatist holds the scales in favour of Brutus (historically, he was not such a noble character). Everybody looked up to him as *sans peur et sans reproche;*Brutus almost made Caesar's assassination respectable, a matter of republican principle. Like such men who are generally admired for their nobility, he is morally self-complacent, for ever congratulating himself on the purity of his motives:

> For I am armed so strong in honesty
> That they [threats] pass by me as the idle wind
> Which I respect not.

He is an idealist and, like most idealists, shows bad judgment throughout. After murdering Caesar he insists on sparing Mark Antony, against the judgment of his fellow-assassins, who then proceeds to turn the tables on them and destroy them. In the quarrel with Cassius before Philippi it is Brutus who shows himself unreasonable; he urges on an immediate battle – against Cassius' more experienced judgment – in circumstances which brought disaster upon them. Indeed, the assassination of Caesar itself was a mistake, apart from the crime: it caused civil war, and did not save the republic, which was the only excuse for it.

Brutus is an idealist, i.e. an idealogue: Napoleon knew their worth in society and in great events – after all, he had been one himself when young and ignorant. But he learned; Brutus was one of those who never learn from experience. William Shakespeare's sympathies were not with such a type; but he does his best for him and writes him an epitaph, which people have taken literally, though placed in Antony's mouth:

> This was the noblest Roman of them all:
> All the conspirators save only he
> Did that they did in envy of great Caesar;
> He only, in a general honest thought
> And common good to all, made one of them.

He assassinated in the cause of liberty and for the good of the people. We are shown by the dramatist what that was worth; nor did Shakespeare bother much about consistency, any more than there is in life.

—— oOo ——

We see all through Shakespeare's plays what his, and the Elizabethans', view of the people was; in this play and in *Coriolanus* they constitute a character in the action.

The tribunes of the people, in the first scene, have nothing but contempt for them, for their ingratitude and changeability, basely transferring their worship of Pompey to his enemy, Caesar. (What else are poor people to do, but fall in with the winning side?) Casca, one of the conspirators on behalf of liberty of the people, describes their servility to Caesar at the offer of the crown: 'the rabble hooted and clapped their chopped hands and threw up their sweaty nightcaps and uttered such a deal of stinking breath . . . that it almost choked Caesar.' The 'nightcaps' detail reveals the contemporary scene, and an Elizabethan mob must have smelt horribly.

After the assassination it is to the wisdom of the people that Brutus, so true to type, appeals: 'censure me in your wisdom, and awake your senses, that you may the better judge.' If he has offended, 'if any, speak: for him I have offended. I pause for a reply.' Their response to this appeal is:

> Let him be Caesar:

> Caesar's better parts
> Shall be crowned in Brutus –

i.e. make Brutus king. He should have been shocked at such a response.

Mark Antony is regarded by Cassius as 'a masker and reveller'; but he knows what the people are, and has no difficulty in twisting them round his little finger, assuring them the while that Brutus and his fellow-assassins are 'honourable men'. He goes on assuring them, while gradually bringing home the horror of the crime and Caesar's good intentions towards them, his generosity and bequests to them in his will, so that in the end the appeal to their emotions makes them weep, and driving home how honourable were the men who had done the deed makes them wild:

> ALL: Revenge! About! Seek! Burn! Fire! Kill!
> Slay! Let not a traitor live . . .
> 1ST PLEBEIAN: We'll burn his [Caesar's] body in the holy place,
> And with the brands fire the traitors' houses.
> 2ND PLEBEIAN: Go, fetch fire.
> 3RD PLEBEIAN: Pluck down benches.
> 4TH PLEBEIAN: Pluck down forms, windows, anything.

William Shakespeare knew his people, ordinary humanity, all too well.

—— oOo ——

His own time thus reveals itself. The conspirators are depicted as muffled up, just as we see them in Gunpowder Plot engravings a few years later. Cassius boasts,

> So often shall the knot of us be called
> The men that gave their country liberty –

'knot' was the regular word for conspirators at the time. Caesar was quite right, by the way, in his judgment of Cassius' type:

> Such men as he be never at heart's ease
> While they behold a greater than themselves.

The play is full of dreams and omens, and though they are authenticated in the sources, they are so much in keeping with the beliefs of the time as to have added much to the dramatic effect. The appearance of Caesar's ghost to Brutus before Philippi not only keeps his spirit before us, but is thrilling in the theatre, and it reminds us of the ghosts that appeared to Richard III before Bosworth. The soothsayer – of whom Caesar, in his generous over-confidence, will take no notice – was frequently to be met with in Elizabethan life: everybody believed in omens, dreams, and foretellings.

We catch another of Shakespeare's regular references to his profession, that appear in every play; at the offer of the crown to Caesar: 'if the tag-rag people did not clap him and hiss him according as he pleased and dis-pleased them, as they use [i.e. are accustomed] to do the players in the theatre, I am no true man.'

Our most perceptive theatre critic, Granville-Barker, says that '*Julius Caesar* is the gateway through which Shakespeare passed to the writing of his five great tragedies', and this play is more carefully constructed than the English chronicle plays. Plutarch, on whose lives of Caesar, Brutus and Mark Antony the dramatist largely relied, 'was a godsend to Shakespeare'. Actually the play has a threefold structure; the first part is mainly concerned with Brutus and his recruitment by Cassius to the conspiracy; the second with Caesar and his assassination; the third with Brutus and Cassius again, their quarrel and reconciliation the most poignant scene in the play.

Why does Brutus receive fuller and more sympathetic treatment than Caesar? Something of Shakespeare's ambivalence towards the dictator may be due to the unfavourable tradition regarding him which had come down in English medieval tradition. But, far more, it must be due to the fact that Brutus' inner conflict, the struggle with his conscience, setting principle above affection and even crime, had more appeal for the dramatist. There is no dramatic conflict within Caesar: he is all too much *there*, a Colossus bestriding the world.

So Shakespeare does him less, and Brutus more, than justice or history warrants.

—— oOo ——

The text offers no problems. E. K. Chambers describes it as 'one of the best printed of the Folio additions' – since there are no quartos; 'a few abrupt short lines may be evidence of cuts.' Ben Jonson made fun of a couple of passages: Shakespeare, writing hurriedly as usual, had made Caesar say, 'Caesar never did wrong but with just cause', which Ben considered 'ridiculous'. In the Folio text this is rectified, possibly by Ben himself, who helped in its presentation to the public. Anyhow, it now reads:

> Know, Caesar doth not wrong, nor without cause
> Will he be satisfied.

Ben made fun, too, of another passage:

> O judgment! thou art fled to brutish beasts,
> And men have lost their reason.

Immediately after, in *Every Man out of his Humour*, Jonson takes this up:

Reason long since is fled to animals, you know.

These are but amusing exchanges between fellows writing for the same Company; it is heavy-footed to speak of Ben's twitting the Master, to whom he was indebted for his introduction to the Company, as showing 'animosity' (Dover-Wilson). Such exchanges alerted performers and audience, and provided fun.

---

1. As I found when putting his farewell speech to his Illinois neighbours in my blank-verse poem 'Abraham Lincoln at Springfield' in *A Life: Collected Poems* (W. Blackwood, Edinburgh, 1981)

Hamlet

1600-1

Hamlet is the most wonderful play ever written, to judge from the fascination it has generally exerted and the amount of discussion to which it has given rise. Most of this has been devoted to moralising about Hamlet's character. Here we must be careful to keep an Elizabethan perspective and remind ourselves that Shakespeare was writing a play, not a text for ethical disquisition. And of course there are inconsistencies and loose ends – as in life.

There is general agreement that the play has a strong reference to its topical background. Dover-Wilson regards it as 'the most topical play in the whole corpus'; but he goes on, 'the main trouble with "historical" critics is their ignorance of history and their lack of historical curiosity.' So this is where the historian can be of use, indeed is necessary. The true historian is a cautious animal: we must be careful not to make crude and simple identifications. A creative writer takes hints and suggestions from his real environment and then makes what he wants out of them.

What an Elizabethan historian knows is that the political scene in these very years, 1600-1, was dominated by the question of the succession to the throne and by the personality of Essex, near to the throne yet tottering unsteadily, hesitantly, to his fall. Again the character of Polonius is important. These three elements were very much at the back of Shakespeare's mind as he wrote. Though not now close to Southampton as he had been earlier, Shakespeare could not but be concerned when his former patron, who had meant so much to him, was Essex's right-hand man. Hamlet is provided with a noble and true-hearted friend in Horatio; and both Verity and Dover-Wilson have seen a personal allusion in the passage (IV.7.80 foll.) devoted to a gallant horseman in Normandy, 'which does not arise naturally out of the context, in which the accomplishment dwelt on is fencing, not horsemanship.' Dover-Wilson points out that Southampton was in command of the horse under Essex in Ireland (as Lieutenant-General, by the way, not Master, a different office).

The contemporary siege of Ostend appears, and there is a lot about the War of the Theatres at the time, the stage and the state of acting.

No doubt *Hamlet is* a highly topical play. As we have seen with *Romeo and Juliet*, Shakespeare resorted to a story which expressed what was working in his mind. He had known the Hamlet story all along from the days of Kyd and Marlowe, from whom there are echoes. Significantly, we have no forward references to Hamlet in Shakespeare's earlier plays, as there are to Troy and Priam and Cressida, to Julius Caesar and the story of Lucrece. Something brought the story of Hamlet to mind, and urged it on, as was his instinctive way.

This early Teutonic story goes right back to Saxo Grammaticus at least, and was known to Shakespeare from an earlier popular stage piece. He refreshed his memory for details by looking it up in Belleforest's *Histoires Tragiques*. Practically all the elements are there. Brother-murder is an archetypal theme – one of the reasons why the play is so gripping. Cain's crime is referred to – among the most frequent of his citations from the Bible, it made an undying impression upon his mind.

Claudius murders his brother, Hamlet's father, to take his throne and his wife. So Hamlet's complex about his mother – revulsion from love – is another archetypal theme, plumbing the recesses of our minds. In it Shakespeare intuited the essential findings of psycho-analysis with regard to the Oedipus complex. Hamlet also felt that the throne was his by right. The significance of his phrase that he is 'dreadfully attended' has been missed: this means in Elizabethan parlance that he is not being given due honour. His uncle stands between 'the election and his hopes'. He is regally Hamlet the Dane; after his death Fortinbras pays tribute:

> For he was likely, had he been put on,
> To have proved most royal.

I cannot refrain from adding, what is insufficiently appreciated, the sheer intellectual brilliance he displays, the scintillation of his wit at all times, both naturally and when he feigns madness. To make an unlikely comparison, I think of the sheer *cleverness* of Falstaff's sallies. There is something personal to their creator in both.

The Danish background was familiar to the Elizabethans, ever since Leicester's players had visited Elsinore in 1587. The finest of lutenists and song-writers, John Dowland, had his career at the Danish Court. English actors frequently visited North Germany; Robert Browne, whose family was wiped out in the plague of 1592-3, had most of his career there.

We do not need to discuss the character of Hamlet, or describe the events of the play – let it speak for itself; merely to illuminate the real background and what it suggested to Shakespeare's mind, where we can.

—— oOo ——

We have had reason to notice the increasing faction-fighting at Court between the Cecils and Essex with his following. Polonius is clearly based on old Lord Burghley, and we can see how close the resemblance is in detail. Lord Treasurer and the Queen's leading minister, he had been Southampton's guardian, whose grand-daughter the young Earl would not marry and had been made to pay for it.[1] The Essex faction detested the politic old man, who was irremovable until his death in 1598; after that it was safe to portray him as Polonius. Hamlet describes Polonius to his face: 'old men have grey beards, their faces are wrinkled, their eyes purging thick amber and plumtree gum . . . together with most weak hams.' Those who are familiar with Burghley's letters in his last years will know that they are full of his querulous complaints about his health, the weakness of his limbs, his gout, his running eyes: 'I am but as a monoculus' (one-eyed), he writes.

One clue to Burghley's hold on power was his remarkable intelligence system. This is clearly rendered in Polonius' interview with Reynaldo, setting him to spy on his son's doings in Paris and report on them. Burghley's elder son, Thomas, had had an unsatisfactory record in France and been similarly reported on; Burghley's famous Precepts, however, were for his clever younger son, Robert Cecil – Essex's enemy. Polonius has a similar set for his son, while his perpetual moralising is Burghley all over – it drove the young men mad, all the more because the old man was all-powerful and irremovable, though prosy and pedestrian. Burghley, indeed, warned Essex as to the recklessness of his course; but he was led astray by ambition and popularity – he was always beloved of the people. As there were touches of this in Bolingbroke, so there are here:

> The courtier's, soldier's, scholar's, eye, tongue, sword,
> Th' expectancy and rose of the fair state,
> The glass of fashion, and the mould of form,
> Th' observed of all observers.

Claudius, the king, gives as a reason for dealing secretly with the threat from Hamlet that he is 'loved of the distracted multitude'.

Contemporaneously, Essex was staggering to his downfall, already foreshadowed, though he could not make up his mind to his final throw. It is true enough that

> on his choice depends
> The sanity and health of the whole state,
> And therefore must his choice be circumscribed
> Unto the choice and yielding of that body
> Whereof he is the head.

Essex was driven on by the young men of his party – such as Sir Charles Danvers, who paid for it with his head.

> Diseases desperate grown
> By desperate appliances are relieved
> Or not at all –

this is what all the young men urged. Essex himself hesitated and hesitated, until it was Southampton who propelled him with: 'Shall we then resolve on nothing?' Dover-Wilson describes Hamlet's 'sense of frustration, of infirmity of purpose, of character inhibited from meeting the demands of destiny, of the futility of life in general and action in particular. His melancholy and procrastination are all of a piece.' Historians know this perfectly describes Essex at the time: he was as psychotic as Hamlet.

He was visibly rocking to his downfall. Shakespeare observed it all from close at hand:

> The great man down, you mark his favourite flies,
> The poor advanced makes friends of enemies,
> And hitherto doth love on fortune tend,
> For who not needs shall never lack a friend.

The first notably to desert Essex was Francis Bacon, who saw what was coming; he was already making up to Robert Cecil, and was to work his passage by taking a leading part in the prosecution of his former friend.

—— oOo ——

Hamlet contains Shakespeare's extensive treatment of the contemporary theatre and his view of his profession and of acting – all fascinating. These years 1600-1 were enlivened by the theatre-war set going by the row between Ben Jonson and Marston, brought to the fore in Ben's plays, *Cynthia's Revels* and *Poetaster*, performed by the Children of the Chapel; against Dekker and Marston's *Satiromastix*, played by Shakespeare's Company. All this was no doubt good box-office, as Shakespeare hints; so we must not take it too seriously, any more than he did.

He himself never wrote for the Boys' Companies; nor did he go in for their comical satires. But he reflects on the situation. 'There is an eyrie of Children, little eyases [a bawdy pun], that cry out on the top of the question, and are most tyrannically clapped for't: these are now the fashion, and so berattle the common stages, so they call them, that many wearing rapiers are afraid of goose-quills, and dare scarce come thither.' Hamlet comments: 'What, are they children? Who maintains 'em?.. Will they pursue the quality no longer than they can sing? Will they not say afterwards, if they should grow themselves to common players – as it is like most will if their means are not better – their writers [i.e. Jonson, who had left off writing for Shakespeare's Company] do them wrong, to make them exclaim against their own succession', i.e. prospects in the profession.

This was plain speaking, and in keeping with his practical common sense. What would be the boy-actors' future when their voices had broken, but as 'common players . . . if their means are not better'? A touch of his own hard experience was there, his old reproach in the Sonnets against the luck

> That did not better for my life provide
> Than public means which public manners breeds.

The public spurred on the controversy. 'There was, for a while, no money bid for argument, unless the Poet and the Player went to cuffs in the question.' For the time, the Boys' Companies carried it off, 'Hercules and his load too', i.e. against the Globe, whose sign that was.

Quarrelsome Ben had left the Chamberlain's Company, to which Shakespeare had welcomed him; that Ben smarted a little is evident from his words,

> Only against them, I am sorry for
> Some better natures, by the rest so drawn . . .

This in itself is a tribute to the man he regarded 'only this side idolatry'. He defended himself:

> Now for the Players, it is true I taxed 'em,
> And yet but some; and those so sparingly
> As all the rest might have sat still unquestioned.

It is significant that, where Ben thought of himself as a poet, Shakespeare aligned himself with the profession by which he lived.

We cannot go in detail into all that he instructs us about acting: here in the *locus classicus*, two whole scenes devoted to the subject, in which he tells us all that is in his mind, a summing-up of years of experience. He had already put into Polonius' mouth, to show that he had no use for it, the too precise classification of plays – 'the tragical-comical-historical-pastoral', etc. His own, like all works of genius, transcended the categories.

Shakespeare's convictions about acting are given at length in Hamlet's instructions to the players: speak the speech trippingly on the tongue, not mouth it; do not saw the air with clumsy gestures, but use all gently, show temperance and smoothness even in the moment of passion – in a word, control. He inveighs against the prating he had observed in tragic parts, the gags which clowns would insert at the expense of some necessary part of the action. It is all summed up in his message that 'the purpose of playing . . . was, and is, to hold as 'twere the mirror up to nature, to show . . . the very age and body of time.'

This was evidently what he himself stood for and had learned to practice, as actor and producer, in the transition from the crude early Elizabethan stage to the mature dramaturgy of which he was the foremost exponent. With artistic and professional success had come at length reconciliation to the necessity he had been under to earn his living the hard way, by public means: let the players be well used, 'for they are the abstracts and brief chronicles of the time; after your death you were better have a bad epitaph than their ill report while you live.' Next follows the marvellous soliloquy of Hamlet, reflecting on the mystery of the actor's art, by which he can produce effects more moving and real than life itself. This is inset within an inset, a kind of double-mirror. Shakespeare owed it to art as well as nature that his mind moved in double-track; Dover-Wilson comments, 'when he used a word, all possible meanings of it were commonly present to his mind.' Hence, too, all the word-play and punning he was given to, and in which Hamlet is such a virtuoso.

More evidences of the time remain in this rich, deep, inexhaustible mine. During these years and for some time to come the struggle continued for Ostend, between Spaniards and the Dutch with English aid, costing thousands of lives:

> We go to gain a little patch of ground
> That hath in it no profit but the name.
> To pay five ducats, five, I would not farm it.

The contest had become a matter of prestige. Hamlet comments:

> to my shame I see
> The imminent death of twenty thousand men,
> That for a fantasy and trick of fame
> Go to their graves like beds, fight for a plot
> Whereon the numbers cannot try the cause,
> Which is not tomb enough and continent
> To hide the slain.

This expressed William Shakespeare's view of the matter: he never was one of the fighting fools, he observed them and put them in his plays.

Indeed, Hamlet meditating in the grave-yard gives a fine opportunity for bitter reflections on the time, the great age gone sour. Here's the skull of a lawyer: 'where be his quiddities now, his quillities, his cases, his tenures, and his tricks?' Another might have been a grand buyer of land in his time, 'with his statutes, his recognisances, his fines, his double vouchers, his recoveries. Is this the fine of his fines, and the recovery of his recoveries, to have his fine pate full of fine dirt?' 'That skull had a tongue in it, and could sing once! . . . This might be the pate of a politician, which this ass now o'er-reaches – one that would circumvent God, might it not?'

The time itself was enough to induce bitterness, the kind of bitterness that went into *Troilus and Cressida*, when one's own friends showed what fools they were: 'fools on both sides', he called them.

Many touches of him occur in this very personal play. We cannot tell whether he had Tarlton in mind in Yorick's skull: 'where be your gibes now? Your gambols, your songs, your flashes of merriment, that were wont to set the table on a roar?' Some think that the reflection on clowns who insist on gagging to the detriment of the play may refer to Will Kemp, who had left the Company the year before.

The quip against 'equivocation' is directed against the unpopular casuistry of the Jesuits. He would be familiar with the many Catholic terms in this, as in other plays, through frequenting Southampton House, which the priests were constantly in and out of – though Southampton's Catholicism was not political, unlike his father's.[2]

A curious passage relates to Elizabethan handwriting. Hamlet says,

> I once did hold it, as our statists do,
> A baseness to write fair, and laboured much
> How to forget that learning.

There follows a satirical account of politicians' formal documents, with all their commas and 'as'es'. What is he tilting against here? The episode of Osric, his affected manner, his inflated, sycophantic speech – all contemptuously held up to ridicule by Hamlet – is a sharp reflection on Court manners, at this moment when Essex and his friends had been driven from it. The depiction of the Court of Denmark shows Shakespeare out of sympathy with it: to him it was rotten. The last years of Elizabeth's reign were indeed sour and faction-ridden.

One need say nothing of all the heart-break in this most moving of all plays: the unbearable reproaches of Hamlet against his mother –

> Refrain tonight,
> And that shall lend a kind of easiness
> To the next abstinence, the next more easy.

Shakespeare knew that well enough from experience. Bitterest of all are Hamlet's words to Ophelia: he is riven with suspicion, torn in two by his situation – and knowledge of psychology tells one of the desire to wound what one loves. Such unbelievable imperceptiveness has been shown in critical comment on this – with no excuse, for Hamlet himself says,

> I loved Ophelia, forty thousand brothers
> Could not with all their quantity of love
> Make up my sum.

Ophelia's madness is so heart-rending, it is like Cordelia's death or Lady Macbeth's obsessive washing of her hands; such is Shakespeare's unparalleled force of impact, that one can hardly bear to see or hear what is going on, he so searches the human heart, and all its crevices of guilt and fear, remorse and grief.

> O, from what power hast thou this powerful might?

A Katherine Hamlet was drowned in the Avon in December 1579; an inquest took place at Stratford early in 1580, when he was rising sixteen. It is unlikely that he would forget that, and with it her name. It suggested Ophelia's end – which has inspired other artists in turn.

We detect him, as always, in his love of rare words ending in 'ive' – conjunctive, splenetive. He never forgot anything; he is still remembering Marlowe's words: 'the whiff and wind of his fell sword' is a reminiscence from *Dido, Queen of Carthage*; the hebona with which Hamlet's father was poisoned comes from *The Jew of Malta*. Reading, as usual, while writing his plays Shakespeare derived some suggestions from Bright's *Treatise of*

Melancholy, and more from Florio's *Montaigne*, a congenial spirit.

The play is full of scraps of ballads, songs and contemporary lore – about ghosts, for example. It is not likely that an Elizabethan like Shakespeare would not have believed in ghosts. Eclipses come into this play full of foreboding and suspicion – and the years 1598 to 1601 were marked by several, both of sun and moon.

—— oOo ——

The best text is that of the Second Quarto put out in 1604, obviously authoritatively to correct the pirated Quarto, a reconstruction from memory by certain actors, printed the year before. The new official version described itself as 'newly imprinted and enlarged to almost as much again as it was, according to the true and perfect copy.' This was a scrupulous description, clearly by Shakespeare himself or by his authority.

Sisson tells us that this Second Quarto 'plainly represents Shakespeare's autograph manuscript, the original material which – with the cuts made necessary by its excessive length – became the basis of the theatre prompt-copy.' This prompt-copy was what Hemming and Condell had available when it came to publishing the First Folio. And this had 'some correction and revision of the original manuscript, in some places almost certainly by the poet himself.' Naturally some cuts had been made, and some additions also. Cuts had to be made for performance, for the play was too long for the normal 'two-hour traffic' of the stage at the time, Shakespeare's mind so overflowed in this work.

There is no mystery about all this, and no need for all the fuss and volumes written about it. In fact there is substantial agreement. Even the too cautious and imperceptive E. K. Chambers agrees that the Second Quarto 'substantially represents the original text of the play. It is a fair text, with little mislineation, light punctuation, and a good many abnormal spellings, and may very possibly be from the author's manuscript; but, if so, numerous misprints suggest that this was not very legible.' This is very likely: we know that Shakespeare wrote rapidly and in old English script, not our modern Italian hand (as Robert Cecil did).

The pirated Quarto, coming from actors, mentioned the play as having been performed in the city of London, as well as in the two universities of Oxford and Cambridge, meaning the university towns. An early tradition has it that Shakespeare acted the part of the Ghost of Hamlet's father – it was a 'kingly part'. An endearing performance was that on board the East Indiaman, by the crew of the *Dragon*, at Sierra Leone for Portuguese and English guests in 1607-8.

---

1. cf. my *Shakespeare's Southampton: Patron of Virginia*, chapter iii, (Macmillan, London, and New York, 1965)
2. ibid. chapter ii

Othello
1604

Othello offers a marked contrast to *Hamlet*; where that has a large cast and much variety of action, this has few characters, with most of the action concentrated on three alone – Othello, Desdemona and Iago. Hardly anything distracts from the main theme, which advances at headlong speed with tremendous impact. It is like an opera; in that, and in its speed, analogous to *Romeo and Juliet* – both, by the way, made subjects of opera.

Shakespeare took his theme straight from a 'mediocre' story of Cinthio, as Bentley describes it; 'brutal and vulgar' Sisson calls it. And see what an unforgettable play – lyrical splendour, a masterpiece of dramatic art. It shows how unimportant 'sources' and all the digging into them are.

—— oOo ——

The tragedy of the heroic but simple Othello and the charming but innocent Desdemona has haunted the world's imagination ever since. But Iago is the most complex and interesting character in the play; this part has chiefly attracted the ambition of actors – it is such a challenge. In a way, Iago is a psychotic, as Hamlet was; it forms another aspect of the universality of Shakespeare's genius that he should have had such an intuitive understanding of abnormal, as well as normal, psychology.

It is often said that Iago, whose villainy causes the tragedy, is an incarnation of pure evil, without motivation. This is not true: he is motivated. He is suspicious by nature, and he thinks that the Moor has colted his wife, Emilia. At one point he suspects Cassio also with his wife. Iago is a Venetian; but Othello has promoted the Florentine Cassio to be his lieutenant over his head, and relegated him, Iago, to be Cassio's ancient, or ensign. So Iago has his reasons for resentment, and he hates the Moor.

But his hatred is more generalised and fascinating psychologically. It has usually been found inexplicable; but though rare, it is understandable. He is one of those beings, not unknown, who hate the sight of other people's happiness. He is not happy himself, he is not happily married: he gives a hint that he suffers the lash of Emilia's tongue. He is not interested in sex, and is envious of the pleasure it gives others. Desdemona's bridal night with her magnificent, and very male, dark lover is described thus by Iago to her father:

> Even now, now, very now, an old black ram
> Is tupping your white ewe.

He regularly describes Cassio's light o'love as a strumpet, and

> it is a creature
> That dotes on Cassio, as 'tis the strumpet's plague
> To beguile many, and be beguiled by one.

Cassio rubs salt in his wound – for Iago's is a wounded nature – when talking of hoping 'to be saved', by saying, 'the lieutenant is to be saved before the ancient.'

There is no love in Iago; he hates humans for being the fools they are; 'thus credulous fools are caught', he says – and they all are caught by their various forms of foolery. Othello is caught by his jealousy and gullibility; Desdemona by her precious innocence; Roderigo is just an ass, and Iago takes his money and jewels off him; Cassio is caught by his weakness for drink. Iago was not a fool about drink or sex, as so many are.

He has utter contempt for humans – a Swiftian character. What is so absorbing is that he carries it so far as to sail right into the wind. He actually warns Othello against jealousy:

> O, beware, my lord, of jealousy.
> It is the green-eyed monster, which doth mock
> The meat it feeds on.

Why? Because he knows that to tell people the truth is an effective way of putting them off the scent. Hitler knew this, and practised it to devastating effect: 'the German people have no idea how they have to be gulled in order to be led', was the epigraph of *Mein Kampf*, which told everybody exactly what he meant to do – and people wouldn't believe it.

'Men should be what they seem', Iago assures Othello brazenly. He even speaks a word to him in favour of Cassio, 'an honest man' – sailing right into the wind again, which makes Othello the readier to believe Iago's insinuations about Cassio and Desdemona. Iago's very cynicism is beguiling. He eggs on Roderigo with, 'Virtue! A fig! 'Tis in ourselves that we are thus and thus'. He has a very Swiftian image in his assurance: 'Ere I would say I would drown myself for the love of a guinea hen, I would change my humanity with a baboon.' His argument to Roderigo again and again is to look after his money, 'Put money in thy purse' – just when he is taking it off him.

And so with his consoling Cassio, when he has disgraced himself with the General:

> CASSIO: I have lost the immortal part of myself . . .
>   my reputation, Iago, my reputation.
> IAGO: As I am an honest man, I thought you had received
>   some bodily wound. There is more sense in that

> than in reputation. Reputation is an idle and
> most false imposition: oft got without merit and
> lost without deserving.

There is always something to be said for what Iago says; nothing for what he does. On the pros and cons of morality he is an able and plausible reasoner – notably in the remarkable scene with Othello in which he sows suspicions against Desdemona. One might suppose that Iago was more rational than other men, as certainly he considered himself, besides being much less of a fool. But such is Shakespeare's intuitive, as well as conscious, knowledge of human nature that Iago too is as much in the clutch of his complex as Othello is in his. Othello is driven mad by suspicion and jealousy; perhaps Iago is already mad – he is hardly sane, certainly not normal – with envy, hatred and contempt.

He and Othello stand out as the two protagonists in this simple, haunting tragedy, Desdemona their sacrificial victim.

—— oOo ——

Again it is like Shakespeare's universality to have prefigured a prime issue of today. As in *The Merchant of Venice* the crux of the action is that Shylock is a Jew, so now the crux is that Othello is a black, or at any rate dark, as a Moor would be. At the crucial moment of his persuasion by Iago of his wife's unfaithfulness, he says, with great pathos, for the trouble it has brought: 'for I am black . . . declined into the vale of years'. This in itself is a source of insecurity, already inclined to suspicion as he is, and makes him think that it was a mistake to think he could hold Desdemona's love.

Her love, too, had been rash, like Juliet's. In 16th century terms it was a grievous fault to have married without her father's approval – so that she too had some responsibility for the tragedy that was provoked. Iago further inflames her father with, 'you'll have your daughter covered with a Barbary horse; you'll have your nephews [Elizabethan for grandsons] neigh to you.'

Her father indeed thinks that the only explanation for such infatuation –

> To fall in love with what she feared to look on!

was witchcraft, love-philtres, charms:

> She is abused, stolen from me, and corrupted
> By spells and medicines bought of mountebanks.

This was cogent to Elizabethans, as we know from Simon Forman's practice for these very purposes. In a year or two he would be supplying love-philtres and charms to Frances Howard, Countess of Essex, to compel the love of James I's boy-friend, Robert Carr. Forman was already well known (Ben Jonson was well informed about Forman, whose name he cites); probably enough Shakespeare thought him a 'mountebank'. Even the handkerchief that did such damage to Desdemona would be recognised for its magic potency by Forman:

> There's magic in the web of it –

it had been given to Othello's mother by an Egyptian, a charmer;

> The worms were hallowed that did breed the silk,
> And it was dyed in mummy –

which Forman, by the way, dealt in.

He also treated people for venereal disease, to which there is a reference *à propos* of Naples. Forman had a good record for treating people during plague, when the doctors fled. Severe plague is again in the background of 1603-4:

> As doth the raven o'er the infected house
> Boding to all.

Iago has a candid passage on servants at the time:

> Who, trimmed in forms and visages of duty,
> Keep yet their hearts attending on themselves;
> And, throwing but shows of service on their lords,
> Do well thrive by them, and when they have lined their
>   coats,
> Do themselves homage.

An historian recognises how true that was to the age.

Iago describes Othello's marriage:

> Faith, tonight he hath boarded a land carrack,
> If it prove lawful prize, he's made for ever.

Portuguese carracks were the treasure-ships from the Indies, several of which the Elizabethans boarded and made prizes of. The voyages, as recounted in Hakluyt, are present behind Othello's account of his experiences:

> And of the Cannibals that each other eat,
> The Anthropophagi, and men whose heads
> Do grow beneath their shoulders.

The description of the Pontic Sea and the Hellespont comes straight out of our reading man's looking into Philemon Holland's translation of Pliny.

—— oOo ——

No references to the stage, after the extended treatment of the subject in *Hamlet*, except for the regular use of the word 'cue'. The play itself suggests, in part, a reversion to the old Morality, with Iago as the stage-villain informing the audience of his intended villainies. A good deal of rhyme occurs, with regular *sententiae* at one point in couplets, presenting Shakespeare's own conclusions:

> When remedies are past, the griefs are ended
> By seeing the worst, which late on hope depended ...
> To mourn a mischief that is past and gone
> Is the next way to draw new mischief on –

very Shakespearean thoughts in their cautious prudence.

Above all, one notices the increasing idiosyncrasy of the vocabulary, oblique words and phrases, the extraordinary expressions. We find 'conjunctive' again from *Hamlet*; phrases like 'sequent messengers' are characteristic, words like 'indign', 'sequestration' for divorce, 'segregation' of the Turkish fleet for scattering, 'equinox' for equivalent, 'exsufflicate'. Who but Shakespeare would write:

> My speculative and officed instruments

or say 'fortitude' for fortification? Equally characteristic is the conjunction of grand words with simple and colloquial: a tempest had so 'banged' the Turks that the 'sufferance' of it could be seen in the fleet. Or, if drink did not rock Cassio's cradle, he'd watch the 'horologe' round.

What it all testifies to is Shakespeare's unparalleled linguistic range, which constitutes a difficulty for modern and foreign readers alike. We need a *contemporary* Shakespeare to make him completely intelligible to both in our time.

—— oOo ——

Two versions of the text have come down to us, a Quarto of 1622, and the Folio of 1623: each helps to complement or correct the other, and both are thought to rest on the same original manuscript. The Folio is fuller by some 160 lines; it has the spelling Æmilia for Emilia, the form Emilia Lanier used in publishing her poem.

The play was performed in the old banqueting hall at Whitehall on All Saints Day (November 1) 1604, and other Court performances are recorded.

Macbeth

1605-6

Macbeth comes immediately after *Othello:* there is no problem about its date. It was sparked off by the shattering sensation of the never-to-be-forgotten Gunpowder Plot of 5 November 1605. Nation-wide shock was felt at its carefully handled revelations, and for the first time a genuine movement of sympathy for the new king and his family, whose extirpation would have led to untold confusion. The dramatist, always alert to what was in the air, was moved to cash in on this. He and his Company already had reason to be grateful to King James I, who had doubled the rate of remuneration for Court Performances (from £10 to £20), more than doubled the number of performances, and given Shakespeare and his fellows the status of Grooms of the Chamber.

So the new play was one on Scottish history, in honour of Banquo, the putative ancestor of the Stuarts, with tributes to his 'royalty of nature', the 'dauntless temper of his mind', while the prophecy is borne home:

> Thou shalt get kings, though thou be none.

A specific recognition of James and his line occurs in Macbeth's vision of Banquo's descendants:

> What, will the line stretch out to th'crack of doom?
> Another yet? A seventh?

Remember that James was James the sixth of Scotland.

> And some I see
> That two-fold balls and treble sceptres carry.

This refers to the union of the two kingdoms with James, while the third sceptre is the claim to the throne of France, which remained in the royal title till George III.

Tributes are made to James personally, who was already, with some complacency, exercising the sacramental function of an anointed king of touching for the King's Evil:

> A most miraculous work in this good king,
> Which often, since my here-remain in England,
> I have seen him do. How he solicits heaven,
> Himself best knows; but strangely-visited people,
> All swoll'n and ulcerous, pitiful to the eye,

The mere despair of surgery, he cures,
Hanging a golden stamp about their necks,
Put on with holy prayers. And 'tis spoken,
To the succeeding royalty he leaves
The healing benediction.

This is a description of the rite, which all the Stuarts exercised – Dr. Johnson himself, as a boy, was touched for his scrofula by Queen Anne. The sacrament was discontinued only by the unsacramental Hanoverians, who properly did not claim the prerogative of divine right: theirs was merely a Parliamentary title.

To the King is also imputed 'a heavenly gift of prophecy', and the play is, in a way, a compliment to one of his chief intellectual interests, demonology, on which he had written a book. A much more sensible book the dramatist had certainly read – Reginald Scot's *Discovery of Witchcraft*, from which he got some suggestions. Actually the 'Weird Sisters' are of Shakespeare's own conceiving: they are not ordinary witches (though it is convenient to call them such), who were common enough in Jacobean England, and still more so with the growth of the ghastly Puritan mentality. We may regard these 'norns' as emanations of evil, the kind of thing the primitive-minded believe in; a modern mind can conceive of them as the hypostatizing, or personalising, of the subconscious, and their 'prophecies' as projections of Macbeth's unspoken desires. As such, they are still apposite and may be accepted imaginatively.

Further evidences of the time and what it suggested to Shakespeare's mind as he wrote are to be seen in the specific references to the Jesuit doctrine of equivocation. This made the worst impression at the time and was pressed home at the trial of Henry Garnet, the Jesuit Provincial, who had learned of the Gunpowder Plot under the seal of confession, but had kept quiet about it. Under examination one need not tell the truth, one could always equivocate. Shakespeare was at one with his countrymen on such matters: an equivocator, he says, is one 'that could swear in both scales against either scale, who committed treason enough for God's sake, yet could not equivocate to heaven.' When the young Macduff asks his mother, 'what is a traitor?', she replies 'why, one that swears and lies. Everyone that does so is a traitor, and must be hanged.'

Shakespeare was never one for going against popular prejudices (unlike Marlowe and Ben Jonson). By this time Southampton, out of the Tower, had become a Protestant. Shakespeare would certainly have met him again, when the King's Men – as the Chamberlain's had been promoted into being – performed before the King, at Wilton in December 1603, where he was staying to avoid the plague. Both Southampton, and his junior, Pembroke, had been present. It was yet another reason for gratitude to James that he had released Southampton and taken into favour the remnants of Essex's former following.

So, once more, the dramatist looked up an appropriate story for his play, and found it in the Scottish section of Holinshed's *Chronicles*. He compressed the events of Macbeth's seventeen-year reign into as many weeks. For his purposes he darkened the character of the historic Macbeth, and whitened that of Duncan, who was by no means so guileless and good in history as in the play. Again, under the Celtic custom of tanistry, the rule of succession to a throne was uncertain, and left it wide open to murder – as one saw contemporaneously in the succession to tribal chieftainships in Ireland. That, historically speaking, Macbeth had some claim to the throne is not noticed in the play: it would not have been in keeping with Shakespeare's aim, which was always to intensify the horror.

The play bears some analogy with *Richard III*, with whose obsessive and haunted mind Macbeth has something in common, and there are echoes of the earlier play in his remorses and self-reproaches. He is, however, a very different character: nothing noble in Richard III, but a certain gleefulness in doing ill; Macbeth has nothing of that, but a flawed and ruined nobility – he is the victim of the Weird Sisters' prophecies or, rather, of the promptings to which their 'prophecies' gave confirmation.

Here Shakespeare speeded up the action to launch the play forward in one grand and simple onrush: nothing of the complex movement of *Hamlet* and *King Lear*. Direct and simple like its neighbour, *Othello*, it yet offers a contrast with it: where that is rich and coloured, *Macbeth* is dark and lurid, full of blood, like the Celtic Northern glooms out of which it comes. Much of the action is by night, torches and guttering candles, knocking at the nocturnally closed gate enough to wake the dead. On the stage this knocking is ominous and thrilling; while the sleep-walking scene of Lady Macbeth is beyond anything, comparable only to the greatest heights of the dramatist's own art, Hamlet's scenes with his mother and Ophelia, Lear with Cordelia at the end of all.

The apparition of the murdered Banquo at Macbeth's feast is hardly less thrilling, and certainly impressed contemporaries. There are two immediate references to it in the very next year, 1607: in *The Puritan* and, more memorably, in *The Knight of the Burning Pestle*:

> When thou art at thy table with thy friends,
> Merry in heart, and filled with swelling wine,
> I'll come in midst of all thy pride and mirth,
> Invisible to all men but thyself . . .
> Shall make thee let the cup fall from thy hand,
> And stand as mute and pale as death itself.

As witchcraft is to the fore in this play so also is the theme of sleep. Immediately after the murder of the King, Macbeth says:

> Methought I heard a voice cry 'Sleep no more!

> Macbeth does murder sleep' – the innocent sleep,
> Sleep that knits up the ravelled sleave of care,
> The death of each day's life, sore labour's bath,
> Balm of hurt minds, great Nature's second course,
> Chief nourisher in life's feast . . .

Shakespeare was recalling the famous apostrophe to sleep of Sir Philip Sidney, but the theme is put to dramatic use, for neither Macbeth nor Lady Macbeth can sleep the sleep of innocence again, and she is driven by her guilt-haunted sleeplessness to suicide.

Short as the play is – and Shakespeare seems to have abridged it for production – it is full of famous lines which have entered into our collective memories:

> After life's fitful fever he sleeps well.

> All the perfumes of Arabia will not sweeten this little hand.

> Nothing in this life became him like the leaving of it.

And one of the most haunting passages relates the action itself to its author's profession:

> Life's but a walking shadow, a poor player
> That struts and frets his hour upon the stage,
> And then is heard no more. It is a tale
> Told by an idiot, full of sound and fury,
> Signifying nothing.

—— oOo ——

In so concentrated a play there is little that is not directly relevant. In the 'Hyrcan tiger' we have another fleck from his reading of Pliny's Natural History, like the reference to the Pontic sea in *Othello*. Tarquin is in mind, as so often; once more there are portents in the air, and

> A falcon towering in her pride of place
> Was by a mousing owl hawked at and killed.

Several references to snakes occur, and the reflection:

> And you all know security
> Is mortals' chiefest enemy.

is a thought characteristic of him.

We have a couple of references to the contemporaneous kerns and gallowglasses, but now these are from the Western Isles – all one Celtic world with Northern Ireland: 'the merciless Macdonald . . . from the Western Isles

> Of kerns and gallowglasses is supplied.'

These were much in the news, for the leader of the Ulster resistance, Hugh O'Neill, had submitted to James I, who was preparing the plantation of Ulster with Scots. There were kern and gallowglass, Macdonalds and MacDonells on either side those narrow waters: to what point their mutual murdering even today?

The play is true in atmosphere to their dark, lugubrious, bloodstained world.

———— oOo ————

The text offers some problems. It has come down to us from the Folio, 'doubtless printed from a prompt-copy', says E. K. Chambers; and this has been cut, perhaps by Shakespeare himself. Greg adds that the stage-directions 'are normal and reveal the hand of the bookkeeper, though some probably originated with the author.' For some later performance another hand, probably Middleton, inserted a few things, but not so much as disintegrating Victorians supposed. Dover-Wilson says that 'modern experts are less pessimistic'; the whole drift of scholarship has been in a conservative direction, to substantiate on the whole what has come down to us.

Simon Forman saw a performance at the Globe on 20 April 1611. It is interesting that he refers to the Weird Sisters not as witches but as 'women fairies or nymphs'. He was most impressed by them, the apparition of Banquo's ghost, and Lady Macbeth's sleep-walking.[1]

Macbeth's reference to Banquo:

> under him
> My Genius is rebuked, as it is said
> Mark Antony's was by Caesar –

shows that Shakespeare was planning forward.

---

1. cf. my *Simon Forman: Sex and Society in Shakespeare's Age*, pages 303-4 (Weidenfeld & Nicolson, London, 1974); American title *Sex and Society in Shakespeare's Age: Simon Forman the Astrologer* (Scribner, New York, 1975)

King Lear
1606

The story of King Lear was familiar to Elizabethans, who for the most part did not distinguish between pre-history and history. To them the story of King Lear and his daughters had the status of authentic history, and both early quartos of the play describe it as a 'true chronicle history'. Only a critical historian like Camden knew better. Shakespeare picked up a detail from his popular *Remains*, which came out in 1605 not long before the play was written, and this he used for the test put to Cordelia, when she reserved half of her love for her future husband.

However, Shakespeare followed Holinshed's account more or less, though still more the old play, *The True Chronicle History of King Leir*, which was also published in 1605. It may be that these two publications inclined him towards the subject. (Llyr is apparently a Celtic name, and Elizabethans mistakenly derived the name of Leicester from it; they thought that it went back to a Caerleir, i.e. Leir's castrum or ceister.) So the story is a very early one. Actually, as we should expect, the dramatist followed the old play more closely than Holinshed. His instinct told him to prefer the poet Spenser's form of the name Cordelia, and he adapted a story from Sidney's *Arcadia* for his under-plot concerning Gloucester and his sons.

The importance of this under-plot marks this play off from the other tragedies. It complicates and enriches, counterpoints and enforces, the main plot, with which it is expertly interwoven. Thus the structure of the play is a complex and Gothic one, as against the classic simplicity of *Julius Caesar* or the romantic unity of *Othello*. Again, the rôle of the Fool in *King Lear*, which the pseudo-classic taste from the Restoration onwards would not tolerate, is also important: as Lear's familiar he brings home to him the truth of his situation and his folly. Wisdom and truth are spoken through the mouth of a Fool, with all the more caustic effect. Once more, Shakespeare's mixing of genres gave him unlimited scope, in keeping with the opulent age in which he lived (compare the effects of Tintoretto or Veronese), as against the restricted taste of the late 17th or 18th century.

Though the cast is not large, the parts are well distributed and several characters are fully delineated in their good or evil qualities. Evil is dispersed throughout the play: Lear's daughters, Goneril and Regan, Regan's husband, Duke of Cornwall, Gloucester's bastard son, Edmund, are all evil. Indeed, Edmund is of a piece with Iago:

> A credulous father, and a brother noble,
> Whose nature is so far from doing harms
> That he suspects none: on whose foolish honesty
> My practices ride easy!

Gloucester is gullible and suffers for his illusions; the chief sufferer for his illusions is King Lear himself. We may be sure that William Shakespeare suffered from no illusions – in fact, we know it, even at the height of his infatuation with Emilia Lanier: he knew all the time what she was.

Exceptionally, after the courtly beginning, the character of the King is fully revealed in the first scene, rashly giving away his kingdom, exposing himself to the bitterest ingratitude, throwing away the devotion of his youngest daughter and his most loyal supporter, Kent. He gets what he asked for, or, rather more: rash and intemperate by nature, later, due to his sufferings, his wits are turned. The rest of the play is devoted to drawing the consequences: he at last, through adversity, learns the truth about himself and others, about life itself. It is the Fool who brings it home to him:

> Thou shouldst not have been old till thou hadst been wise.

It might be regarded as the moral of the play in one sentence.

Unlike lesser spirits, and contrary to many critics, Shakespeare is never afraid to drive home the moral of what he has exposed – indeed, it would have been un-Elizabethan of him not to do so. These often take the form of sententious rhymed couplets, such as Elizabethans regaled themselves or plastered their houses with. Under the description Shakespeare's 'gnomic verse' this is currently depreciated – again, without knowledge of the age of which it is characteristic. As in *Othello* these *sententiae* are given prominence, and evidently speak for the poet himself, tell us what his conclusions were.

It is the Fool who advises Lear (and us):

> Have more than thou showest,
> Speak less than thou knowest,
> Lend less then thou owest,
> Ride more than thou goest (i.e. walk),
> Learn more than thou trowest (i.e. know),
> Set [i.e. stake] less than thou throwest:
> And thou shalt have more
> Than two tens to a score.

That evidently spoke for Shakespeare, and stood him in good stead.

Later in the play similar saws of wisdom are given to Edgar:

> When we our betters see bearing our woes,
> We scarcely think our miseries our foes.
> Who alone suffers suffers most i'the mind,
> Leaving free things and happy shows behind.
> But then the mind much sufferance doth o'erskip,
> When grief hath mates, and bearing fellowship.

Here speaks the sociable Shakespeare, the family man; such didactic words of wisdom were much to the taste of an Elizabethan audience.

Similar touches reveal his thought to us. Gloucester, blinded, says, 'I stumbled when I saw'; there follows a very Shakespearean thought:

> full oft 'tis seen,
> Our means secure us, and our mere defects
> Prove our commodities.

That is, our resources make us feel secure and careless, when our very defects may prove to benefit us. How like his prudence, always keeping a weather-eye open! And we are given the consoling reflection, often proved true:

> the worst is not
> So long as we can say, 'This is the worst.'

Or again,

> Striving to better, oft we mar what's well.

His scepticism is like that of Montaigne, a comparable spirit of the time, *divers et ondoyant*. It enables him to make reflections through his characters which are, in a sense, in inverted commas and yet his own – on others, on men in general, and on *la condition humaine*. It is Lear mad, who tells blinded Gloucester: 'A man may see how this world goes with no eyes. Look with thine ears: see how yon justice rails on yon simple thief. Hark, in thine ear: change places, and – handy-dandy – which is the justice, which is the thief?' In a beggar running from a farmer's dog, you may behold the great image of authority: 'a dog's obeyed in office'. And the conclusion? –

> Get thee glass eyes,
> And, like a scurvy politician, seem
> To see the things thou dost not.

'Politicians' never get a good word in Shakespeare: only good rulers, and good people. It is given to the cynical Edmund to reflect on the foolery of people so that, when things go wrong with them, often through their own ill conduct, they impute it to the planets, 'as if we were villains by necessity; fools by heavenly compulsion; knaves, thieves, treachers [i.e. traitors], drunkards, liars and adulterers' through the influence of the stars. Plenty of people thought like that – Shakespeare's message is that it is open to all to be more intelligent and responsible.

Many indications denote the background. Shakespeare had read Samuel Harsnet's book, *Declaration of Egregious Popish Impostures*, which had come out three years before, in 1603. Professor Harbage[1] calls it an 'excursion into pseudo-demonology'. It is not: it is a fascinating exposure of the claims of contemporary Catholic priests to exorcise demons from women, and as such a revealing investigation of the phenomena of female hysteria and male credulity and imposture. It was this useful reading that suggested to Shakespeare the names of the spirits that haunted the hovel on the heath, according to Edgar, feigning madness, who had taken refuge from the storm there with Lear, Kent and the Fool.

Edgar himself, in this world wheeling round, with madness in the air, Lear's wits becoming unsettled and the elements raging, takes on the folklore character of Tom o'Bedlam – about whom the age produced a mysterious, but marvellous, anonymous poem. Such beggars were a feature of the time:

> The country gives me proof and precedent
> Of Bedlam beggars, who, with roaring voices,
> Strike in their numbed and mortified bare arms
> Pins, wooden pricks, nails, sprigs of rosemary;
> And with this horrible object, from low farms,
> Poor pelting villages, sheepcotes, and mills,
> Sometime with lunatic bans [curses], sometime with
>   prayers,
> Enforce their charity.

And the serving-men of the time? Edgar pretends to have been one, 'proud in heart and mind; that curled my hair; wore gloves in my cap, swore as many oaths as I spake words, and broke them in the sweet face of heaven; one that slept in the contriving of lust, and waked to it.' He then offers a warning that betrays William Shakespeare himself: 'let not the creaking of shoes nor the rustling of silks betray thy poor heart to woman.' One has known heterosexuals whose senses were as keen to that alert. Perhaps one may see him personally too in the comment:

> Love's not love
> When it is mingled with regards that stand
> Aloof from the main point.

Many more indications portray the age out of which Shakespeare's creations sprang. We have the stage itself in Edmund speaking of Edgar, 'and pat he comes like the catastrophe of the old comedy: my cue is villainous melancholy, with a sigh like Tom o'Bedlam. O, these eclipses do portend these divisions!' Those years were marked by a number of eclipses, which were regarded as portents at the time. Putting people in the stocks makes an appearance – in the porches of many country churches we used to see the village-stocks, useful to lock delinquents in. But it was shocking of Regan's husband to put her father, the King's messenger, the Earl of Kent, in the stocks. Gloucester protests:

> Your purposed low correction
> Is such as basest and contemned'st wretches
> For pilferings and most common trespasses
> Are punished with.

An hierarchical society knew what was proper in these matters. Again, it is given the Fool to speak common sense about society: 'he's a mad yeoman that sees his son a gentleman before him.'

An interesting piece of information, not usually known, crops up when Gloucester is told by his bastard son, Edmund, that his legitimate brother had intended to murder their father:

> his picture
> I will send far and near, that all the kingdom
> May have due note of him –

as is the habit of the police today with wanted criminals. Kent neatly tripped Goneril's horrid steward, Oswald, by the heels with 'you base football player'. Football was but a low street-game then, not the organised mass-orgies of today which give such opportunities for the civilised masses to express themselves in their behaviour.

The play is filled with snatches of contemporary songs and ballads, bits of folklore and such. One notices, as in so many of the plays, Shakespeare's consciousness of snakes: were the Cotswolds particularly a haunt of them – as Salisbury plain evidently was of geese? The description of the tall cliff at Dover now known by his name reminds us that the Chamberlain's Men had been there the summer before he wrote the play.

Shakespeare's addiction to grand words is what we notice all along, and it is not just a matter of scansion: a man reveals himself in the words he chooses. Goneril tells King Lear to 'disquantity' his train, i.e. to reduce. Edgar, instead of saying 'a follower of the stars', says 'sectary astronomical', and it comes in a passage of prose. Edmund, suggesting that his brother cautiously retires for a bit, words it 'have a continent forbearance.' We have 'cadent tears', 'festinate' for speedy, 'questrists' for followers. Even the 'catastrophe' of the old play merely meant its end.

—— oOo ——

There is no other play like it – one can only call it epical. The elements themselves, storm and rain, heath and hovel, mad and men pretending to be mad mingle together in a roaring, howling symphony. Madness on the stage is extraordinarily exciting, as Shakespeare learned from Kyd's *Jeronimo*, and as we experience from Hamlet's affected madness. For one thing, it removes all restraint upon the tongue: anything can be said, and with a more cutting edge. For all that we may compare *King Lear* with *Hamlet* as the twin peaks of Shakespeare's achievement in tragedy, the two plays are very different and in some ways at opposite poles. Hamlet is introspective and *innerlich*: there are no bounds to the exploration of that dark interior. King Lear is, in one sense, extrovert; his character is clear from the first, and he brings his tragedy on his own head. Hamlet has his burden imposed upon him from without, through no fault of his own: our sympathies are thus more deeply engaged with him. *King Lear* is intensive too, but far more extensive: it shows us a world afflicted by evil. Because of the sheer scale of the work Charles Lamb has often been cited, with approval, saying that the play is impossible of representation on the stage. This is absurd: however epical our own imaginations may be, it was written for representation on the stage by the most experienced dramatist we have ever had.

Hazlitt concluded, 'all that we can say must fall far short of the subject, or even what we ourselves conceive of it.' Precisely – the best of reasons for letting the play speak for itself.

—— oOo ——

The two texts that have come down to us reveal something of what went on behind the scenes. For the Quarto printed 1608 has some three hundred lines not in the First Folio, which was obviously based on the prompt-copy, cut for production. On the other hand the First Folio has over a hundred lines not in the Quarto. This gives us a glimpse of the practical chopping and changing that went on in Elizabethan production – flexible adaptation to circumstances: no sacrosanctity. Unlike the French producer of today who held it sacrilege to omit a single line of Shakespeare's!

E. K. Chambers describes both texts as 'substantially [sensibly cautious expression] derived from the same original.' So editors have the job of conflating the two, and modern editions are happily longer than the original printed texts.

The earliest recorded Court performance was 'before the King's Majesty at Whitehall upon St. Stephen's night in Christmas holidays', i.e. 26 December 1606. One would like to know what King James made of it.

---

1. Introduction to the Pelican edition of the play (1970), which, the professor is also able to tell us 'is a sad play, as all tragedies are sad'!

Antony and Cleopatra

1607

There could hardly be a greater contrast than there is between *Macbeth* and *Antony and Cleopatra* – the former dark and smelling of murder, the latter brilliantly lit by all the colour of the Mediterranean and the gorgeous East. Then this play is the only one of the great tragedies to be a love-tragedy; in that it casts the mind back to *Romeo and Juliet*, though neither Antony nor Cleopatra has the excuse of those young and immature lovers. Antony, in fact, has grey hair, and Cleopatra – who had had a child years before by Julius Caesar – is past her youth. The story carries on from *Julius Caesar* – and Antony unexpectedly refers to 'mad' Brutus, showing what he thought of his illusory doctrinairism. But Antony suffers no less for his own dominant illusion, the illusion of love. It seems that Shakespeare by this time had none – at any rate, of sexual love: that theme is not so important again in the plays.

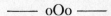

Shakespeare got his story from Plutarch, who gives us the character of the actual woman in history: her political intelligence and gift for languages, the devouring ambition she derived from her Macedonian-Greek stock. Nothing of this in Shakespeare; and, since we are looking for what reveals him, we should note the characteristics he gives her that are not in Plutarch. With the historic Cleopatra sex was but a means to political power. In the play her aim is simply to exert power over one man, Antony. And well she knows how to do it. When Charmian advises,

> In each thing give him way, cross him in nothing:

Cleopatra replies:

> Thou teachest like a fool: the way to lose him.

So she is contrarious, she holds him on tenterhooks – as with a recent English king who thought the world well lost for love. But was it? Antony did not think so in the end. Nor apparently did Shakespeare; in a moment of truth Antony admits,

> Would I had never seen her!

He himself describes her as one

> Whom everything becomes, to chide, to laugh,
> To weep: whose every passion fully strives
> To make itself in thee.

She uses these as instruments; Antony tells Enobarbus: 'she is cunning past man's thought'. The latter glosses: 'we cannot call her winds and waters, sighs and tears; they are greater storms and tempests than almanacs can report.' She was seen once, this queen, to

> Hop forty paces through the public street
> And, having lost her breath, she spoke, and panted,
> That she did make defect perfection,
> And, breathless, power breathe forth.

The clue to Cleopatra is her very *foreignness;* she casts a spell by her contrariousness, her changing moods, her undependability; passionate and temperamental, she let Antony down at the crisis. He knew her faults and failings, yet could not help himself – like Shakespeare years before with his temperamental half-Italian mistress: 'Whence hast thou this powerful might?' to compel him against all the evidence about her. [1]

—— oOo ——

The play has not the dramatic intensity of the other high tragedies: its action is more dispersed and various, and its interest is almost as much political as it is amorous. Whole scenes are devoted to the political issue between Octavius Caesar and Antony; Antony and Caesar's noble sister, Octavia, loyal and sensible, whom Antony deserts for 'his Egyptian dish'; discussions among the rival followings and battles in the field. It is not until the end that the action speeds into the grand finale; or, rather, there are two of them, Antony's downfall and defeat – his death is postponed for a last meeting with Cleopatra – and then the unforgettable way she chooses death, turning it into triumph.

Several strokes reveal the Antony we knew from *Julius Caesar*, where he was described as 'a masker and reveller'. In the later play he revels with Cleopatra in the streets of Alexandria, masquerading as common citizens, night walkers. What a way for a Triumvir, ruler of one-third of the Roman world, to behave! No wonder Octavius Caesar, much younger, but altogether more mature, disapproved. Antony has a weakness for drink and, like such people, eggs on the young Caesar, who declines:

> I could well forbear't.
> It's monstrous labour when I wash my brain
> And it grows fouler.

Antony persists:

> Be a child o'the time . . .

But Caesar excuses himself:

> . . . I had rather fast from all, four days,
> Than drink so much in one.

Antony goes on

> Till that the conquering wine hath steeped our sense
> In soft and delicate Lethe.

Such men are not made to inherit the earth.

He is generous, as such types are; but he is a great fool to be led by the nose by a woman, and to follow her flight from the sea-battle at Actium when they might perhaps have won. Defeated, he runs mad and rails at her, with the insults such people exchange when things go wrong between them:

> This foul Egyptian hath betrayed me . . .
> Triple-turned whore, 'tis thou
> Hast sold me to this novice, and my heart
> Makes only war on thee . . . etc.

Octavius Caesar is no novice, and he holds with none of this nonsense. It is usual for sympathies to run with the lovers, a soft option, and not to appreciate Caesar at his true worth. Critics find him 'unattractive': literary folk find it difficult to understand the true political type with a mind to rule, as Hazlitt did and so many others over Henry V. Octavius is a man in full control of himself, as a ruler must be, and moreover is reasonable, moderate and just. He did not wish the war, or a breach with Antony, and was more than willing to meet him half-way. But Antony fell down on his duty and broke their mutual compact, while his wife Fulvia and their friends actually attacked Octavius.

He is ready to forgive and forget and, on Fulvia's death, to cement friendship by giving his sister Octavia, whom he much loves, to Antony as wife.

> CAESAR: There's my hand.
> A sister I bequeath you, whom no brother
> Did ever love so dearly. Let her live
> To join our kingdoms, and our hearts, and never
> Fly off our loves again.

Antony jilts her, and goes back to Cleopatra. Moreover he is jealous of the younger man, the 'novice'. A soothsayer warns him,

> Near him [Caesar], thy angel
> Becomes afeared, as being overpowered . . .
> If thou dost play with him at any game,
> Thou art sure to lose . . .

Octavius Caesar carries the charisma of the deified Julius: Antony is bound to lose going the way he does. We need not go into the pathetic boasting of what he once was, when he has lost out. Suffice it to say that Caesar is magnanimous; when he hears that Antony is dead, he says:

> The death of Antony
> Is not a single doom, in the name lay
> A moiety of the world.

In pronouncing his panegyric, Octavius laments

> That thou my brother, my competitor,
> In top of all design; my mate in empire,
> Friend and companion in the front of war . . .
>   that our stars,
> Unreconciliable, should divide
> Our equalness to this.

Such are the tragedies of high politics, a matter for more mature pity, when all is said, than the misfortunes of elderly lovers, asking for the fate they brought upon themselves.

Their fate gives opportunity for much fine poetry, and I agree with M.R. Ridley – who was sensitive to such things – that 'the peculiar glory of this play is . . . in its poetry.'[2] Many passages of such grandeur are familiar – the description of Cleopatra in her barge upon the river Cydnus, or the too often quoted 'Age cannot wither her'; and Antony's words on being told that Cleopatra had died, with his name on her lips:

> Unarm, Eros, the long day's task is done,
> And we must sleep . . .
> Eros! – I come, my queen. Eros! – Stay for me,
> Where souls do couch on flowers, we'll hand in hand,
> And with our sprightly port make the ghosts gaze:
> Dido and her Aeneas shall want troops,
> And all the haunt be ours.

The master could always fetch up from the depths of his inspiration this magical verbal mastery at such moments, but never more so than in this play. Ridley concludes that here is 'Shakespeare's topmost achievement in dramatic poetry, that kind of poetry which apart from its context is little remarkable, but in its dramatic setting is indefinably moving.' We would merely emend this to say that it is, apart from its context, both remarkable and moving.

—— oOo ——

In a play of such Oriental colouring, not many touches of the contemporary background are discernible, but, significantly, more than usual of the personal. A reference to the author's own profession appears in every play; here, along with the ballad makers who, Cleopatra foresees, will make rhymes on her and Antony (they certainly did) –

> the quick comedians
> Extemporally will stage us, and present
> Our Alexandrian revels: Antony
> Shall be brought drunken forth, and I shall see
> Some squeaking Cleopatra boy my greatness
> I' the posture of a whore.

Evidently the boy-actor who played the part of Cleopatra – his inches were fewer than Antony's – had not a squeaking voice; and how professional he must have been to play such a part!

Shakespeare portrays the masses in his usual terms. Octavius describes Antony reeling the streets at noon and buffeting with slaves that 'smell of sweat'; Cleopatra foretells that they will be played as puppets in Rome:

> mechanic slaves
> With greasy aprons, rules and hammers shall
> Uplift us to the view. In their thick breaths,
> Rank of gross diet, shall we be enclouded,
> And forced to drink their vapour.

Elizabethan crowds, indeed people in general, were very smelly; grandees at Court, the Queen and Leicester, smothered themselves in scent – and William Shakespeare certainly had a sensitive nose. His consciousness of snakes (whatever Freud would think about that) is naturally more in evidence than ever; two extended passages are devoted to the subject, and Cleopatra's asps have their part to play.

A few lines here and there give us his reflections on what he had observed. We have learned

> That he which is was wished until he were:

this means that the man in power is popular, until he gets there. Octavius is speaking, with his political insight. He goes on,

213

> And the ebbed man, ne'er loved till ne'er worth love,
> Comes deared, by being lacked.

This is a highly elliptical way of saying that the defeated candidate, never appreciated till he is no longer worth supporting, is all the more popular for being missed. How often we have seen that too! As for the people –

> This common body,
> Like to a vagabond flag upon the stream,
> Goes to and back, lacking the varying tide,
> To rot itself with the motion.

He had observed people's behaviour over Essex from close at hand:

> I see men's judgments are
> A parcel of their fortunes, and things outward
> Do draw the inward quality after them.

The dilemma posed to Antony's chief follower, Enobarbus, is fascinating:

> Mine honesty, and I, begin to square [quarrel].
> The loyalty well held to fools does make
> Our faith mere folly.

That was what Francis Bacon had thought as he watched the folly of Essex's conduct. Enobarbus speaks an aside:

> Sir, sir, thou art so leaky
> That we must leave thee to thy sinking, for
> Thy dearest quit thee.

He deserts the falling Antony – and then finds himself conscience-stricken, and repents:

> Yet he that can endure
> To follow with allegiance a fallen lord,
> Does conquer him that did his master conquer,
> And earns a place in the story.

In the end Enobarbus did. Everybody remembered Bacon's conduct against him; however prudent, Shakespeare cannot have regarded it as a matter for commendation. Enobarbus is given a better exit.

Once more we observe Shakespeare's scepticism about the way in which things are likely to turn out:

> We, ignorant of ourselves,
> Beg often our own harms, which the wise powers
> Deny us for our good: so find we profit
> By losing of our prayers.

And again:

> What our contempts doth often hurl from us
> We wish it ours again. The present pleasure,
> By revolution lowering, does become
> The opposite of itself.

Touches of bawdy reappear, naturally in this play in which sex has a decisive role – though we have none of the joyous rollicking stuff of earlier plays. People have seen signs of sex-nausea in those from *Hamlet* and *Troilus and Cressida* to *King Lear*, with no sex interest at all in *Macbeth*. Now Cleopatra addresses her eunuch with,

> I take no pleasure
> In aught an eunuch has: 'tis well for thee
> That, being unseminared . . .

perhaps we should spell this, unsemenared. When it is a question of playing billiards:

> As well a woman with an eunuch played
> As with a woman.

The splendid passages of poetry have often been cited; here we will call attention only to the extraordinarily oblique and often elliptical language. On hearing unwelcome news from Rome, for 'it offends me: be brief', Antony says; 'Grates me – the sum.' The movement of Shakespeare's mind linguistically is, surely, very strange? When drifting clouds efface a fancied picture, it is simply, but elliptically, 'the rack dislimns'! Dogs die of some disease; here they die of 'languish'. And, within a few lines, Antony imagines Eros 'windowed' in Rome watching her master with 'pleached' arms, bending down

> His corrigible neck, his face subdued
> To penetrative shame.

Extraordinary language, though the clue to it, as always, is that Shakespeare thinks visually – and rather superciliously.

We might add that the incredible splendour of the language of this play

– rich as Veronese – is unsurpassed. In truth it is incomparable: the *ne plus ultra* of English speech, beyond which there is no going.

—— oOo ——

The text, from the Folio, is a good one and, it is agreed, from the author's manuscript. Its mislineation is due to Shakespeare economising space by running on half-lines to fill the rest of the line. Sometimes he punctuated carefully, sometimes not. His rapid handwriting evidently gave printers difficulty.

In 1607 Daniel considerably revised his *Cleopatra* in the light of Shakespeare's play, trying to make it more dramatic. Earlier he had been influenced by *Richard II* in revising his account in the *Civil Wars*, to which Shakespeare in turn was indebted. (So the *Parnassus* play's flout at Daniel for 'base imitation' does not get the situation quite right.) It is worth adding that Emilia Lanier knew Daniel through their common patroness, the Countess of Cumberland. Towards the end of the year Barnes's *Devil's Charter*, 'renewed, corrected and augmented', borrowed Cleopatra's asps for his purposes. We may note that earlier the poet Barnes had been one of Southampton's circle, with him in Normandy in 1591, and dedicating his first poems to him.

---

1. Agatha Christie, a devoted Shakespearean with her exceptional insight, was convinced that in Cleopatra, like no other character in Shakespeare, he was recalling someone he had known, his half-foreign Dark Lady.
2. *Arden Shakespeare* edition (1967), Introduction, pages liv and lv.

Coriolanus
1608

The content of *Coriolanus* is almost entirely political, and its interest concentrated upon the character of the chief protagonist. We might say that there are two protagonists in the large cast the play requires – Coriolanus, and the People. The dramatic conflict is essentially between him and them: the varying, changing relationships, reluctant admiration for the man to whom Rome owed so much, his pride and his contempt for them, the mistake of submitting himself to them for election while refusing to flatter them and talk the necessary humbug, their turning against him, artfully encouraged by their tribunes – and the train of fatal consequences.

What can have turned Shakespeare's mind in this direction? He found his subject in his reading of North's Plutarch, as with *Antony and Cleopatra*, and he used a passage in Camden's *Remains*, that for Menenius' fable of the belly, as he had used another in *King Lear*. But sometimes external events, as we have seen, led him to his subject.

In May 1607 agrarian disturbances in the Midlands affected Warwickshire, where Shakespeare was now a landowner. Most of the trouble was over enclosure; but Shakespeare's friend, William Combe, reported to Cecil, now Lord Salisbury, the widespread complaints at the dearth of corn, 'the prices rising to some height, caused partly by some that are well stored refraining to bring the same to the market out of a covetous conceit that corn will be dearer.' Prices reached their topmost that year.

This is the issue that starts off the first scene. The citizens are mutinying against the governing class – so here we have a modern theme, that of class-conflict. The First Citizen says: 'What authority surfeits on would relieve us – if they would yield us but the superfluity while it were wholesome . . .' (At this time, at Stratford the provident dramatist had a considerable store of malt in his big house, New Place.) 'They ne'er cared for us yet, and their store-houses crammed with grain; make edicts for usury, to support usurers . . . and provide more piercing statutes daily to chain up and restrain the poor.' This refers to the severe Elizabethan Poor Law established by the statutes of 1598-1601.

The corporate wisdom of the people speaks through the First Citizen; they regard Coriolanus as their chief enemy, 'a very dog to the commonalty . . . Let us kill him, and we'll have corn at our own price.' The Second Citizen suggests that Coriolanus' services to the country be taken into account. The First replies that what won him fame he did merely to that end: though softies ('soft-conscienced men') said it was for his country, 'he did it to please his mother and to be partly proud, which he is, even to the altitude of his virtue.' Here the people have a point – and it is his pride that proves fatal to him.

The patrician Menenius tries to explain to the plebeians:

> For your wants,
> Your suffering in this dearth, you may as well
> Strike at the heaven with your staves as lift them
> Against the Roman state –

as it might be a bureaucrat in Whitehall explaining that nothing can be done about inflation. And he expounded to them the function of the belly in the body – the rôle of consumption in the economy.

Coriolanus has rendered supreme service to Rome by saving the state, so he has been prevailed on to stand for consul. The tribunes of the people – in modern terms, the democratic leaders – harp on his pride, instigate the people against him, and manage to entrap and ruin him with them. They are, recognisably, envious of the great man – as an eminent historian said of American democracy, 'their instinct is to lop the tallest'. And Coriolanus is too tall, an obvious target. The tribune, Junius Brutus, has a contemptuous description of the returning hero's reception – he is no more enamoured of the people than Coriolanus is; but he is not a cynic: they are –

> the kitchen malkin pins
> Her richest lockram 'bout her reechy neck,
> Clambering the walls to eye him. Stalls, bulks, windows
> Are smothered up, leads filled, and ridges horsed
> With variable complexions, all agreeing
> In earnestness to see him.

It is clearly an Elizabethan, not a Roman, crowd:

> Matrons flung gloves,
> Ladies and maids their scarfs and handkerchers
> Upon him as he passed.

Two officers discuss the prospects of the election. The first: 'That's a brave fellow; but he's vengeance proud, and loves not the common people.' The second replies: 'there hath been many great men that have flattered the people, who ne'er loved them; and there be many that they have loved, they knew not wherefore.' The first puts his finger on Coriolanus' trouble: 'but he seeks their hate with greater devotion than they can render it him, and leaves nothing undone that may fully discover him their opposite.' That being so, he should never have submitted himself for election by the people he despised.

Overpersuaded by the patricians of his order, he reluctantly appears in the garb of humility. But this is what he says when a citizen reproaches him with not loving the common people: 'You should account me the more virtuous that I have not been common in my love. I will, sir, flatter my sworn brother, the people, to earn a dearer estimation of them. 'Tis a condition they account gentle,' i.e. this is what they expect of gentlemen. 'And since the wisdom of their choice is rather to have my hat than my heart, I will practise the insinuating nod and be off to them [i.e. take off his hat] most counterfeitly.'

Not a very promising election-speech: though a hero, Coriolanus was a bad political candidate:

> Better it is to die, better to starve,
> Than crave the hire which first we do deserve.

Yes, indeed ('er' was always pronounced 'ar', as still with 'serjeant' today).

The tribunes, who are demagogues (like the tribunes of today, shop-stewards) have no difficulty in driving such a man into the open, to say what he really thinks of a state of affairs,

> where gentry, title, wisdom,
> Cannot conclude but by the yea and no
> Of general ignorance.

Here is what William Shakespeare really thought: such a state of society

> must omit
> Real necessities . . .
> Purpose so barred, it follows,
> Nothing is done to purpose.

This is far-seeing, as we should expect of his insight into human nature and society: long-term interests would be sacrificed for soft options, and nothing done to purpose.

> The multitudinous tongue – let them not lick
> The sweet which is their poison:

that is, do not give way to the people's demands – for example, for ever pushing wages up for less work – against their own well-being in the end, to produce inflation and unemployment. Such democratic weakness, Coriolanus says,

> bereaves the state
> Of that integrity which should become it,
> Not having the power to do the good it would
> For the ill which doth control it.

All this is as true as ever today – it brings home again the continuous application of Shakespeare's thought. He understood, too, that

> . . . manhood is called foolery when it stands
> Against a falling fabric.

Today it is thought eccentric to see clearly how things are going – but the fabric breaks down nevertheless. A figure who stands out heroically against the solvents of society and tells people home-truths they will pay no attention to is already alienated, as Coriolanus was, and may be driven into exile as he was. When the people mutiny against him, his reaction is:

> I would they were barbarians – as they are,
> Though in Rome littered: not Romans, as they are not –

not worthy of their country's history. In such a society he is already an inner exile.

—— oOo ——

So, driven out, he goes over to the enemy, and takes refuge with the Volscians, from whom he had saved Rome. The scene in which, disguised, he enters the house of his opponent, Aufidius, and is embraced by him, makes a fine ominous scene. We are shown the servingmen there, in realistic prose-dialogue, no other than the populace in Rome, as changeable and as stupid. They look forward to the renewal of war – a contemporary reflection on James I's peace with Spain from 1604. 'This peace is nothing but to rust iron, increase tailors, and breed ballad-makers', says one. 'Let me have war', says another. 'It exceeds peace as far as day does night . . . Peace is a getter of more bastard children than war's a destroyer of men.' 'Ay', says another wiseacre, 'and it makes men hate one another.' Then the popular wisdom scores a point: 'Reason – because they then less need one another.'

This was true of Jacobean society. Elizabethan England had held together in the long struggle against Spain; with peace, it tended to fall apart, the cracks and strains of class- and religious-conflict to come into the open.

Coriolanus, driven into exile, then led the Volscians to victory and had Rome at his mercy. He could have burned the place over their heads, as he meant – again in keeping with modern psychology, the recognisable reaction of a love-hate complex: the destruction of what one loves.

He is prevented by his love for his mother, Volumnia. Much is made by critics of the beauty of this character and the touching nature of their relationship. She is in fact a stern Roman matron, a kind of female Cato, and is much to blame for the fault in her son – what makes him virtually another of Shakespeare's psychotic characters. She had brought him up harshly, without tenderness; she had urged him to expose himself to the people, and she ruined him by prevailing on him to spare Rome. A solitary soul like Coriolanus should have lived solitarily, to himself alone.

But that would have been contrary to Shakespeare's deep social conviction, his family spirit. In the end, it was not in Coriolanus' nature to

>   stand
>   As if a man were author of himself
>   And knew no other kin.

In this severe, classic play we come across charming touches that reveal the author:

>   O, let me clip ye [embrace you]
>   In arms as sound as when I wooed, in heart
>   As merry as when our nuptial day was done,
>   And tapers burned to bedward!

This must have meant much to the writer when he repeats it later, like a home-coming to Stratford:

>   more dances my rapt heart
>   Than when I first my wedded mistress saw
>   Bestride my threshold.

The more numerous and detailed stage-directions from the author's hand would indicate that some of the play at least was written in the country. Apart even from the reflection of local circumstances in the inception of the play – the dearth of corn, popular disturbances, etc. – we find,

>   forth he goes,
>   Like to a harvest-man that's tasked to mow
>   Or all or lose his hire.

Hare-coursing comes in; and we have a noticeable medical reference such as is to become more frequent from now on. 'The most sovereign prescription in Galen is but empiricutic and, to this preservative, of no better report than a horse-drench.' We can tell that, in his later years, he profited from talk with his son-in-law, Dr. John Hall, whom Susanna, his intelligent elder daughter, married in 1607.

A London reference corroborates the date: the 'coal of fire upon the ice' refers to the great frost in the winter of 1607-8, when the Thames was frozen over and fires were lighted upon it. We have yet another reference to his profession, as in practically every play:

> Like a dull actor now,
> I have forgot my part, and I am out,
> Even to a full disgrace.

—— oOo ——

This is Shakespeare's second classic play, and the style is in keeping – none of the glowing colours of *Antony and Cleopatra*. It is more like *Julius Caesar*, though it has more variety in the colloquial talk of the Roman citizens and the comic exchanges of the serving-men. The language is the elliptical, overcharged language of the later plays. The blank verse has a considerable proportion of feminine endings. We note the fondness for the rare, rather than the obvious, word: for 'fearless' this writer will say, more visually, 'shunless'. Ben Jonson made fun of one of these odd phrases:

> He lurched all swords of the garland,

meaning, he robbed. In *Epicoene*, next year or so, Ben made somebody say:

> You have lurched your friends of the better half of
> the garland.

I expect that this gave them both a good laugh; for us it corroborates the date.

—— oOo ——

The text is a fair one, as it appeared first in the First Folio, but with many of Shakespeare's mislineations, as in its predecessor, and probably for the same reason – the author saving space over half-lines. We have indications of his idiosyncratic spelling and that the manuscript from which the play was printed was not easy to read. We know from the signatures to his will that Shakespeare's handwriting, like many authors', became rather illegible.

Timon of Athens
1608-9

Timon followed straight upon the heels of *Coriolanus* with which it has much in common. From North's Plutarch Shakespeare took over the stories of Timon and Alcibiades, and resolved to combine them for his next play. The situation was repeated from *Coriolanus*: both Timon and Alcibiades were alienated from their native city; Alcibiades was banished and returned to conquer and spare it, Timon banished himself.

The dramatist may also have looked up Lucian's version of Timon's story, perhaps in Latin; certainly not in Greek, for Greek was hardly at all taught in Elizabethan schools, and most of the names in the play are Latin.

The theme, as with most of the tragedies, is the revelation of his own nature to the protagonist, as with King Lear, whether the self-discovery is adequate and convincing or not. With Timon it is not: he goes from one extreme to another, from prodigality and profuse liberality to the misanthropy induced by the discovery of the falseness of friends, the undependability of people who will accept one's hospitality and gifts, without giving anything in return, their unwillingness to come to one's help in time of need, the insincerity and hypocrisy of flatterers in one's prosperity, desertion in adversity, ingratitude – a subject on which Shakespeare was peculiarly sensitive.

Timon learns all this from bitter experience; he should have known it before, but what he finds suddenly and totally changes him, like a conversion, into a misanthrope. Apemantus, who is another Thersites from *Troilus and Cressida* and a complete cynic about men already, tells Timon the truth about himself: 'the middle of humanity thou never knewest, but the extremity of both ends.' And further:

> If thou didst put this sour cold habit on
> To castigate thy pride, 'twere well; but thou
> Dost it enforcedly.

So Timon's profuseness was a form of pride, and even of patronising others: he gets what is coming to him. On the other hand, he is capable of telling Apemantus the truth about himself too:

> If thou hadst not been born the worst of men
> Thou hadst been knave and flatterer.

His reviling of men is but the other side of the coin.

So all illusions are exposed in this singularly disillusioned play, the first half of which is devoted to this theme – Timon's illusion (like Lear's).

The play begins with a strong scene, in which the poet and the painter prepare to present their works to the lordly Timon as patron. This is highly contemporary; Shakespeare could have heard this sort of patter at Southampton's or some other great house. The painter inquires of the poet: 'You are rapt, sir, in some work, some dedication to the great lord.' The poet replies, with the bogus self-depreciation one knows so well,

> A thing slipped idly from me.

The poet commends the painter's work with: 'this comes off well and excellent.' The painter coyly disclaims praise: 'indifferent'. The poet then responds with a piece of outrageous flattery, the interest of which to us is that it tells us what Elizabethans looked for in a portrait – evidently speaking lifelikeness, plus art and grace:

> Admirable! How this grace
> Speaks his own standing! What a mental power
> This eye shoots forth! How big imagination
> Moves in this lip!

The painter is constrained to admit:

> It is a pretty mocking of the life.
> Here is a touch: Is't good?

The poet assures him:

> I will say of it
> It tutors nature. Artificial strife
> Lives in these touches livelier than life.

Elizabethans used the word 'artificial' in praise, meaning 'artistic'; these exchanges give us an idea of their aesthetic standards.

This is followed by a banquet at which Timon entertains his lordly friends. We are given a nice parody of Court-flattery, which Shakespeare had had every opportunity of overhearing: 'Might we but have that happiness, my lord, that you would once use our hearts, whereby we might express some part of our zeals, we should think ourselves for ever perfect.'

Apemantus, the cynic, knows perfectly what this is worth and expresses his disbelief in men's assurances, in the *sententiae* of his grace. Timon is already in debt; his faithful steward is driven to distraction to raise the wherewithal for such bounty, such senseless extravagance. Bankrupt, Timon tries to cash the assurances of these friends for help to tide him over. Each refuses with a different excuse. Timon invites them to a last banquet, where the covered dishes contain nothing but smoking hot water and stones, with which he pelts them and drives them away. He then departs into the wilderness of solitude and misanthropy.

All this may be seen as a comment on the ostentation and vulgar extravagance, which boomed with the new régime. The financial strain of the war, with Elizabeth and Burghley's watchfulness, had kept things within bounds; with peace and prosperity they passed beyond them. Neither James I nor his Queen had any idea of money; coming from poor Scotland, England was their milch-cow. The magnificent series of Court-masques – for which Ben Jonson was the poet and Inigo Jones the painter – had now begun and cost fortunes. It is interesting that Timon provided a masque with his first banquet.

The costly banquets of James's favourite, James Hay, were notorious; he was popular, too, because – though he got something like £200,000 out of the state – he ended up, Clarendon says, with not a stitch of land. He had spent it all. Many of his sort were forced to sell their lands to keep up with the improvident Stuarts. Timon is forced to this course: 'Let all my land be sold.' His steward knew the situation too well, but Timon would not listen – and there were many like that:

> His promises fly so beyond his state
> That what he speaks is all in debt: he owes
> For every word. He is so kind that he now
> Pays interest for't: his land's put to their books.

As for promises, the painter is able to tell us, 'Promising is the very air o'the time . . . To promise is most courtly and fashionable; performance . . . argues a great sickness in his judgment that makes it.' One academic critic asks, Why was Timon such a fool? But there were many people like that, and Shakespeare knew well that most of humanity were fools, of one sort or another. He puts the knowledge into the mouth of one of these lords, who describes Apemantus as 'opposite to humanity', precisely because he expresses the truth.

In the absence of war people's minds were dominated by money, and religious bickering (that could not be presented on the stage, but we can be sure what Shakespeare thought of it). The first colony went out to Virginia to start Jamestown in 1607; instead of cultivating the soil, they gave themselves up to digging for gold, and were shortly starving. The year 1608 saw a gold-craze over there; the report came home, 'no talk, no hope, no work but to dig gold, wash gold, refine gold, load gold.'[1] Meanwhile, the fools starved, and were forced to dig for roots for sustenance.

Timon digs for roots in the woods by the sea-shore – and finds gold. He holds forth on the subject:

> Gold! Yellow, glittering, precious gold!
> . . . Thus much of this will make
> Black white, foul fair, wrong right,
> Base noble, old young, coward valiant . . .

> This yellow slave
> Will knit and break religions, bless th'accursed,
> Make the hoar leprosy adored, place thieves
> And give them title, knee, and approbation
> With senators on the bench.

True enough: money has provided a golden (today paper) route to the House of Lords. Old Lord Burghley had written in his Precepts that nobility was but ancient riches: he knew well enough, it was his own case.

—— oOo ——

A severe outbreak of plague marked much of 1608-9; it is no less marked in the background of the play, with several references. When the news gets round that Timon has discovered gold, it brings the wolves round the door once more, poet and painter, lords and senators, Alcibiades and his whores. To the senators come to greet him, thus Timon:

> I thank them, and would send them back the plague
> Could I but catch it for them.

He wishes Alcibiades upon them as their plague, and for his own epitaph leaves:

> Seek not my name. A plague consume you wicked caitiffs
>   left!
> Here lie I, Timon, who alive all living men did hate.

To Alcibiades' whores his wishes are:

> Give them diseases, leaving with thee their lust.
> Make use of thy salt hours. Season the slaves
> For tubs and baths; bring down rose-cheeked youth
> To the tub-fast and the diet.

Venereal disease was rife in Jacobean London; anyone who knows Simon Forman's case-books will recognise the authentic note in this:

> Be as a planetary plague when Jove
> Will o'er some high-viced city hang his poison
> In the sick air.

The scalpel is quite unsparing:

> Down with the nose –
> Down with it flat; take the bridge quite away.

The dramatist, William Davenant, who liked to think that he was an Oxford by-blow of William Shakespeare's – John Aubrey thought so – lost his nose from syphilis.

There is even more of this kind of thing, an exposure of society from top to bottom – even blameless academics come in for a swipe:

> the learned pate
> Ducks to the golden fool –

as it might be Left-wing academics in our time prostituting their services to press-lords.

All this is expressed, as critics have noted, with 'passionate conviction'. What accounts for this, the increasing bitterness – one cannot mistake it – of these plays from *Hamlet* and *Troilus and Cressida*, that is, from 1601 onwards? E.K. Chambers, who enjoyed the liberal illusions of pre-1914 civilisation, was appalled. 'In each alike we find the same readiness of bitter criticism, the same remorseless analysis, probing and dissecting, as with a cruel scalpel, the intimate weaknesses and basenesses of man-kind. In each, ideals are shattered, heroes are discrowned and stripped of their heroism, until it is with difficulty', he adds innocently, 'that our sympathies, so essential to the sense of tragedy, are retained.' But is this so? It is more important to recognise the truth of the picture.

—— oOo ——

The text offers a fascinating problem, as it was inserted in the Folio in the space intended for *Troilus and Cressida*, temporarily held up by copyright difficulties. *Timon* represents the author's rough draft; from it we can see how he worked – visualising scenes and completing them as he felt inclined. Thus the beginning and end of the play are complete, and contain fine poetry. The middle of the play remains in rough draft, with Shakespeare jotting down his first thoughts sometimes in prose, sometimes in irregular blank verse, at others in rhymed couplets. We know that Ben Jonson wrote his verse first as prose – as his schoolmaster, Camden, had taught him – and then turned it into poetry. This is most unlikely to have been Shakespeare's way. As Hemming and Condell, who knew, tell us: 'his mind and hand went together; and what he thought he uttered with easiness' . . . where Ben Jonson was notoriously constipated.

Our leading authority on the printing of the Folio, Charlton Hinman, says that *Timon* represented a 'not yet finally revised text, a version antecedent to "foul papers", as an author's last draft of a play is rather misleadingly called.' I agree: though orthodox, it is a rather absurd phrase.

---

1. cf. my *The Elizabethans and America*, page 192 (new edn, Greenwood Press, London, 1978, and Harper, New York, 1959)

SHAKESPEARE'S
ROMANCES

We have observed how effectively, and how subtly, the very practical and successful man of the theatre responded to its demands, often with something new; but also how this most sensitive register of the age picked up what was in the air and being talked about. Thirdly, we have his own personal circumstances to consider, as with any writer, his inner development and inflexion, his own affections and choices that give a man's writing its individuality and character.

All these come together to form a last phase which it is convenient to subsume as 'the Romances'. We have seen that all through – at least since he matured and found his own style – Shakespeare broke the rules and transcended the boundaries. Indeed, in *Hamlet*, he specifically expressed disrespect for the rigid categories beloved of dull, prosaic people, Poloniuses. *Richard III*, for example, is melodramatic but also has elements of tragedy; some of the comedies tremble on the edge of the tragic, others are farces; some of the history plays are tragedies. Plays like *All's Well* and *Measure for Measure* all critics have been hard put to it to define, let alone categorise. The truth is that it is totally impossible to circumscribe him.

Now, in this last phase, he achieves something new – and again different. Though these four plays end happily enough, they have much that is melancholy and wistful, backward-looking and nostalgic, some tragedy mixed with comedy, some brutal realism with the pathos and sentiment, much poetry and music. Above all, these last plays are atmospherical; it is the atmosphere, touched with magic, that they have in common.

Externally, and dramaturgically, the old master was responding to the new demands of the Blackfriars theatre: new stage-conditions, indoors, more scenery and music, a more select audience demanding surprise, sentiment, fantasy, the improbable and unreal. This must have chimed with his own nature and aptitude, which had always leaned to the romantic (with his first mentors, Spenser and Sidney), not with Jonsonian realism and satire. Now, for the Blackfriars audience, he found kindred spirits among the younger generation to take up this side of his own more catholic and multifarious work: Beaumont and Fletcher, Massinger.

From the life of the time something came too: these plays are full of the sea, of sea-ventures and voyages, of losses and wrecks at sea, of travellers and movement – as were those years with the founding of Virginia (with which Blackfriars was in touch, through William Strachey), the colonies being sent out, the incursion in strength into the Mediterranean, the new voyages via the Cape to India.

These plays are full of findings as well as losses, lost children and wives found again, reconciliation and forgiveness, at the end perhaps farewell to his art. We can only speculate from what circumstances in his personal life these things came, or to what they answered in his own dual experience of life and theatre. The historian may point out that they coincide with his return to family life at Stratford, with which he had never lost touch, whatever other experiences he had had in London. There, at home, life was being renewed for him in the birth of a little daughter (named Elizabeth, with what memories!) to his own daughter, Susanna, who took after him; and there was his faithful, silent wife waiting:

Ubera, tu mater, tu lac vitamque dedisti.

Pericles

1608

After the abortiveness of *Timon of Athens* something new was demanded, and Shakespeare produced it with *Pericles*. In spite of the unsatisfactoriness of the text that has come down to us, the play was exceptionally successful: we have plenty of evidence of that. We must remember too the bearing of external circumstances upon a professional dramatist with a strong box-office sense.

The subject of Pericles was, as usual with Shakespeare, in the air at the time. Among other publications the story came to mind with a new edition in 1607 of Lawrence Twine's *The Pattern of Painful Adventures*. Shakespeare took a few touches from this into his play, but far more important to him was the version of the story which he read up in John Gower's *Confessio Amantis*.

Shakespeare, very much a reading man, read his Chaucer; but Chaucer's contemporary, Gower, was visible to the dramatist in the neighbouring church of St. Saviour's, which dominated Southwark. His youngest brother, Edmund, another actor, was buried in the church in December 1607, with a knell which presumably the prosperous older brother paid for. Within the church the foremost visual image was the splendid monument of the old poet – who had been a benefactor of the church in his time – dating from the reign of Henry IV. There he lies in effigy, full length under a Gothic canopy, his head resting upon his three chief works, one of which is the *Confessio Amantis*, which was Shakespeare's chief reading for his play.

With his usual observancy, he was very conscious of monuments and tombs. In the play Pericles says, on the way to recognising his lost daughter Marina:

> yet thou dost look
> Like Patience gazing on kings' graves –

it is thought that he had some such sculpted figure in mind. This is likely, for Southwark was where the famous monumental workshops were located (whence his own monument at Stratford would come in a few years).

For his play he thought up something new indeed, and gave it an archaic framework, with John Gower as Chorus, most of his speeches in antique English and octosyllabic couplets like his own. These introduce the first acts; the fifth has Prologue and Epilogue in rhyming pentameter. Many rhymed couplets occur in the play – the trouble is that an unintelligent reporter, with a pedestrian mind, reported the first two acts. Even here we have recognisable Shakespearean touches, in words and phrases.

The function of Gower's speeches goes back to the Chorus of *Henry V* (with additional propriety, for that was Gower's period), introducing us to the action and leaping over space and time. The figure of the poet Gower clinches the scheme of the play.

—— oOo ——

Its subject is the extraordinary adventures of Pericles – as in the emphasis of Twine's title, *The Pattern of Painful Adventures*. Ben Jonson thought it 'a mouldy tale' – and it certainly was ancient, going back to Apollonius of Tyre, whom Shakespeare had known about from much earlier. But the public loved it: Pericles fleeing from the Court of Antiochus, after guessing the guilty secret of his incest with his daughter; his travels by sea, in the course of which his daughter, Marina, was born to his wife, Thaisa, whom he had won at the Court of Pentapolis; the wife's presumed death in childbirth, her coffin thrown overboard, which yet arrives on land, with Thaisa awakening out of her trance to become a Vestal at Ephesus; Marina's rescue from pirates, and her more admired rescue from the brothel at Mytilene; Pericles's meeting with his lost daughter, and the eventual recognition and reunion of all three at Ephesus, with a husband found for Marina in the Governor of Mytilene.

Lost and Found might be a subtitle for the play, and such a farrago of adventures needed a Chorus to fit them all together and tell us where we are – otherwise *we* should be lost.

The sea is everywhere in the play, as again in *The Tempest*, with a rôle also in *The Winter's Tale*. The reason is not far to seek. Jacobean London was filled with news of the first English colony, at last, in America and the voyages thither, to New England as well as to Virginia. Hundreds of leading figures subscribed to the Virginia Company (Southampton was to become its Treasurer), i.e. they became 'venturers' in contemporary terms (most of them lost their venture). These later plays of Shakespeare bear evidence of his reading not only of Hakluyt, as earlier, but of the pamphlets giving news of the ventures across the Atlantic. Voyages, the sea, storms and tempests, shipwrecks, the sea-shore, pirates, crews – the later plays are full of it all; nor is it surprising: the most sensitive register of the time noticed, as Dr. Johnson observed, everything.

Nor is there any difficulty about date: it is obvious. The reprint of Twine's novel came out in 1607; Shakespeare's brother was buried in Gower's church in the same year; the Venetian ambassador saw the play not later than 1608; and in that year George Wilkins cashed in on the success of the play with his novel, *The Painful Adventures of Pericles, Prince of Tyre*. A pamphlet of 1609 bears further witness to the success of the play:

> Amazed I stood to see a crowd
> Of civil throats stretched out so loud . . .
> So that I truly thought all these
> Came to see *Shore* or *Pericles*.

George Wilkins has an interest of his own; for, like Shakespeare, he knew the Montjoys and their house in Silver Street, and gave evidence also in the law-case concerning their daughter and son-in-law. The young couple, whom Master Shakespeare had betrothed, came to lodge in the tavern which Wilkins kept in Turnmill Street.[1] This was frequented by theatre-folk, and he himself tried his hand, with little success, at writing plays as well as this novel.

The more we know about these people the more we see how they relate, and things come together. Common sense and research are what is needed, not conjectures *in vacuo*.

------ oOo ------

Everything shows that a turning point was reached, not only in Shakespeare's work but in his life. Even the unimaginative Chambers was 'subjective' enough (his own phrase for it) as to posit a possible breakdown for the dramatist at this time. But we do not need to be subjective: consider the objective, external circumstances.

After the successful production of *Pericles*, the theatres were closed on account of plague from July 1608 for eighteen months. One cannot over-estimate the disturbance plague periodically created for contemporary life, but especially for theatre people. With plague raging in London, and the theatres closed, it is likely that Shakespeare retired to the country, and to a full renewal of family life. From these decisive years, 1608-9, he would have been based at Stratford: when he gave evidence in the Montjoy suit in 1612 he had to come up from the country; a second set of interrogatories could not be put to him, for he had gone back again.

At Stratford his mother died in 1608; but a new life was forming around the young couple – the intelligent Susanna and the good doctor, her husband – and Shakespeare's grandchild, Elizabeth, was born this year.

The intermission of playing gave opportunity for the discussions that took place prior to a further decisive event, the resolution on the part of the Burbages and Shakespeare to take over Blackfriars as an indoor playing-house. This was a step of growing importance for the future. Blackfriars had a smaller, more sophisticated upper-class audience, which paid better; it had had, from the Boys' Companies, a tradition of music. Shakespeare now became a part-owner of Blackfriars under the new dispensation; but it also offered a new challenge, and new opportunities, for his writing. It was natural that he, always ready to move with public taste, should experiment, now that he was to write for two audiences, that at the Globe and the other at Blackfriars. This is evident in the plays of his last period.

The experiment of *Pericles* was a great success, for the public was given everything: not only romantic adventures, and surprising recognitions, but a dumb-show, something like a masque, a dance, a tilt, and a great deal of music: some of it lost, the song Marina sings, for example. Several times music is invoked:

> The rough and woeful music that we have,
> Cause it to sound, beseech you.
> The viol once more; how thou stir'st, thou block!
> The music there!

This is to aid in bringing Thaisa back to life, but it is called in at other junctures.

Altogether, it was spectacular, as well as new.

For all its newness, much is recognisable. The brothel scenes and characters, the Bawd and Boult, are after the fashion of *Measure for Measure*, and the generous helpings of bawdy would have been another factor making for success. Some of them are commonplace gags, others stamped Shakespearean:

> Your bride goes to that with shame which is her way to go with warrant.
> Faith, some do, and some do not.
>
> There was a Spaniard's mouth watered, and he went to bed to her very description [Marina's].

We find the phrase, 'the deed of darkness', Shakespeare's word for it before.

Another regular touch we have noticed is Boult's, 'What would you have me do? Go to the wars, would you? where a man may serve seven years for the loss of a leg, and have not money enough in the end to buy him a wooden one?' The name of 'the great pirate Valdez' comes from the Spanish commander whom Drake captured from the Armada of 1588. A touch of the time occurs when the knights tilt and King Simonides says to his lord:

> We will withdraw into the gallery.

This was just how Queen Elizabeth viewed the tilts, from her gallery looking down into the tilt-yard below.

—— oOo ——

The text of the play that has come down to us is most unsatisfactory, and we must put that down to the disturbed circumstances that followed its successful production. Above all the severe plague of 1608-9, closure of theatres, Shakespeare's absence from London. His Company began by protecting their rights in their success by blocking its publication in 1608.

Next year a publisher got hold of a text of the play, put together by one or two reporters, and published it, the first two acts badly reported, and much of it badly printed. It seems that they got hold of an original draft of the last three Acts, and this is probable enough, for such 'reporters' who reconstructed plays for a pittance from a publisher were recognisably actors in the play. (Hence the 'bad' Quartos, which are sometimes helpful to editors in fleshing out the text.) There was such a demand for it – perhaps all the more on account of the theatres being closed – that another printing was called for the same year; and yet a third in 1611 – six altogether before the nasty Puritans (to whom the play has a reference) closed the theatres altogether.

Hemming and Condell did not print the play, for all its success, in the Folio of 1623 – evidently they had no text of it available. The simplest explanation is always best, and the exceptional circumstances of 1608-9 make it understandable. Sad as it is, we are grateful for the play as it is, as with *Timon*, rather than none at all.

---

1. cf. Prior, Roger 'The Life of George Wilkins' (in *Shakespeare Survey 25*, page 137 fol. (Cambridge University Press, Cambridge, 1972)

Cymbeline

1609

Cymbeline is both experimental and reminiscent. The new idiom of romance, with a strong fairy-tale element, needed to be worked at to achieve a satisfactory creation, set a new model. Shakespeare took exceptional pains with this one; it is indeed laboured, an amalgam of diverse elements rather than a creative fusion. Sisson notes the pains that Shakespeare took in the variety of sources he looked up or called upon – Holinshed, Geoffrey of Monmouth, Boccaccio; but, most striking are the numerous echoes from his own early work. Evidently in the long intermission that the plague gave he had time for reading and reflection at Stratford.

Sisson notes that the play 'combines all the well-worn themes, motives, devices and conventions that Shakespeare had used before, translated into the new idiom . . . Finally Shakespeare and his Company lavished upon *Cymbeline* the elaborate devices of the Court Masque to add spectacular effect to its attractions.'

We must remember that, since much of it is comedy, its incongruities should be taken comically, as if in inverted commas – Cloten's decapitation and his head brought on as a stage-property, the sudden surprises and sensational improbabilities. Shakespeare was writing with his tongue in his cheek. Of course there are serious elements too – Iachimo's intrusion upon Imogen, which Shakespeare added for himself to the folk-tale love-wager theme, can hardly be regarded as comic. It is a reminiscence from *The Rape of Lucrece*.

Something new was demanded for the public, for the two publics now, of Blackfriars as well as the Globe; so the old master is trying his hand out at a dual-purpose play. In performance one or other of these elements can be – indeed, must be – cut down; the masque-like theophany at the end, with the descent of Jupiter, would have been for Blackfriars with its more elaborate scenic devices. So far from it being 'sacrilege' to sacrifice a word of Shakespeare's in production, that experienced theatre man would not object to cutting, as we can tell from the evidence of some texts where we find relics of alternatives provided.

—— oOo ——

These last plays have long and detailed stage-directions, which would indicate that Shakespeare was writing at home in the country. The long closure of the theatres, from July 1608 to December 1609, gave him plenty of time, and *Cymbeline* is over-long. The triple recognition at the end is closely similar to that of his recent *Pericles*. He had been re-reading, or was recalling *The Rape of Lucrece* and *Titus Andronicus*. The comic clod, Cloten, had been dressed in Posthumus's clothes, and Imogen, taking his body for that of her husband, cries,

> O Posthumus, alas,
> Where is thy head? where's that? Ay me! where's that?

All this is to be taken comically. When asked by the invading Romans for his name, she gives Richard du Champ. This is a characteristically indirect salute to Richard Field, the Stratford printer of the two poems – all the more appropriate now that Shakespeare had become part-owner of the theatre in Blackfriars, where Field's press (and his French wife) held out.

All his life Shakespeare was apt to think of Tarquin – he was a very sexy man himself, and the image of rape must have given him a kick as well as the audience. We have Cleopatra once more in glory on the Cydnus, and the story of Tereus and Philomela which sparked off *Titus Andronicus*. The 'Arabian bird' appears from *Antony and Cleopatra*, and 'the worms of the Nile' (but why does he so often refer to snakes as 'worms'?). Yet another apostrophe to gold and the ill effects of its cults refers back to *Timon*. The charm of innocent country life in the mountains of Wales, lived by old Belarius and Cymbeline's unknown sons, as opposed to the falsity and treacheries of Court life, re-appears from *As You Like It* or even goes right back to *Henry VI*.

For the elements of his story he had those old stand-bys, Holinshed, *The Mirror for Magistrates* and the *Faery Queene*. He hardly needed Boccaccio or anything else for the familiar folktale of a husband wagering everything on his wife's fidelity. (After his own variegated experiences in London he had come back to a faithful wife of his own at home.) A new element in the play is the character of the Doctor, who instructs the wicked Queen – another dissembling, deceitful Tamora – in the use of drugs. Shakespeare's son-in-law could have instructed him about that.

Iachimo – the Italian adventurer who instigated the husband, Posthumus, to take the wager upon Imogen's fidelity and gets into her bedroom in a chest, to report everything – is another, more light-weight Iago.

Here we have a curious feature in the reflection on Italians:

> What false Italian,
> As poisonous-tongued as -handed, hath prevailed
> On thy too ready hearing?

This accounts for Posthumus' onslaught on womankind:

> Is there no way for men to be, but women
> Must be half-workers? . .

> Could I find out
> The woman's part in me! For there's no motion
> That tends to vice in man but I affirm
> It is the woman's part. Be it lying, note it,
> The woman's; flattering, hers; deceiving, hers;
> Lust and rank thoughts, hers, hers; revenges, hers;
> Ambitions, covetings, change of prides, disdain,
> Nice longing, slanders, mutability –

we cannot but recognise the experience with his half-Italian mistress portrayed in the Sonnets. Posthumus goes on, curiously:

> I'll write against them.

This very year 1609 saw the publication of the Sonnets, and only a year or so after, Emilia Lanier's replication with its attack on men, inserted in prose, before her own long quasi-religious poem. (Certainly ambition had been a consuming passion with her, and all those other characteristics 'noted' were recognisable too.)

We do not need to repeat the windings, sudden turns and surprises, the improbabilities, which disgusted Dr. Johnson. Once more, the dramatist did not mind improbabilities any more than the audience did, and he was out to give them what they wanted. The play has a double, or even triple, plot and all admit the experienced skill with which so many threads are drawn together at the end. As against the fairy-tale background from remote British history – Cymbeline (Cunobelinus), a Cloten as a supposed Duke of Cornwall, a world beyond Severn, Wales and Milford Haven, as a port of disembarkation from Italy! – the characters are real and possess veracity. Cymbeline is a kind of silly Lear, easily taken in by a dissembling wife, real enough; though Posthumus is too credulous, there are such types as he and Iachimo; Imogen has always been found moving, so too the faithful Pisanio.

—— oOo ——

The language in which the play is written can only be described as extraordinary. Shakespeare had always had a lordly way with words, a fondness for rare and grand, impressive words. Increasingly, he does what he likes with them: he will frequently use nouns as verbs, and sometimes a preposition, 'beneath', for example, as a noun. Instinctively he uses a visual word rather than an abstract one. Posthumus puts aside the thought of another wife:

> give me but this I have,
> And cere up my embracements from a next
> With bonds of death!

The words 'cere up' come to mind for he sees the waxen shroud, and the idea of sealing is behind the thought of wax. He always had been double-minded: hence all the double-talk and punning throughout his work, which Dr. Johnson considered *his* fatal Cleopatra. The habit grew upon him until he expresses himself, not only elliptically, but so obliquely as to be devious – it is sometimes difficult to know what he means. The very first words of the play are:

> You do not meet a man but frowns. Our bloods
> No more obey the heavens than our courtiers
> Still seem as does the King's.

Only Shakespeare would use the word 'bloods' for moods, and the rest is obscure: it implies that the courtiers do not agree with the King's mood (in exiling Posthumus for marrying Imogen).

In Cloten's comic duel, his sword missed its thrust. This is the way it is expressed: 'His steel was in debt. It went o' th' backside the town', i.e. like a debtor, it took a back road. Iachimo praises Imogen to her face, in contrast with others, thus:

> It cannot be i' th' eye, for apes and monkeys,
> 'Twixt two such shes, would chatter this way and
> Contemn with mows the other; nor i' th' judgment,
> For idiots, in this case of favour, would
> Be wisely definite.

We know that he wrote rapidly; evidently his pen could not keep up with his thought. We may infer too that his manuscripts were hard to read, and gave both transcribers and printers much trouble.

Here is a thought he puts in concrete, visual terms, because he *sees* it:

> The love I bear him
> Makes me to fan you thus; but the gods made you,
> Unlike all others, chaffless.

Iachimo simply means that he was testing Imogen, and she was faultless, but the image behind the word 'fan' is that of winnowing, and she is without chaff. Note, too, that the image is from country life. Even a quite simple thought is thus worded:

> Frame yourself
> To orderly solicits, and be friended
> With aptness of the season;

i.e. make your requests in order and at apt times. For 'give an account' Shakespeare will say 'words him'; for 'tell about', 'story him'. Or what about a passage like this, when Imogen is persuaded that Posthumus has been unfaithful to her away in Italy? –

> To think, when thou shalt be disedged by her
> That now thou tirest on, how thy memory
> Will then be panged by me.

'Disedged' is Shakespeare's coinage, and it has a visual element in it, for it means dulling the edge of sexual desire. 'Tirest' is double-talk, for it suggests both preying on, like a bird of prey, and also tiring of her. 'Panged' is a verb coined from the noun 'pang'. The psychological subtlety behind it is that when she and her husband had been together when first married, Imogen had chastely moderated his pressing desires.

But what a writer! And how difficult for the modern reader! There is everything to be said for modernising him.

This is not to say that there are not passages of fine poetry, and others of the most effective simplicity: he can do both, as he chooses. We are given two beautiful songs – Fidele's, the name Imogen takes, one of the most moving he ever wrote, with its burden of farewell:

> Fear no more the heat o' th' sun,
>   Nor the furious winter's rages;
> Thou thy worldly task hast done,
>   Home art gone and ta'en thy wages . . .

—— oOo ——

In this remote fairy-tale world there are still touches of the time. The story is put into the framework of a conflict between Rome and ancient Britain, over the payment of tribute. This gives the cue for a couple of patriotic statements like those of John of Gaunt and Faulconbridge earlier. (How much of the past is taken up into this reminiscent play!)

> Our countrymen
> Are men more ordered than when Julius Caesar
> Smiled at their lack of skill, but found their courage
> Worthy his frowning at.

(Visual again.)

> Their discipline
> Now mingled with their courages, will make known
> To their approvers they are people such
> That mend upon the world.

This was true enough, after the long struggle with Spain for a place in the sun, and with the English colonisation of North America now beginning to gain some momentum.

Lesser evidences of the time occur in a whole scene devoted to playing bowls, a favourite game with Shakespeare (and rather upper-class then). The stupid Cloten goes on about being free to utter what oaths he likes – a reference to the recent Jacobean statute against Oaths, which made for further difficulties when it came to printing the plays. As for stage-apparel, we hear of 'cloak-bag, doublet, hat, hose' – so the clothes worn were Jacobean. So were the rushes on the floor, and the equipment, of Imogen's bedroom. Here we may note again Shakespeare's interest in the work of his neighbours in Southwark, the sculptors who made so many chimney-pieces for great houses as well as monuments:

> The chimney
> Is south the chamber, and the chimney piece
> Chaste Dian bathing. Never saw I figures
> So likely to report themselves. The cutter
> Was as another nature, dumb; outwent her,
> Motion and breath left out.

In taking the bracelet off the sleeping Imogen, to confirm his false story to Posthumus, Iachimo breathes:

> O sleep, thou ape of death, lie dull upon her.
> And be her sense but as a monument,
> Thus in a chapel lying.

Cymbeline's son, Arviragus, in an exquisite passage strewing flowers on Fidele's body, thinking her dead, says that the robin, bringing moss, shames

> Those rich-left heirs that let their father lie
> Without a monument.

This, however, would not happen to him: the faithful family called upon one of the Southwark sculptors for the monument at Stratford.

Most interesting is the way the play is conceived to pay compliment once more to King James and the new dynasty. Why should the Roman forces land (where they never did), and the action come to pivot, at Milford Haven? – Because that was where Henry VII had landed in 1485, James I's great-great-grandfather through whom he came to the English throne. The combination of England with Scotland made it the 'British' throne, and there was concurrent talk of the 'imperial' theme.

The play ends with an oracle. 'When as a lion's whelp shall . . . be embraced by a piece of tender air; and when from a stately cedar shall be lopped branches . . . which shall be jointed to the old stock then shall Britain be fortunate and flourish in peace and plenty.' The interpretation:

> The lofty cedar, Cymbeline,
> Personates thee; and thy lopped branches point
> Thy two sons forth . . .

Cymbeline, of course, was James, also with two sons, Prince Henry and Prince Charles, and an only daughter (like Cymbeline's Imogen), Princess Elizabeth, whose marriage was much in the air at the time. When it came about in 1613 to the Elector Palatine – from which the present royal house descends – the plays of the veteran dramatist occupied one-half of the repertory at the celebrations. 'Jointed to the old stock' referred of course to the Tudors. As for 'peace and plenty', the best thing to be said for James I was the peace that he, *Rex pacificus*, maintained until·practically the end of his reign.

The text in the Folio offers no great problem, it is reasonably good, and is thought to have been from a scribe's transcript of Shakespeare's difficult hand for the prompt-book.

The Winter's Tale
1610-11

The Winter's Tale is a singularly beautiful, an inspired play, from beginning to end, where *Cymbeline* gives the impression of having been laboured. The new play is not long, and seems to have been written at Stratford in one onrush in the winter of 1610-11. With this play the dramatist completely mastered the new genre and, together with the next, *The Tempest*, produced two masterpieces, for other writers to follow. John Fletcher, who was to succeed him as dramatist-in-chief to the Company, was already working along these lines with his *Philaster*; much influenced by the old master, he was to make the new genre his own.

Shakespeare had a subject that he knew would appeal, from the success of Robert Greene's romance, *Pandosto*, which provided the story and the ground-work for him. The novel, written in the exciting year 1588, had been recently republished, under a new title, in 1607. It is ironical to think, after what had happened between Greene and Shakespeare at the beginning of his career, that he was now, at the end of it, writing with Greene's work beside him. The dramatist followed the outlines fairly clearly, but added Autolycus and the country folk, a realistic rendering from the shepherd life of the Cotswolds, sheep-shearing feast and all.

The subject of Leontes' psychotic jealousy of his wife, Hermione, inspired him and immeasurably more is made of it – half the play, in fact. The characters of the Queen's faithful lady, Paulina, and the King's no less trusty Camillo, are portrayed in depth and win our complete sympathy. Autolycus, the enchanting, thieving pedlar, is one of Shakespeare's happiest inventions. The Queen herself is a moving creation and, in her regal dignity in circumstances of injured innocence, has much in common with Catherine of Aragon, in the last play of all, *Henry VIII*. The hearts of the sentimental have always been taken – as probably Shakespeare's was – by his girls, Imogen and Miranda and, in this play, Perdita. There is even an Emilia, but she has only the part of a waiting-woman.

Simon Forman saw the play at the Globe on 15 May 1611 and gives us a full account of it. He was particularly interested, as he would be, in Leontes' jealousy and his sending to the Oracle at Delphi to know the truth as to his suspicions; in the bringing up of the King's abandoned child by a shepherd and her ultimate discovery; and the character of Autolycus, who was much in Forman's line. It was performed at Court on Gunpowder day, 5 November 1611 and again among the entertainments for the marriage of Princess Elizabeth to the Elector Palatine in 1613.

He picked most of his names out of Plutarch or Sidney's *Arcadia*, and Autolycus from the beloved Ovid; oddly enough, a Florizel occurs at Stratford.

The character of Leontes dominates the first half of the play – one of the most original and intuitive Shakespeare ever created. In it he intuited the nature of schizophrenia, in its modern diagnosis, and portrayed precisely how it works. We have the alternation of perfectly sane with mad speeches – the latter difficult to write, but authentic and convincing. The jealousy is the more deep-seated because Leontes and Polixenes had been such close friends in their youth. Under the compulsion of his psychosis – Paulina recognises the symptoms from the first and calls them his 'lunes' – the King's mind works with the formal reasoning and cunning of schizophrenics, cleverly picking up every indication to buttress his complex and corroborate his suspicions.

The first Act, in which all this is developed, is one of the most compelling Shakespeare ever wrote, with an ominous atmosphere, the foreboding of what is to come. As was usual with him throughout his career, he increased the tension by emphasising former friendship and fondness – not only, as we have seen, for dramatic impact but also for the revelation of the depths in human beings and the extremes they will go to, under stress. Polixenes diagnoses the case:

> This jealousy
> Is for a precious creature; as she's rare,
> Must it be great; and, as his person's mighty,
> Must it be violent; and, as he does conceive
> He is dishonoured by a man which ever
> Professed to him, why, his revenges must
> In that be made more bitter. Fear o'ershades me.

Shakespeare's imagination saw more deeply into human nature than any rationalist psychology. And, actually, events in everybody's mind at the time bore him out. Leontes sent his Queen to prison, where she was supposed to have died. Elizabeth I's father, Henry VIII, not only sent her mother and her cousin – Anne Boleyn and Catherine Howard, both his Queens – to the Tower but beheaded them. Leontes lost his wife, and his only son and heir died. This is what happened to Richard III after the murder of the Princes in the Tower: his son, for whose succession it had been done, died and then his Queen. Leontes was hardly more stricken by fate, and by remorse, than Richard.

The Queen is cited before a court of justice, as Catherine and Henry appeared before the court at Blackfriars. Her speeches, in their dignity and sense of outrage, look forward to Catherine in *Henry VIII*: she too was an alien, receiving no sort of justice in the country into which she had married:

> The Emperor of Russia was my father:
> O that he were alive, and here beholding
> His daughter's trial!

At that moment the lords arrive with the declaration of the Oracle that Hermione and Polixenes are blameless, Leontes' suspicions false. He refuses to believe it. Upon the heels of this his sick son dies; the Queen faints and is borne away, Paulina returns to tell him that she has died. These blows confirm the Oracle, and Leontes is struck with remorse and grief.

His conversion is highly sensational; but everybody knows that there are such sudden conversions.

—— oOo ——

Act IV is introduced by Time, a Chorus, as in *Pericles*, to leap over time and tell us the events of the intervening years:

> Impute it not a crime
> To me, or my swift passage, that I slide
> O'er sixteen years . . .
> since it is in my power
> To o'erthrow law, and in one, self-born hour
> To plant and o'erwhelm custom.

The author makes up to the audience in his usual courteous manner (unlike Ben Jonson):

> Of this allow,
> If ever you have spent time worse ere now;
> If never, yet that Time himself doth say,
> He wishes earnestly you never may.

The pastoral element takes over. The Queen's child, Perdita, born in prison, is carried overseas – like Marina in *Pericles* – where she is brought up by a shepherd, who, from the jewels and trinkets brought with the child, knows something of her story. Here she is, of course, wooed by Florizel, Polixenes' son and heir.

All that is charming enough, but enchantment enters the play with Autolycus, his petty thievings from Clown and shepherds, the way the country folk fall for his wares, his cozening tricks and his songs, the sheep-shearing feast they all attend. Perdita and Florizel are watched by Polixenes and Camillo, thus skilfully bringing the two halves of the action together. The poetry is breath-taking, from the moment Autolycus enters, singing:

> When daffodils begin to peer,
> With heigh! the doxy over the dale,
> Why then comes in the sweet o'the year,
> For the red blood reigns in the winter's pale.

And Perdita takes up with

> daffodils
> That come before the swallow dares, and take
> The winds of March with beauty; violets, dim,
> But sweeter than the lids of Juno's eyes
> Or Cytherea's breath; pale primroses
> That die unmarried, ere they can behold
> Bright Phoebus in his strength; bold oxlips and
> The crown imperial; lilies of all kinds . . .

Amid the English flowers, we should notice how, as always, the classical images and comparisons spring naturally to mind from his early education.

Along with school at Stratford, from the very first – Plautus, Ovid and Seneca, with *The Comedy of Errors* and *Titus Andronicus* – there is the Warwickshire and Cotswold background that comes into several of the plays, from *The Taming of the Shrew* on. Here we have authentic, loving observation: 'Let me see – what am I to buy for our sheep-shearing feast? Three pound of sugar, five pound of currants, rice – what will this sister of mine do with rice? [One throws rice at weddings.] But my father hath made her mistress of the feast, and she lays it on.' She has made nosegays for the shearers, who can all sing the three-men songs of the time – only one Puritan among them, 'and he sings psalms to hornpipes.' This is to suggest that he is a cuckold.

The country fellow doesn't know whether he has got money enough to pay for it all. 'Let me see – every 'leven wether tods – every tod yields pound and odd shilling – fifteen hundred shorn, what comes the wool to? . . I cannot do't without counters.' How often Shakespeare must have observed that in the country round about or at Stratford market! As in *The Two Gentlemen of Verona*, years before, the Whitsun pastorals are recalled:

> Methinks I play as I have seen them do
> In Whitsun pastorals . . .

The girls press around Autolycus for fairings: 'I love a ballad in print, a'life, for then we are sure they are true.' In contrast to the juke boxes of today, they can all sing: 'We can both sing it. If thou'lt bear a part, thou shalt hear: 'tis in three parts . . . We had the tune on't a month ago.'

It is the authentic voice of traditional rural England, which some of us can still remember.

—— oOo ——

Though the play is full of romance and pastoral delights, the passion and pain of jealous emotion, grief and sensational surprise, it never loses touch with the ground of reality. Here is a homely scene:

> when my old wife lived, upon
> This day she was both pantler, butler, cook,
> Both dame and servant; welcomed all, served all;
> Would sing her song and dance her turn; now here
> At upper end o'the table; now i'the middle;
> On his shoulder, and his; her face o'fire
> With labour, and the thing she took to quench it
> She would to each one sip.

Does it represent a home-coming? It sounds like it.

Perhaps here, too, is a no less authentic recollection:

> Besides, you know,
> Prosperity's the very bond of love,
> Whose fresh complexion and whose heart together
> Affliction alters.

We have a passage between Shepherd and Clown on the familiar theme earlier of gentility, and how one becomes a 'gentleman-born'. (The dramatist took out a coat-of-arms in his father's name.)

The device of the living statue had been used before by Lyly and Marston. The reconciliation, the forgiveness and renewal are beyond anything: perhaps equalled only by Lear's eventual recognition of Cordelia. We have noticed Shakespeare's interest in monuments: this is 'a piece many years in doing and now newly performed [i.e. finished] by that rare Italian master, Julio Romano, who – had he himself eternity and could put breath into his work – would beguile Nature of her custom, so perfectly he is her ape.' Once more we observe the aesthetic taste of the time – naturalness, lifelikeness, reality and grace. It is appropriate that Julio Romano should have been the one artist Shakespeare names; for Julio, though Raphael's pupil, reacted away from classicism into a highly personal style, extreme, erotic, violent. Evidently a congenial spirit.

The episode of the bear, pursuing Antigonus off the stage, is thought to have been suggested, along with the dance of the twelve satyrs, from Ben Jonson's masque of Oberon, performed at New Year 1611. The language of the play, though it contains as many rare and *recherché* words as ever, is nothing like so convoluted as that of *Cymbeline*; it has more direct and forceful speaking and more poetry.

—— oOo ——

The text is an excellent one as it appeared in the Folio, it is thought from the transcript made by the Company's experienced scribe, Ralph Crane. Stage-directions were cut, however, and in place we find, exceptionally, act-scene divisions with a list of the characters for each scene.

The Tempest
1611

The Winter's Tale was followed by an exquisite masterpiece, *The Tempest*, which was played later the same year on Hallowmas night (1 November) before the King at Whitehall. It has not the power and drama generated by the theme of the former; but its poetry is no less, and its interest even richer and more diverse, particularly in what relates to the New World.

For, with the formation of the Virginia Company, the foundation of Jamestown, the voyages going out to the American coast, there was mounting national interest in these ventures. Shakespeare had a considerable number of friends actively involved; he read the Voyages and Travels, as he had read Hakluyt, along with the news pamphlets. In 1609 the flagship of the small fleet going out with reinforcements for Virginia, the *Sea Venture*, met with a tornado off Bermuda, ran in on the rocks a wreck and yet, miraculously, not a life was lost. Jourdan's pamplet, *A Discovery of the Bermudas*, otherwise called the *Isle of Devils*, alerted Shakespeare to the subject in 1610.

His full knowledge of the event, in circumstantial detail, came from William Strachey's manuscript account of the wreck, and its redemption, which came back to Blackfriars, dedicated to some 'Noble Lady' Shakespeare would have known. Strachey himself was more interesting: a literary man who had contributed a sonnet for Ben Jonson's *Sejanus* (in which Shakespeare had acted), been a shareholder in the Children of the Revels when they occupied the Blackfriars theatre, and was frequently in and out of that fascinating precinct. The details of the tempest conjured up by Prospero's arts for his purposes closely follow those given by Strachey, to the St. Elmo's fire-ball running down the rigging. Events that follow in the play are sparked off by those that happened in the island, and other suggestions come from Shakespeare's reading. Dr. Johnson noticed that he was a 'diligent reader'.

Contemporaries thought that the uninhabited island, 'the still-vexed Bermoothes' – the constantly storm-vexed – was given over to devils, as Jourdan's pamphlet shows, and to enchantment. Thus the first, and dominant, theme of the play is magic – fascinating to a world in which 'Dr.' Dee and 'Dr.' Forman were notorious, but in the nature of things not so dramatic as that of human conflict. For, Prospero's magic has determined the outcome beforehand and at every juncture he controls the action through the operations of his sprite, Ariel. (Just as Dr. Dee needed his medium, Kelly, in order to operate.)

The island is several times described, with its qualities. Even Caliban, who was its possessor before Prospero came and enslaved him, is moved to poetry:

> the isle is full of noises,
> Sounds and sweet airs, that give delight and hurt not.
> Sometimes a thousand twangling instruments
> Will hum about mine ears; and sometime voices
> That, if I then had waked after long sleep,
> Will make me sleep again.

He is the most original creation in the play, one of Shakespeare's most remarkable, and is the upshot of reading and reflexion. He is based on the various accounts of the American Indians coming home from the New World.

> When thou cam'st first
> Thou strok'st me and made much of me; wouldst give me
> Water with berries in't; and teach me how
> To name the bigger light, and how the less,
> That burn by day and night.

This is entirely in keeping with the *True Report* of the new-found land of Virginia by Ralegh's agent, Thomas Hariot, who had shown the Indians the stars and planets through his perspective glass.

> And then I loved thee,
> And showed thee all the qualities o'the isle,
> The fresh springs, brine-pits, barren place and fertile.

The primitive possessor of the land had been ready to worship the newcomer; and when the baser elements of the ship's company come a-land, Caliban is pathetically ready to venerate and serve them, a jester and a drunken butler:

> I prithee, let me bring thee where crabs grow;
> And I with my long nails will dig thee pig-nuts;
> Show thee a jay's nest, and instruct thee how
> To snare the nimble marmoset; I'll bring thee
> To clustering filberts, and sometimes I'll get thee
> Young scammels [sea-mews] on the rocks.

The rascally Stephano and Trinculo respond by making the poor primitive drunk – and fire-water proved the ruin of the American Indian. Caliban, however, led them on to make an attempt on Prospero's life.

More important than this mutiny is the conspiracy in which Antonio, who had usurped Prospero's place as Duke of Milan, tries to inveigle

Sebastian into killing his brother Alonso, the King of Naples. These grandees had been on board the ship which, approaching too near the island, had foundered in the storm raised by Prospero, though he had brought them safe to land for his purposes.

In historic fact there had been a mutiny against the governor during that winter on Bermuda, the leader of which had been hanged on a tree – and the tree occurs in the play. And a dangerous conspiracy blew up during the starving time in Virginia, led by two treacherous Germans, who received their comeuppance.

—— oOo ——

It is given to Gonzalo, 'an honest old councillor', to put forward the ideal of blissful communism, which Shakespeare had read about in Florio's Montaigne; and he leaves us in no doubt what he thought of it.

> I'the commonwealth I would by contraries
> Execute all things; for no kind of traffic [commerce]
> Would I admit; no name of magistrate;
> Letters should not be known –

one is reminded of Jack Cade years earlier –

>   riches, poverty,
> And use of service, none; contract, succession,
> Bourn, bound of land, tilth, vineyard, none;
> No use of metal, corn, or wine, or oil;
> No occupation; all men idle, all.

The women were all to be innocent and pure. Yet

> All things in common Nature should produce
> Without sweat or endeavour: treason, felony,
> Sword, pike, knife, gun, or need of any engine,
> Would I not have. But Nature should bring forth,
> Of its own kind, all foison [harvest], all abundance,
> To feed my innocent people.

One cynical hearer of this nonsense inquires:

> No marrying 'mong his subjects?

Another concludes:

> None, man, all idle: whores and knaves.

So much for Montaigne's illusions about primitive man; Shakespeare depicts the 'man in a state of nature' of the political philosophers as a Caliban. At no time in his career had he any use for illusions about life and the human condition, and no one has ever had deeper insight into it.

This is not to say that his view was a cynical one: the purpose of Prospero's bringing these men to the island was their redemption, his forgiveness, and reconciliation. Shakespeare knew the truth about human nature, both sides to it; we cannot doubt that Prospero speaks for him:

> the rarer action is
> In virtue than in vengeance.

—— oOo ——

Magic was much in the air at this time, with a king on the throne who was an authority on demonology, and Prospero was a properly mysterious character: a Magus, or *mage*. His power depended on his books – and we remember the magical importance that both Dee and Forman attached to their books. Caliban alerts Stephano and Trinculo:

> First to possess his books; for without them
> He's but a sot, as I am, nor hath not
> One spirit to command . . .
> Burn but his books.

Instead, Prospero raises up hunters and hounds and, with Ariel, sets them on this nasty crew. They call the hounds by their names: 'Hey, Mountain, hey!' 'Silver! there it goes, Silver.' 'Fury, Fury! there, Tyrant, there! hark, hark!' 'Hark, they roar!'

> Let them be hunted soundly. At this hour
> Lie at my mercy all mine enemies:
> Shortly shall all my labours end, and thou
> Shalt have the air at freedom. For a little
> Follow and do me service.

To do this scene, and several others, justice – perhaps to realise this play as a whole – one needs the resources of film. Here we are reminded of Shakespeare's enthusiasm for the hunt, from the very beginning.

He may have intuited his own farewell to his art in Prospero's renunciation of his:

> I'll break my staff,
> Bury it certain fathoms in the earth,
> And deeper than did ever plummet sound
> I'll drown my book.

This comes at the end of the marvellous speech:

> Ye elves of hills, brooks, standing lakes, and groves . . .
>   You demi-puppets that
> By moonshine do the green sour ringlets make,
> Whereof the ewe not bites; and you whose pastime
> Is to make midnight mushrooms, that rejoice
> To hear the solemn curfew . . .

All that goes back to the country lore he loved, of Mercutio's evocation and *A Midsummer Night's Dream*.

The youthful love of Ferdinand and Miranda – that went to Victorian hearts and filled so much of their commentary – we may take for granted: it is charmingly rendered, as was that of Florizel and Perdita. Of more special interest is that the reason for Caliban's subjection and servitude was his attempt to rape Miranda. Contemporary travellers, not having had a course in anthropology, were shocked by the laxity of morals in the New World. (The Puritans would put that right – by decimating the Indians.)

We take for granted, too, a complete scene given up to the master's old habit of verbal play and punning – even apart from its appeal to the contemporary audience, it was necessary to fill up the interstices of the action. We should observe that the language of the play, filled with beauty, is perhaps simpler again than *The Winter's Tale*, and far more so than the laboured convolutions of *Cymbeline*. The play is, as the island was, full of music, and the marriage of the lovers is adorned with a formal masque, which must have appealed at Blackfriars. Goddesses descend to bless them; more endearing are the country reapers who dance:

> You sunburned sicklemen, of August weary

(was he writing that August, one wonders?)

> Come hither from the furrow, and be merry:
> Make holiday, your rye-straw hats put on.
> And these fresh nymphs encounter every one
> In country footing.

The songs are exquisite, as ever. 'Full fathom five' – the 'five-fathom' goes back to *Romeo and Juliet*: in 'Come unto these yellow sands . . .' the phrase 'the wild waves whist' goes right back – after all these years and all the work between – to Marlowe. (And what might not *he* have achieved, too, if only he had lived!)

It is all as if Shakespeare were rounding things up.

In the Epilogue, speaking in the person of Prospero, he is speaking doubly, as so often, partly for himself:

Now my charms are all o'erthrown,
And what strength I have's mine own,
Which is most faint . . .

Then, propitating the audience, as all along:

Gentle breath of your's my sails
Must fill, or else my project fails,
Which was to please.

—— oOo ——

The text in the Folio is an excellent one, with more elaborate stage-directions than for any other play, for apparently he was writing away at home in the country. One wonders whether the passage describing Caliban as a 'mooncalf' suggested the remarkable satiric poem of that title to Shakespeare's prolific countryman, Drayton, who certainly was indebted to *A Midsummer Night's Dream* for his delightful 'Nymphidia'. Ben Jonson observed of Caliban, 'if there be never a "Servant-monster" in the fair – who can help it? he (the author) says; nor a nest of antics [fantastics]. He is loth to make Nature afraid in his plays, like those that beget *Tales*, *Tempests*, and such-like drolleries.' This is grumpy, rather than really bad-tempered, and Ben more than made up for his quips by the magnificent generosity of his tributes to the Master in, and his help over, the Folio edition of his plays.

INDEX